D1083820

THE LETTERS OF JOHN CLARE

JOHN CLARE
1793-1864

Painting by William Hilton, R.A.
National Portrait Gallery

THE
LETTERS
OF
JOHN CLARE

EDITED BY
J. W. and ANNE TIBBLE

NEW YORK
BARNES & NOBLE, INC.

First published in Great Britain 1951
Reprinted 1970
Published in the United States of America, 1970 by
Barnes & Noble, Inc.
105 Fifth Avenue, New York, N.Y. 10003

SBN 389 01021 9

Printed in Great Britain

To Edmund Blunden
who gave Clare his true place
as a poet

There is something in the madness of this man that interests me more than the sanity of Lord Byron and Scott.—WORDSWORTH, of Blake

Perhaps no more should be asked of an editor than the highest possible standard of accuracy in the presentation of the text and a commentary on it sufficient to identify all the persons, places, and circumstances referred to.—*Times Literary Supplement* review of *Journal to Stella*, January 1948

CONTENTS

ACKNOWLEDGEMENTS

Our greatest debt is to Mr. R. W. Brown, the chief of the Northampton Library. He it is who has been largely responsible for the collection of Clare documents there, and who permitted our access to the ninety-six letters of the Brooke-Taylor manuscripts, giving us, with his assistants, help and advice throughout our task of transcribing.

Secondly, our thanks are due to the curators of the Peterborough Museum, for offering every facility for copying letters from the Clare manuscripts in their care; also to the librarians of the Norris Library, St. Ives, Huntingdon, the Bodleian Library, and the British Museum.

Thirdly, we are grateful to all those who have so kindly lent letters or transcripts: Mr. M. Buxton Forman, Mr. R. N. Green-Armytage, Geoffrey Harmsworth, Esq., Sir Ambrose Elton, Mr. E. J. Rudsdale of the Wisbech Museum, Miss Eleanor Nicholes, Mr. R. W. King of Bangor University College, Messrs. J. Thornton and Son, Mr. Allan B. Stirling, Messrs. Myers and Co., the Rev. Michael Etherington, and Mr. J. E. Kite.

Lastly, we are indebted to all those who have submitted to queries, and spent time answering them: Mr. Geoffrey Grigson, Mrs. Garfoot-Gardner (for much patience in giving 'local' information), Miss Russ of the Bristol Reference Library, Mr. G. A. Hill of the Bath Municipal Libraries, Mr. G. L. Day, Miss Yseult Parnell (for work in Somerset House), Dr. Cyril Turner of the City of Leicester Mental Hospital, the librarian of the Mitchell Library, Glasgow, Mrs. Xenia Wood (the descendant of Mrs. Emmerson), the Right Hon. Lord Radstock, Mrs. Stallebrass and Mr. Fred Clare, the District Probate Registrar of Bristol, Messrs. Sotheby and Co., Messrs. John

ACKNOWLEDGEMENTS

Grant of Edinburgh, the Rev. Lucian Cary, Mr. John L. Harvey, the late Mr. F. A. Downing, Mr. E. V. Miller, Assistant Keeper of Printed Books at the British Museum, Dr. Julian Park of the University of Buffalo, Mr. E. Byrne Hackett of New York, Mr. Bliss of the Henry Huntington Library in California, the Librarian of the New York Public Library, Professor Jack Simmons, Dr. Hoskins, Miss Bennett and her assistant Librarians at the University College, Leicester, Miss Margaret Traynor, and Mr. E. Boult, of the Institute of Education, University College, Leicester.

J. W. AND ANNE TIBBLE

University College, Leicester
1950

INTRODUCTION

SINCE Clare, with faith that he could find his public, wished both his 'autobiography' and his letters to 'creep into print', there is satisfaction in knowing that the present volume, after a hundred and twenty-five years' waiting, is given to his readers at last. A debt has been paid: an unhappy ghost perhaps appeased.

If Clare's editors have accepted too readily the sanction he gave to his publisher, John Taylor, to 'use liberty and do as you like', it may be set down in extenuation that he left them no easy task.

In those jungles of manuscripts in the two main collections of Clare's papers at the Northampton Public Library and the Peterborough Museum, beautiful manuscript books like 'The Midsummer Cushion' (showing what Clare could do when, as so rarely in his life, chance helped necessity) lie side by side with volumes of essay-scraps; poem-drafts are mixed up with letter-drafts and autobiography; sometimes four or five drafts, only slightly variant, of poems and of letters remain. All these circumstances contribute to confound an editor, and lead him from his duty.

It may be useful to record here what we know of the whereabouts or fate of Clare manuscripts. Apart from the two main collections at Peterborough and Northampton, there are smaller collections in the Bodleian, the British Museum, and the Norris Library at St. Ives, Huntingdon.

Of Clare papers that may remain 'at large', first and foremost are the letters to Mrs. Emmerson. The sentimental, religiously hortatory, but scrupulous replies to these are in the British Museum. Not a clue has so far yielded anything hopeful concerning Clare's to her. Mrs. Emmerson, dying before the

13

Married Women's Property Act, left no will. Thomas Emmerson, in 1855, left no mention of Clare letters. It therefore seems increasingly likely, that in spite of Mrs. Emmerson's intention to publish them, the many Emmerson letters have been destroyed.

Since George Darley burnt all his unpublished papers, no letters to Darley remain, except the one which strayed into the Taylor letters and so to Northampton, and the unsent one of 1830, at Peterborough.

The Radstock letters remain untraced, as do most of those to E. V. Rippingille, Van Dyk, Behnes Burlowe, Cunningham, and Elizabeth Kent, and also, apart from one in the British Museum, those important Inskip Asylum letters of 1841-9.

The Symons manuscript, the extent of which is unknown, seen by Arthur Symons for his Selection of Clare in 1908, was in the possession of E. D. Brooks of Minneapolis, till his death in 1917; it was then thought to have been bought for the Henry Huntington Library. But, though the New York Public Library has one Clare letter and the Houghton Library one letter, the Henry Huntington Library now has no Clare manuscripts at all. All trace of the Symons papers seems, for the moment, to have vanished.

Some of the 'Nature' letters, of which Clare intended to make his 'Biographies of Birds and Flowers', are in the hands of a New York private collector, together with some poems.

Manuscripts which have passed through Messrs. Sotheby's hands in the last twenty years include the important ninety-six letters of the Brooke-Taylor collection, printed in this volume, those lent to us by Mr. M. Buxton Forman and by Mr. Green-Armytage, and three letters to Cunningham, bought by Messrs. Elkin Mathews, resold, and, to date, lost sight of. The Cary letters, seen by Mr. R. W. King in 1925, purchased by Messrs. Birrell and Garnett from Sotheby's in 1929, have also, so far, eluded discovery; finally, at least eight known others remain in the hands of booksellers.

In the following volume of letters, then, the major number comes from the Brooke-Taylor Northampton manuscripts. These comprise most of the letters sent by Clare to Taylor and Hessey between 1819 and 1837. Another group comes from the Beattie manuscripts, also part of the Northampton collection, and containing the Asylum letters, sent and unsent. Still another group contains those letters handed by Taylor to Frederick Martin for his work in 1865, printed by Mr. Edmund Blunden in *Sketches in the Life of John Clare* (1931), and also housed at Northampton. Apart from the eight Holland letters in the Norris Library at St. Ives, the one to Weston among the Bloomfield papers in the British Museum, the odd one of the lost Inskip letters also in the British Museum, the draft-letter to Allen in the Bodleian, those scattered up and down the manuscripts in both Northampton and Peterborough collections, the rest have been collected from miscellaneous sources outside, all of which are recorded in the alphabetical index of correspondents and letters at the end of this book.

The present volume is, then, a representative collection; 249 in all, perhaps half Clare's known letters. Except for those printed in *Sketches in the Life of John Clare*, the extracts given in *John Clare: A Life* (1932), the Inskip letter of 1824, and the Cary excerpts, they are published here for the first time. The Emmerson letters, if found, would, with the rest at large, merit a second volume of like size.

It is hoped that not too great a strain will be put upon reader and student by printing these letters, unpunctuated and uncorrected—as exactly as possible as he wrote them. We 'take liberty' to present Clare as he was.

There are unavoidable inconsistencies inherent in such a decision. During his long near-submergence in Helpstone's cultural and intellectual backwaters, with no one at hand with whom to discuss standards and methods of precision, Clare admitted that he gave 'no brush of correction' to letter-writing. There were abortive efforts to tidy spelling, under the 1820 encouragement of success, and again, in 1826, under the sting of Taylor's statement that he could not bring out *The Shepherd's Calendar* because the manuscripts took so much time editing. But both these efforts can be observed petering out. Clare wrote both 'dont' and 'don't'; sometimes 'Ill', sometimes 'I'll'; now 'somthing', occasionally, later, 'something'; most often he used 'then' for the comparative conjunction and adverb, but at times the standard 'than'; participles and past tenses he frequently spelt '–d', but after about 1826, '–ed'; 'coud' and 'woud', about that date, more frequently became 'could' and 'would'; 'ie' and 'ei' remained unsorted to the end; 'possess', 'necessary', 'lately', and 'disappointment' were also bugbears which came in for different treatment on different occasions. His sentences are often long and rambling; his syntax occasionally faulty to the orthodox; his verbs should sometimes be plural to agree with their plural subject; but, to post-Mallarmé-Stein-Joyce-reading eyes, almost always he is magnificently unambiguous.

We are aware, too, of inadequacies that may become apparent as the reader progresses. There was, in Clare, until the self-reckoning that began about 1824, almost Keats's 'proverbial negligence' in the matter of dates. Only therefore by inside clues and conjecture can many of the letters in the crowded periods 1820–3, in 1827, and again in 1831–2, be put in sequence. It is hoped that no important lapse has occurred there. Where seals have been cut away, where there is a gap in the manuscript, or where an obvious slip of Clare's makes the sense shaky, liberty has been used to supply a word or word-ending, [ ].

Clare was twenty-four when these letters begin, at the outset of his meteoric rise to fame. There is therefore little of the story of his early poetic growth here. This he embodied in the account of his life which he sent to Taylor in 1821, and which Mr. Blunden published in *Sketches in the Life of John Clare, by Himself* (1931). Whether, as has been thought, Clare wrote and finished a second fuller account seems to us doubtful. If he did not progress beyond the 'I have nearly finished my Life' of the letter to E. V. Rippingille, of May 1826 (unfortunately not in our collection), only the vigilant piecing together of the fragments (many of which were printed in *John Clare: A Life*), together with the *Sketches*, can give the complete account of his early life. There is, too, little of his four London visits in the following letters. The account of these, besides what Mr. Blunden has already printed, needs assembling in full from the vast Peterborough fragments. The most significant records of his two Asylum periods are, of course, absent too. They are to be found, besides the 'Journey out of Essex', in *Poems of John Clare's Madness*, edited by Mr. Geoffrey Grigson (1950). But

16

the letters of those periods provide an invaluable commentary on poems like 'I live in love, sun of undying light . . .' 'Invite to Eternity', 'I Am', and others of his greatest. When the 'Autobiography' or 'Life' as Clare severally calls it, up to the 1824 London visit, and the correctly printed 'Journal' of 1824–5 and the 'Journey out of Essex' are added to these letters, then the full, first-hand account of Clare's life will be available.

In Clare's letters there is, because of the immediacy he felt necessary to the truth of writing, something of the same 'living' quality as in his poetry. True, he was, as he wrote to Cary (30 December 1824), 'far from a close reasoner in prose'. This 'living' quality is particularly evident in the drafts of unsent letters, all those not definitely marked 'sent' in this volume. But in all his letters, sent and unsent, the reader is allowed to see Clare's mind at only one remove from the unceasing flux of internal thought. Here he may watch all the hopeful beginnings decline, through struggle and inevitable disillusion, into schizophrenia. He will perceive Clare's joy, in the prospect of the spirit's freedom success might bring, disintegrate slowly, during years of frustration and poverty, into—astonishingly!—fore-accepted madness. These letters illumine the process. They outline Clare's decision, after the lionizing of 1820 had ceased to deceive him into thinking a living might be made out of his writing, to remain steadfast to his inspiration, to take the consequences. Whether he could, with the common sense (or divided loyalties) of a J. H. Reynolds, have renounced or reduced his poetry, to support his family more adequately as a normal labourer, it is idle to debate. Shoe-making and poetry nearly drove Bloomfield mad. The idea of achieving independence by writing looked so possible in the light of that same common sense that it died hard in Clare, of course. There were L.E.L., Mrs. Hemans, Cunningham, Hogg, and many others with the power to make money. Had not Crabbe, not so long before, found Burke? Had not Burns cleared 'Two or three hundred'? True, Clare did not always succeed in getting paid even what he was owed. But the difference in tone in the letters, after Clare's first prolonged mental illness of 1823, the gathered and reaffirmed determination to stand by what he called the truth of love, 'love's eternity', even though such a decision meant poverty, failure, misery, and ultimate madness for himself—all this, which the perceptive reader will glean from these letters, throws new light on the poet hitherto regarded as a spontaneous minor lyricist incapable of any body of imaginative statement concerning his poetic purpose.

Every writer of stature probably has to take decisions similar to Clare's, without knowing how formidable the consequences may be. Like Blake, Clare found himself against the current of his world. He had not Burns's physical exuberance and shrill brawling delight in baiting Holy Willies. He was physically frail. He had not Hogg's self-saving vanity. His nostalgia suggests, perhaps, an ominous rigidity of mind: until we remember that the Helpstone of his childhood *had* gone for ever in one of the most violent changes in English history.

Gilchrist, a sound, disinterested judge, unlike Drury, always stressed Clare's intelligence and balance. He said he discerned no unbalance. In these letters of between 1817 and 1837, we find abundant commentary on his mental condition, ranging from the 'confounded lethargy of low spirits' alternating with 'hopes to stand on my own bottom as a poet', to the 'my future prospects seem to be no sleep—a general debility—a stupid and stunning apathy or lingering madness . . .' But there is also a continuous background of evidence that Clare was well aware of his life as a whole, of his poetic aim, and of the odds against him.

Mr. Geoffrey Grigson has noted, in by far the most percipient account of Clare's mind yet written, that the quality of a mind, once overtaken by madness, is changed. There is no longer any sanity. The controls, once broken through, are swept away. Clare's appeals for help echo between the years 1822 and 1827: to Mrs. Emmerson, Taylor, Dr. Darling. But Mary Unwins and Polly Thomsons—friends who can take so much of the burden—are rare. Mrs. Emmerson, despite her great kindness and friendship, was not Clare's mental companion. There was an immense social gulf between them that was never bridged. The enigmatic Taylor stayed the course, in a real, if limited, sense, but not the kindly, pompous Hessey.

And all had their own difficulties in no small degree. With Patty, though Clare was loyal enough to keep her his second

18

wife even in madness, there may have been, in the deepest
sense, no 'consummation' of the marriage. In spite of their nine
children, and Clare's love for them, there was little in Patty
that could absorb any of that deep universal love that was in
him. What is important to perceive, after Mr. Grigson's analysis, is the utter loneliness surrounding the clear vision that
led up to Clare's collapse in 1837. Incidents that later become
tangled in crazy delusions are seen afar like mirages down the
horizons of the years. The suspicions and cautions of other
'identities' are observed pressing on his, which clung so
tenaciously to eternal love and trust. His loss of pride in his
own exquisitely sympathetic 'identity' is painful to witness.

And the cleavage is clear. The letter of March 1831, quite
different from some of those immediately following, has the
ring of complete clarity. In 1831, Clare still knew his state of
mind—though Taylor, Mrs. Emmerson, Dr. Darling, in that
early-nineteenth century era of retributive religion, had for
years been persuading him his ills were due to drink and over-
eating. He himself had gaily fostered the first myth by such
statements as: 'I am damnation drunk' (3 April 1821). He had
written a long letter and did not *sound* drunk! There is the
damning £7, which 'grins at my Folly on the greasy manteltree at the Bell', in 1823: a lapse in 1827, in elation over the
long-delayed *Shepherd's Calendar*. But after 1824, obviously
little was spent on drink. Against the statement that psychotics
do not know their impending fate, there is an array of evidence
that Clare, as close as 1831, saw, and recognized, like Swift,
but in complete isolation, whilst still sane, his approaching
madness. The first mention of the word is his.

Soon after that, there are signs of growing unawareness, a
failure to remember. He no longer knows his own condition, as
he did, in his periods of recovery before. But the amazing thing
is, as well as the deepening of the poetic impulse, the un-
alterable attachment to eternal values. This gives the Asylum
letters, even the very latest, their deceptive serenity, their
nearly sane resignation, perhaps their uniqueness: 'Dear Sir—
I am in a Madhouse I quite forget your name or who you are.
I have nothing to communicate or tell of &'—then the jerk
backward, the betrayal (he had said as early as 1820 his mind

was the 'disappointment' as well as the ecstasy)—'why I am shut up I dont know.'

It has been said that Clare is a small poet, belonging to another sphere than Wordsworth: that 'Wordsworth's incessant effort to comprehend experience would itself have been incomprehensible to Clare'. Clare's letters show him failing to develop what may be called 'discipline': failing, too, to arm his mind against worry, against increasingly heavy responsibility, against his ideals. Witness his over-grateful leaning on Taylor's friendship, letters, literary judgements: his advice nearly always contradicted in the next breath: 'excuse my conscieted meddling': witness his humility in his letter to Powell, and those to Alaric Watts. But witness, also, his determined loyalty to Taylor, even through Taylor's delays and loss of interest. Witness his agonized attempts to keep the peace among his squabbling supporters. Trouble and human misinterpretation moved him too much, as the assailants of the everyday world moved Virginia Woolf too much. Clare could not, as Mrs. Woolf did, cast his life away: he 'loved the time too well'. A decision like his—to stake all on spiritual freedom—cowed Blake only sufficiently to send him further into the land of shifting symbols. But this daring to be true to the life in him, driving the creative artist always deeper, even though not intellectually stated, is seen to be in Clare's letters with more deliberation than in the poems. Perhaps, as one critic in 1949 suggests, it says as much as 'the mighty harmonies' of poets already fully recognized as great.

LETTERS OF JOHN CLARE
1818–1837

LETTERS OF JOHN CLARE
1818–1837

To Isaiah Knowles Holland*

Addressed: To a Gentlen.an Unknown.
[sent]

[1817]

To The Gentleman (a Stranger to me) Who has taken the *trouble* (as I am Informed) to Enquire after a *Clown* who as yet *Slumbers* in *Obscurity* and perhaps whose *merits* deserves no better *Fate*—For his *Condesension* & notice I return him my most hearty *thanks* & *Acknowledgements* & if he thinks it worth his while to *come over* (as I understand he intended) I shall think myself much *honoured* by his *Company.*

I remain &c

JOHN CLARE

To Holland

Addressed: The Gentleman at Mrs Clarks Northboro.
[sent]

[1817]

SIR

I have sent you the tale† as promisd I would have corrected it but repetitions are irksome & tireing & I could not set myself to it—you will excuse it

---

* See Biographical Memoranda.
† 'The Fate of Amy': *Poems Descriptive of Rural Life and Scenery* (1820).

23

The verse you hinted—I have corrected in this manner

The flowers the sultry summer kills
Springs milder suns restore
But innosence that fickle charm!
Blooms once—& blooms no more.

As trifling Anecdotes are ever pleasing to Literary curiosity
—I send you the origin of the tale—
I heard it related (some years ago) by an old Woman in this
manner—'The poor Girls name was Amy' said she '& as fine a
Girl as ever was seen she livd at "Garners Farm" (now call'd)
& at this time belonging to Mr Clark But she was ruin'd by a
base young man & went early one morning from the house (half
drest) (Curiosity remarks her red pettycoat which she had on
when found) to the Pond below in the Close which' says the
simple narrator 'was call'd when I was a child "Amys Pond"
& she lov'd the fellow so much that she could not rest afterwards but was often seen walking round the pond in her red
pettycoat even in the daytime!—till latley—' here the old lady
ended thumping her stick several times on the ground to confirm
its reality & boasted her remembrance as witness
    You will see by this that I have deviated away from the
original--I once when a boy had the tale in another manner as
near to the truth as possible—under the title of the 'Haunted
Pond'—it as now lost or I would have sent it—but this crampt
the imagination (truth in my opinion in poetry always does)—I
therefore wrote it in the manner you see it gave my imagination
free scope—
    New pieces as soon as Written you shall have for perusal—
                Sir
          With the greatest Respect
              Yours &c
                   JOHN CLARE

The incorrectness will be excused as it was wrote hastily this
morning when I had no leisure for thought

To Holland

[sent]

[1817]

Rev. Sir

I send all the pieces[1] I can find you shall have the rest as soon as ready & all I write for the future—All that hurts me is the Nessesity of taking to hard Labour again—after all my hopes to the Contrary—A Clergyman of the Church of England propos'd raising a Subsn for me but as he spoke very coldly of pieces I sent him my proud spirit declin'd the offer & despis'd such unintentional humanity when at the same time Like the Poet Marvell I had not Sixpence to bless me

When I know the fate of my book you shall have a Lampoon on that Learn'd & humane Gent.* who while he offer'd to foster the branch with promises was actually crushing the blossom of Genius in oerwhelming Ruin—

Yours

JOHN CLARE

To Holland

[sent]

[1817]

Sir

I Return one of the Books—Shenstone is a Good Poet but his Pastorals (as I think) are improperly called so the rural Names of Damon Delia Phillis &c & rural objects Sheep Sheepfolds &c&c are the only things that give one the slightest glimps of the Species of Poetry which the Title claims—

Putting the Correct Language of the Gentleman into the mouth of a Simple Shepherd or Vulgar Ploughman is far from Natural—Pope for Harmony of Numbers surpasses all I have ever seen—Your Criticisms of the 'Trifles' sent would oblige

---

[1] See page 330, note 1.

* Undoubtedly the Rev. Mr. Twopenny, of Little Casterton, of whom Clare's lampoon begins: 'Twopenny his wisdom is, and Twopenny his fame is . . .' (*Life*). But in the prose notes for his 'Autobiography' Clare says it was not he himself who sent the poems to Twopenny, but Edward Drury, the Stamford bookseller.

—'The Jewell of All' 'To an April Daisy' & 'The Winds' are
the Productions of a Moment & as such are always the best in
my Opinion—Seemingly happy Suggestions & easily attaind—
Yours
JOHN CLARE

To Holland

Addressed: Revd. Mr Holland, Northbro.
[sent]

[1818]

SIR

I return 'Burns' & am greatly Obligd to you for the kindness—its my Opinion that he's an Exelent Poet & far Exceeds
Ramsay[1] I have sent an Imitation (at least in the Measure. no
other ways I know of) of 1 his familiar Epistles—I was charm'd
with the Manner of Expressing his homespun thoughts & have
attempted accordingly—You are a Gent: of Learning Your
criticisms of Pieces I send you will be thankfully recieved—
Your Opinion of this is requested if you please to grant the
Condscension—I ask not for Flattery Just as you think Sir I
wish you to Speak

I look up to you as the first Encourager of My Obscure
productions & heartily wish I had known you sooner I send you
the 'Epistle'[2] & intend to send every thing I write in future
tho it may be very Insignificant as I am going to reasume my
Hard Labour—if Poets in General had no better Encouragement to write then I have at present—I think they must be
mad to pursue it—I intend to bid a farewell to Muses for the
present Sir your Exertions in my behalf will always be lookd
on with Gratitude—Your presenting the pieces I send you
among your Learned Acquaintance might be to my advantage I
am in no fear but you will act for the best—If fate Ordains me
the fortune to present a 2 Ext: to the Public—I shall ask the
favour of a Dedication from you I look not at Riches—Tis
Sense & Learning that gains my Esteem
Yours
JOHN CLARE

To John Taylor[1]*

Addressed: John Taylor, 93 Fleet St., London
[*sent*]

Taylor's date: 'I believe Nov 24 1818.
Gilchrists Ded. is dated Nov 22 & it arrived
the day before this'

DEAR SIR

I was very pleased with the dedication which Mr. Gilchrist wrote for me on Sunday but after a little Consideration percieved it was too Refined & Elegant to flow from the pen of a Clown & as such unsuitable for the Book Altogether. Therefore I have done one in my own way above which your Taste will model in shape most Suitable

I am
Yours
With Respectfull
Regard
JOHN CLARE

P.S. Mr. Drury has not yet recieved the Book you promised & I am very anxious to see it particularly the 'Memoir'

[There follows:] A Dedication To the Right Honourable Charles William Lord Viscount Milton . . . [not in P.D.]

To Edward Bell Drury*

[1819]

MR DRURY

Please to take Notice that the following Verse in 'Evening' is a Plajaring

Nor do I earnestly beleive
Such things could ever be
But superstition does decieve
Far wiser folks than me

---

* See Biographical Memoranda.   † See Biographical Memoranda.

After is this

> *But superstition still decieves*
> *& Fancys still prevails*
> *While stooping genius een beleives*
> *Her evil [slandering?] Tales*

A Gent: of Casterton shewed me the passage in 'Poems in England' by a Native of the West Indias' How I come to hit a parallel almost in the same words is unaccountable as I never saw the Book in my Life—All corrections I send while they can be corrected as desird to be punctually noticd—Did you mind Corrections in 'Noon'[1] Last Letter

A Poet at Exton is Started up your Information wether good or bad as soon as possible—Wether he pubs on the Spectackles of Books become an Imitation or writes from Nature Original —Inform me—

'Poems on Several Subjects'
By S. Messing'[2]

Yours

JOHN CLARE

To Taylor

[*sent*]

About 20 December 1819

SIR

The Meeting is several months old & the one in the Book varies a great deal from my improved one which I here send you, which is very little different however from what it was when first Written

THE MEETING[1]

Here we meet too soon to part . . .

To Holland

[sent]

[1819]

SIR

I Return your Book with my thanks I have many New Pieces but no time to Copy them—My First Attempts at Poetry are nearly Published—They have this Title 'Pastoral Sketches' in Poems Songs Ballads & Sonnets by John Clare 'A Northamptonshire Pheasant' Printed for Taylor & Hessey London—I could have wishd to begin a Correspondence with you from Casterton[1] but dare not venture for fear of Offending I am now writing 'The Woodman' in the manner of Burns' Saturday night you Recollect giving me the hint The last verse concludes in a Dedication to you I hope you'll alow its Insertion[2] I send it in Letter—You was my first & best Friend & as such I shall always Esteem you—Drury wishd me to mention that when you next came to Stamford he should be happy to have the pleasure of your Company

Yours Ever

JOHN CLARE

P.S. Return to Casterton on Wednesday I could wish an Answer by Return—I would have sent the Last Verse of the Woodman[3] but cannot Reccolect it at present but you may expect the whole Piece the first Opertunity

The Following Pieces are either Written or now Writing—

Pause before the Battle[4]
Woodman[3]
To Solitude[3]
Many Songs & Ballads[4]
Thunder Storm[3]
Winter[3]
Autumnal Day[4]
Autumn[3]
Ways of a Village[4]
To a Sprig of Barley[4]
Royce Wood[4]
Dissapointment[3]

29

SIR

I hope you will Excuse my Scraps of Paper but you know it is a Scarcity with me

J.C.

To Holland

[sent]

[1819]

SIR

I send the Concluding Verse & Dedication of the Woodman If you will not agree to its insertion it must be notic'd as the Piece will be at London in a few days—

Holland to thee the humble ballads sent
Thee who for poor mens welfare oft has prayed
Whose tongue did ne'er belye its good intent
Preacher as well in practice as in trade
(Alas too often moneys business made)
O May the wretch thats now in darkness living
The Bibles comforts hear by thee display'd
And many a Woodmans family forgiven
Have cause to bless thy guiding hand that led the
*   way to Heaven*

I return 'Pope' & thank you for the kindness of lending it me—I have a Sonnet adress'd to you but dont know whether it will come out in the Book this time I have not a Copy or would send it

JOHN CLARE

Any Poet Rural or Pastoral which you have to Lend would be taken as a great Kindness—Have you Bloomfields 'Banks of Wye'[1]—he is coming out again this Winter but what Poem I dont know—

I have all his Works but the above

JOHN CLARE

To Holland

[sent]

Dated by Holland: '1819. on the eve
of the first pub. of his Poems'

SIR

Lord Milton is come home would you do me the favour to
acquaint him with the Publication of 'Trifles' You are a
Gentleman of Learning Your word will go a great Way in such
matters & as I can find no one in the circle of my acquaintance
& Friendship that appears better qualified for the Undertaking
I eagerly solicit your Condesencion & rest assured of your
agreement thereto—Please to hint the Dedication if he will not
agree to it I am undone but I am in no fear as to that When
you come to Inform him that I am the son of the Lame Man at
Helpstone Please to hint Likewise the Intention of Sending me
to the National School to enable me to act in the Capacity of a
School master which has dropped from the Want of Friends—

P.S. the sooner done the better as I am affraid Drury will
Interest himself in that matter[1]

A Shabby Booksellers[2] Word will be no advantage to me as
Self Interest is the Cause—What copies you take to Lord
Milton please to write over again as they are the only Copies
& he may lose them 'The Suprise'[3] & 'Epistle to a Friend'[4]
will be sufficient—Return the 'April Daisy' 'Jewel of All' 'To
the Winds' 'Sonnet' 'To Hope'[4] &c what you have done
with—send your remarks for.correction I am going to Casterton
& it will be an amusement

A Gentleman in Stamford has kindly offerd to Put any of my
Pieces to Music which I may oblige him with—'The Jewel of
All' I think will suit him Your Opinion—

                                              Sir
                                              Yours
                                        JOHN CLARE

To Octavius Gilchrist[1]*

[sent]

[January 1820]

SIR

I return 'Wordsworth' & acknowledge the favour with many thanks I have been very idle this week—I have nothing to send you the frost having kept me in the Corner which is a very bad place at least for me to lay ryhmes together in—however rather than forfeit a promise wi Mrs G. I have continued to bodge up a few 'Songs' & 'Ballads' which I send on a seperate sheet—I have troubled you wi a note for Mr Taylor it is to request a few 'Books' to give to my friends before they are published[2]—I Beg the favour 'Lord Byron' that Vol which has the smaller poems Mrs G. knows it.

I Remain
Sir
wi the greatest Respect
Your humble Servant
JOHN CLARE

[There follows:]

TO POESY.
O Sweetly wild & witching poesy . . .

To Gilchrist

Note on other side: 'Red brompton Stock for Mrs Emmerson seed 1826'[1]

[sent]

[January 1820]

SIR

I return 'Byrone' 1 Vol & beg the Favour of the other a little longer wishing to read 'Child Harold' a Second time I am anxious to Enquire—What says the 'London Mag?'[2]

Sunday was a bad day or I should have been happy to gratify Curiosity many trifles begun but never finished—have done

* See Biographical Memoranda.

nothing this week—only erected a 'Castle in the Air' having
got a new M.S.S. Book from D—I dasht it wi a 'Title Page'

'Songs Ballads & Gossip Stories'

but have not entered a line into it further nor dont know when
I shall—I have seen 'Title Page' 'Dedication' & 'Glossary' of
my book Taylor wishes for no Dedication I have therefore with
a gloomy resolve agreed to it & Crosd it out altogether—if
your parcel contains anything for me I beg leave to caution
you not to send it to Drurys—if any books come open the
Parcel if you think well & if one be thought worthy of Mrs
G's acceptance she will oblige me by taking it—the rest you
may keep while convenient to send them—the humble ambition
of gratitude if it may be called so will be gratifyd by offering
her small tribute—Respect to you—in a Book

Sir
Your Humble Servant

JOHN CLARE

To Taylor

[sent]

Stamf January 17 1820

DEAR SIR

I thank you for the Books you have sent me they are such
as I long wisht to see—Mr Drury has a great No of M.S.S.
which he is arranging & will I suppose forward to you before
long I have in contemplation a 'Poem' on another Self-murder
(as Amy*) measured 10.s. Intituled 'Cross Roads' has any
hit of it before if so hint it to M.D.† You said nothing Respecting the 'Peasant Boy' perhaps your silence is better than your
advice in this matter—I am become weary of it & shall give
it in I have 'Lodge house'‡ 'Soldiers Return'‡ 2 tales Ready
for your Inspection & Remain
Your humble Servant

JOHN CLARE

---

* 'The Fate of Amy': *Poems Descriptive of Rural Life and Scenery.*
† Drury.   ‡ Unpublished.

To Gilchrist

[sent]

January 21, 1820

SIR

I intended to send you a Copy of my Poems but am very poorly & cannot get over to Stamford for one but I will send you the verses I meant shoud accompany it.

JOHN CLARE

[There follows:]
Address to a Copy of 'Clare's Poems' sent to O. Gilchrist. Esqr.

To thine and mine our topmost friends . . .
[3 stanzas (unpublished)]

[Then there follows:]
THE JEWEL OF ALL
Ye gay blinking daisies ablooming so sweetly . . .
[3 stanzas (also unpublished)]

Not willing to brake a promise i send it patcht up by memory & had I known it was so bad i woud not have mentioned it— I think Taylor has a Copy.

To Gilchrist

[sent]

Winter Helpstone.
[1820]

SIR

I am happy to think I can return Mrs G. a favour I have done it accordingly I am very near being laid up what with the anxiety of the fate of the Book & a bad winter cough it has nearly confined me to my bed tho it is not a little that will do it Friday was a bad day & my old conveyance was stopt—but as soon as I got your letter I made shift to crawl over to Stamford when Drury had but 3 copies, but I was resolved not to be disappointed I have presented a Copy with a few Rhymes to the Lady which I hope will be acceptable & in return beg a 'foolish request' of you as I have no copy by me I have sent the verses I intended should accompany it & to gratify my vanity hope you will paste it on the flyleaf of yours & tho hardly worth the cost I have fust it up to be in hopes of a gilded coat

Your humble Servt

JOHN CLARE

SIR

Thinking you might want to forward this to the lady I sent it by my mother to-day,

J.C.

An ansr to say it came safe will be acceptable

J.C.

To Taylor

Addressed: Messrs. Taylor and Hessey, Fleet St,, London.
[*sent*]

Helpstone Feb. 24 1820

SIR

Just to acknowledge the Hon. Lords[1] Kindness I send this note and you may tell him I have not Goldsmith Cowper I have but it is not half his poems being *Wartons*[2] pocket one. I often wished to see Haleys[2] but his lordship will know best when you inform him I cannot tell you about Miltons yet but shall when I get to London as I am coming with O.G. soon so you may wait till then when I shall have better News still to tell you about Burghley. Drury and I are not very good friends Then I have something to say to you but cannot while I come you may see by my writing what a taking I am in.

Adieu but not without telling you what ever luck I meet with in this world I shall look to you as the cause and as such I wish to reward you in some way or other.

JOHN CLARE

To Taylor

Addressed: Messrs Taylor & Hessey, 93 Fleet Street, London
[*sent*]

Helpstone Wednesday
[March 1820]

DEAR TAYLOR

Excuse the warm expression—according to promise I send
you a note to tell you of my safe arrival home[1] & glad enough
I am for I was weary of noise & bustle I send you 'Solitude' The
'Lodge house' next time Lord M. flatters me I doubt in saying
many parts of it please him much as I found a note to that
purpot when I got home my book is to be sent me in a weeks
time give Mr Hessey a hint of the fiddle & if you please you
may send me the Head of Lord Radstock[2] as you proposed give
my sincere Respects to Keats[3] & tell him I had a great desire
to see him & that I like his first Vol of Poems much I coud
point many beauties in my thinking if I had time but as soon
as I got home I found the tables in the Hut coverd with Letters
18 in No 10 of which I found it nessessary to answer so you will
excuse the hasty scrawl—I must not however forget to tell you
to give my respects to Messrs Reynolds[4] Woodhouse[5] Percival[6] Hilton[7] Dewint Mrs D & little Girl & all whom I may
forget in great haste

Your humbl Servt

JOHN CLARE

(With Speed) Send 2 or 3 Copies of 2nd Edit as Lady F.[8]
wants 2 directly

To Taylor

Addressed: Messrs. Taylor & Hessey, 93 Fleet St., London.
[*sent*]

March 19. 1820

DEAR TAYLOR

I recieved the parcel by coach this day but the other is
miscarried & I fear lost will you take the trouble to question

the waggoner about it the next time hes in London—as to
Drury I think we are under no obligations to him for anything
I should always wisht him to have been a partner in the things
I publish but as he cannot speak well of me when he has no
longer hopes of interest in my concerns I think I can have done
with him altogether in my next which I shall not esitate to do
I was mentioned by somebody in Stamford Town Hall this week
(it is from good authority) & Drury I suppose answered him
strictly 'no more Clare for me' you know thats enough I think
he is paid very well for his journeys to Helpston & I think to
pay myself with resentment is to wipe out his name at the
bottom of the next book—If you & I was to part tomorrow I
dont think you woud find reasons to say anything against me
as he does shoud you I never set no price on my writing to
him I always humoured him with new pieces as soon as he wrote
& went to Stamford weeks and weeks only on his account when
I had more need been at work still I dont wish nor mean to
speak ill of him to no one I shall always respect him as long
as I live but when he got his agreement upon foot I quickly
grew jealous of his fidelity and resolved to keep my pieces more
to myself you will no doubt say this thought was timly put in
practice after the hints I gave you at London I doubt you will
think I trouble you with letters but the 'Lodge house' was just
posted off when I got your letter speaking of the parcells—
You Talk of cutting me about in 'Solitude' I can only say have
mercy I have provd your judgement & patiently submit—my
lodge house I think will be above your thumbs & Keats' too it
as undergone the Critiscism of my father & mother & several
rustic Neighbours of the Town and all aprove it you will agree
they beat your polite Critics in that low nature which you never
prove but by reading & which them & I have daily witnessed
in its most subtle branches so much for this—you will laugh at
my conceit but dont humour it by looking over what you may
think faults—I always heartily wish for your plain judgement
about everything you know that—now for something else there
is a murmur in Stamford about putting in force a subscription
for me of 100 Guineas I told O.G. at the fair but he knew
nothing of it tho the person that told me had it from the Mayor
himself. tell O.G. your self that if he would have the goodness to

put a paragraph in Drakards 'News' it would soon be put forward you might hint it as your own opinion—if Lord R would do this in the London papers instead of his huffs perhaps it would produce me a benefit—This hint is for your opinion— now I will give you my opinion—if by subscription I could get £1000!!!! dont be struck I should be satisfied and should want not a farthing more £50 a year would keep me capital & I should have no dread to look forward this is not the case now I even shudder to peep at whats to come I cannot write a line in this suspence & never shall while I percieve my doom To turn out good or bad Excuse my freedom it is always my way to unbosom my thoughts to friends which I believe as such tho I know I have paid dearly for it by turning to you at a venture I dont hesitate to say anything just as I think I speak to you & always shall

Farwell

P.S. Respects too Messrs Hessey Hilton Mr & Mrs Dewint & little girl Reynolds Keats Woodhouse & all who I may forget Pattys best respects to you & wishes very much to send a piece of Bride Cake tho she thinks it will [cost] you too much carriage but I shall venture out I could say much more if paper & time would hold out

Yours

JOHN CLARE

Sunday
Helpston

To Gilchrist

[sent]

[April 1820]

DEAR SIR

The bearer is 'Ben Close' he will bring the Book Case & I think safe—Lord Milton sent for me on Monday to meet him in the fields—round oak spring but you know I was with you what he wanted me for I cant say but I think it was to choose a bit of ground for a cottage mother gave his servant the letter I told you of & the next day his servant came with some books

viz 'Pope' 'Dryden' & Johnsons Dicty the 8vo abridged 14/-
the poems are pocket size one 'Wartons Edit & the other
'Cookes'—you have some more of my anecdotes—& if you
intend to interleave a copy as you proposed of my poems dont
be long as I am in the kip for writing such trifles now—I cant
think of no more things in my life so this must finish

Yours &c &c

JOHN CLARE

I have received my $\frac{1}{4}$s Pension[1] from Mr. Adams I am desired
to come to Stamford every $\frac{1}{4}$ to take it there—I think I must
be bound to write an Ode to the Marquis as I am certainly his
Laureat now by profession—Please to put James Simpson in
mind of a good fair jar of Ink—you must mind I am quite set
up as to money matters & you as well know I shall not be much
friendly with work till[2] it lasts

J.C.

I have had rare news from Lord R he has turned out honourable he has collected nearly £100 so I hear from Taylor this
morning A Guest from Trinity Hall Cambridge[3] paid me a visit
yesterday & came purposely. Flattering verses teems in upon
me fast inspired with £1 notes these are pieces you know I
must praise & I intend not to be sparing of it now I am got
idle dont wait for more anecdotes

Ever yours

JOHN CLARE
Thursday Morn

To Chauncy Hare Townshend*

[sent]

Helpstone 1820
[March]

SIR

You will doubtless be surprised at my writing after you so
soon† but it is to give a grateful acknowledgment for the favour

* See Biographical Memoranda.
† Townshend, then a student at Trinity Hall, paid his first visit to Clare in
March 1820.

you left behind Tho I doubt your fine Sonnet flatters me too
much be as it may I have vanity to be proud of such notice who
would not I am afraid your journey met with little satisfaction
to repeat it if it did I should be glad of a longer Interview at
some future period—I have little more to say at this time only
when you have time to communicate anything to me as to
advice in my unknown change of life I shall think myself
honoured with the kindness

Yours

JOHN CLARE

Please to direct for John Clare Helpstone left at Octavius
Gilchrist Stamford

To James Augustus Hessey*

*Addressed: Messrs. Taylor and Hessey Booksellers
to his Royal Highness Prince Cobourgh,
93 Fleet Street, London.*
[sent]

Helpston April 2 1820

DEAR HESSEY.

I am happy in having for the first time an oppertunity of
addressing a letter to you in ans^r to yours accompanying the
fiddle parcel which I resieved last night (1st of April) I had not
time to put it in tune but I can agree with your opinion readily
that I think it is not got worse with age I shall not fill my letter
with thanks neither to you nor Mr. Taylor for his present as I
am obliged to do to others tis fulsome flattery downright I shall
only tell you I esteem both gifts gratfully and believe that your
fiddle will remain with me as a standard for life tho I shall not
despise my old one I may lay it on the shelf but cannot sell it
as it is like an old Friend when I behold it. it reminds me of what
is past many pains and pleasures mingled together in banished
days—I have found out the No 35 Fleet Street it is Mr
Hoar[1] a Banker as I have been so pesterd with fussing puffs
from booksellers chiefly country I thought this was one and

---

* See Biographical Memoranda.

some time shall send M.T. a copy of his letter with my
Ans^r which for the first time I purposly copied

Lord Radstock has promised me 'Curries Burns'[2] did you
know of it it is a good book I think and will be as valuable a
present as his Lordships first 'Blair' dont forget to hint that
I am highly pleased at the mention he made of such a present
in his last letters for I do asure you Expectation is on the look
out for it every day here I must stick Mr Hilton tell him I
dont know what hes about with my pictures I am a blunt fellow
and if he is likewise short questions will please him best which
I think he is and the most unlike a Londoner I saw all the while
I could not help feeling a sort of friendly gratification at my
first interview he appeared to me like a neighbour of the
Country and when I was told it was Hilton the Painter I was
more supprised then ever as I had heard of him much at Stamford my foolish opinion of these Celebrated London Writers
and Painters was that there was something different to other
men and if M^r H and D took notice of my staring at them so
strictly I dont wonder at it as I did it as a matter of curiosity
to find where the distinction was which the fact is I could not
see you will readily excuse my silly remarks it is only for your
own eye I shall never get that polish which some recomend
to me I cant abide it I write to you and T. as I shoud do to a
Country friend I tell you my most simple opinions of things
that strike me in my own rude way as I shoud have done 3 or 4
years back—dont mention to Hilton what ive said only give
my respects to him and Mr Dewint his wife and little girl
some folks tell me my letters will creep into print and that it is
a serious benefit for me to try to polish and only tell them I
must then make an apollagy to creep after them as a preface
and all will go right—what a polished letter this would be if
it was printed!!!—and my last wild thing to Taylor theres two
specimens for ye.—but as I am in one of my half fits of good
humour I must consider before my papers filled what I have got
to say of information as you will have a long roundabout of
silly blunders and nothing else—I must tell you tho Taylor has
took all the pride away that I had in the poetical line of judging
that I have this last fortnight wrote a good many sonnets 2 of
which to 'Taste'[3] and 'Poetry'[4] I like best I have begun a

Long Poem on Spring[5] but cannot finish it I send Taylor the
only prospectus left he very much desired it so make him pay
for the letter

yours etc.

JOHN CLARE

I have looked in all Drurys letters but not a word T. mentions
in them I had a good mind to send them but though they would
not pay for carriage O.G. wants a prospectus you must not (if
he mentions it) say you had one from me so latly as I said I
had none which I then thought.

N.B. if Lord R. says anything of Burns tell him you have it
as I shoud like it from your shop when you can send it and it
will be a good copy.

To Chauncy Hare Townshend

[sent]

Helpstone April 10 1820

MY DEAR SIR

I shall be very happy to have another opportunity of seeing
you agen & shall certainly not let it slip if possible—I just got
your note as I was starting from Stamford having gone there
yesterday—I left word with Mr. Drury to inform you that I
woud return agen to Stamford on Friday night on purpose of
meeting the pleasure of your company an hour or two—but
recollecting the hazzard of forgetfulness on his part I sent you
the letter after I got home to ensure a certainty of seeing one
whom I shall ever esteem not with a jargon of worded flatterys
but with a heart that feels proud as well as grateful for your
friendship & indebted with additional obligations for every
token of its continuance

Yours etc etc

JOHN CLARE

P.S. I have long been looking for the pleasure of 'Jerusalem'*

* Townshend's fiery poem on the City's destruction, in *Cambridge Prize Poems*
(1817), alongside Macaulay's 'Evening', was being republished with others of
Townshend's poems.

but now think mine will be out first you may have seen them advertised 'The Village Minstrel etc' in 2 Vols which as soon as I get my hands on them shall find the way to 'Trinity Hall' & I hope you will give me the benefit of your partial criticisms on the long poem as I intend to continue it in 'The Ways of the Village' if the present succeeds I have engaged in a matter of song-writing & as a secret to a friend its a thing that gives little pleasure being a matter of course for a livelihood—that poets are always poor is proverbial & that I shall ever belye the proverb is little to be expected—still if they take with the public they will do me good & if not they will do the new publication very little harm—so the consequence is trifling come what will & my postscript is getting longer then my letter I had better put a stop to it so farewell and God bless you

Yours
J.C.

To Taylor

Addressed: Messrs. Taylor and Hessey, 93 Fleet St., London.
[*sent*]

Helpstone [April 1820]¹

DEAR TAYLOR,

You will not write to me so I must take the trouble to force you if I can how is the 2nd Edit going on when do you intend to publish a new vol. The matireials are all ready the M.S.S. are come safe from Milton and O.G. has got them now as soon as he has done with them he sends them to you I suppose with the Chauser and etc. of yours I have recieved a ¼s Pension from burghley I am writing an Ode to the Marquis as I think I must certainly be his Laureat now by profession have you got a Copy of the unpublished M.S.S. which you have if not can you spare the M.S.S. as I think a great many of the pieces with a little alteration might do well at least they may be too good to be lost I have happen of good luck since I heard of you having in this last day or two got about £11 I have had a gentleman from Cambridge purposly to see me he says I am admired at Coledge much and thats not bad News is Mr. Hilton dead

and gone you know what lies in that question reccolect as I am
renounced all work for this month or 6 weeks if you could wish
to have [any] of the old M.S.S. altered nows the time as I am
not in Q to write originally get the old M.S.S. copyd out if you
like D. dare not trust 'em again with me I am getting a deep
shifty designing scoundrel so be upon your guard and have your
eyes open—I sent to D. for the book I told you but he would
not let me have it then he is more out of my favour than ever—
you must do what you can with him he has got too many pieces
to be lost in fact I know not what he has got—you say nothing
more about the 'Lodge House'* I could say a good deal about
here but my paper wears a weary—I have been teribly plagued
with the muses since I saw you I think I have wrote 50 Sonnets
—wether they are inspired by those ladys I cant [say] I am
almost afraid that some evil spirit is fond of personifying them
to torment me—Expect the 'Review'✝ in next Quarterly
Goodbye
JOHN CLARE

To Taylor

[sent]
Helpstone April 19 1820

MY DEAR TAYLOR

I have no fault to find with you only this you have made me
sit down to write a second letter as I had just wrote one for
you when the letter of yours came in I have now to answer it
but my revenge is satisfied to make you pay for 'em both I am
glad you declind publishing the Subscription & I am sorry I
said anything about it—your reasons are the best apology for
not doing it be what they may so dont say anything to O.G.
about it & let it all drop altogether you know I am always
easily turnd—I am proud enough to think I shall not want your
remittances of the money in your hands any more—you know
it is a bad way of making us‡ of it in the bud so dont humour
me so much it was only conjectured by Mrs Emerson to Lord R
so as I wanted money which I certainly did but I dont like to

* Unpublished.   † Gilchrist's, of *Poems Descriptive*.   ‡ Use?

spoil what is intended for my future happiness—but thats
past—I'm rich now remember—& very idle—& worse in health
than you can conjecture or than myself am aware of—I walk
round the Lordship 3 or 4 hours a week go & make wild
arbours in the middle of the woods ready agen summer & cut
marks on the barks of trees to find my way to it agen—be sure
you find some work for me in patching up old pieces I should
like to serve you some way or other & I think that is the easiest
   you will find O.G's remarks in the book you know what I
said—let your remarks be free give me what you really think
bad or good on all occasions & I am satisfied—you say you
hope all will be made strait with D. I am glad to hear you I shall
not hear better news then that I like Drury I have felt very sorry
since things have been as they are but I would not go to see
him till you & he had got a right understanding together—
besure you take care of all M.S.S. as you have & may recieve
as they will often be the only copies tell me next time only
dont lose none I think you had better conseal all my papers
now & not gratify people that comes with a sight of them as it
will take off the freshness that the new vol should come out
with—give me subjects that may strike you to write on I
have got 'Nutting'* in view is it a good subject think you
   To make you some amends for the trouble of reading these
letters I send you my last written piece

ENGLAND

England with all thy faults I love thee still
My country & while yet a nook is left
Where english minds & manners may be found
Shall be constrained to love thee

Cowper

[There follows 'England my country mong evils enthralling'†]
   tell me how Drury & you settles as I may not be mistaken—
has captain Sherwill‡ been to town latley when he comes to

---

* *The Rural Muse*, 1835.
† Unpublished.
‡ Captain Markham E. Sherwill, author of *Ascent to the Summit of Mont Blanc*
(1825), and of *Poems* (1832), had importuned his acquaintance, the newly made
baronet, Sir Walter Scott, about a donation for Clare. Scott gave Sherwill £2 for
books, but declined to write his name in them.

you again he will bring a parcel for me from Sir Walter Scott tell him to direct—'left at bull inn M Deeping' as I may know where to find it—what think you by 'England' I think I shall stand a chance for the Laureat Vacancy next time it turns out!!!! I had something else to say but have quite forgot—

Farwell

JOHN CLARE

P.S. you have a little pocket edit of 'Ramsay' I should vastly like it—I dont know wether I shall return Keats Endymion think as you will I begin to like it much—. heres a description of woody glooms—

> —*in buried paths where sleepy twilight dreams*
> *The summertime away*—

To Taylor

Addressed: Messrs. Taylor & Hessey, 93 Fleet Street, London.
[*sent*]

Helpstone May 1820

DEAR TAYLOR

Having little more than nothing to do this day I must do mischief by robbing you of L. s. d. for this letter be as it will I will cheapen it to you as much as I can by sending most of it in ryhme—I have been trying songs & want your judgment only either to stop me or to set me off at full gallop which your disaproval or applause has as much power to effect as if spoken by a magician the rod of criticism in your hand has as much power over your poor sinful ryhmer as the rod of Aaron in the Land of Egypt—I understand also by the by that Hilton is nearly done the 'Phiz' when you send it send a good long Letter as long as ever you are able to send & as much as you are able to say. Forgive your idle corespondent I forgot I was writing to a man of business—

Farwell

J. CLARE

[There follows:]
Swamps of wild rush beds & sloughs squashy traces . . .*
* The Village Minstrel.

I measured this ballad to-day wi the thrumming of my mothers wheel if it be tinctured wi the drone of that domestic music you will excuse it after this confession

J.C.

This is my favourite
[There follows:]

SONG

*Where the dark ivy a thorn tree is mounting . . .**

I think I hear you wisper if its a favourite song of Clares its none of mine—but lets hear these things some future oppertunity dont let some folks spoil your judgment by approving pieces which you have rejected remember your trust

> *If there's a weapon fate prepares*
> *That worst of pangs surrounds*
> *If theres a thorn her terror wares*
> *That pricks the bitterest wounds*
> *Tis when a worthy breast does bleed*
> *In sad misfortunes hour*
> *& hearts woud help a friend in need*
> *That hant it in their power*

Tis only a jingling thought that tormented me in your letter so take it wi the rest.

[There follows:]

CHUBS LAMENT FOR NANNY A PASTORAL†

Oh faithless love Ive met thy scorning . . .

I had almost presumption enough to send a double letter of these songs but if they are worthless this sample is sufficient to prove it—

Yours
JOHN CLARE

---

* *The Village Minstrel.*   † Unpublished.

To Chauncy Hare Townshend

[*sent*]

Helpstone May 1820

DEAR SIR

I must trouble you with an answer to say I have received the parcel safe & I must give you my grateful thanks for it my father sees the benefit of the plasters imediately & I hope that they may succede 'The Minstrel'* is a sweet poem & far as I have read a many thoughts occur which are in my 'Peasant Boy' I doubt the world will think them plagarisms, therefore I must alter or cut them out altogether, but nature is the same here at Helpstone as it is elsewhere—I am now employed in writing songs for a musicseller in Town If I succeed it may perhaps be to my advancement If I dont there is not much risk to run—so I am careless as to these matters I shall be glad of your advice whenever you shall give it I shall be happy to see you again at Helpstone likewise your first visit found me in a glowering desponding condition that often gets the sway but when I have been inspired with a pint of 'John Barleycorn' & in one of my sunshiny moments you would not know me I am a new man & have too many tongues tho your visit did not find it, still I can be cheery but in my sullen fits I am defiled with the old silence of rusticity that always characterized me among my neighbours before I was known to the world. I was reckoned a 'glumpy half sort of fool' amongst em you will excuse all this it is only to make apology for the ill behaviour that might seem predominent at our first interview—excuse likewise my writing so soon, had I neglected perhaps it might have been too long before I had pluckt up my spirits to address you—I am obliged to answer every friend imediately while gratitude is·warm, otherwise indolent neglect woud defer too long to be thought as such—you will look over my faulty correspondence. Letter writing is a thing I give no brush of correction or study too—tis just set down as things come to

* James Beattie's.

my 'tongue's end'. I am affeard I shall weary you with my stupid scribbling, therefore I must conclude with acknowledging myself to be your

gretfull St

JOHN CLARE

To Taylor

Addressed: Messrs Taylor and Hessey. 93 Fleet. St. London.
[*sent*]

Helpstone May 16 1820

DEAR TAYLOR.

Being very much bothered latley I must trouble you to leave out the 8 lines in 'Helpstone' beginning 'Accursed wealth' and two under 'When ease and plenty'—and one in 'Dawnings of Genius' 'That nessesary tool' leave it out and put * * * * * to fill up the blank this will let em see I do it as negligent as possible* D–n that canting way of being forced to please I say—I cant abide it and one day or other I will show my Independence more strongly then ever you know who's the promoter of the scheme I dare say—I have told you to order and therefore the fault rests not with me while you are left to act as you please.

Yours

JOHN CLARE

To Taylor

Addressed: Messrs. Taylor & Hessey, 93 Fleet St., London.
[*sent*]

Helpstone May 20 1820

DEAR TAYLOR,

You seem surprised at my scribbling of late but you have none to be surprisd at what D sent you are the silly stuff of my

---

* Lord Radstock had written to Clare and to Taylor complaining that certain passages in 'Helpstone' and 'Dawnings of Genius' contained 'radical and ungrateful sentiments'. Mrs. Emmerson had also written to Clare advising the removal of the 'highly objectionable' passages. Cf., however, Clare's letter to Hessey of July 1820; and also letter to Taylor of 16 January 1821, concerning omissions in Second, Third, and Fourth Editions of *Poems Descriptive*.

young days generally speaking some songs sonnets & ballads included—What will you be when you come in for the tail piece now at O.G. you may be surprisd then & more so when I tell you all of them or nearly are the productions of this winter—'my good old chuckey' you are blind in my manners and plans of writing when I am in the fit I write as much in one week as would knock ye up a fair size vol—& when I lay down the pen I lay it down for good a long while—reccolect the subjects are roughly sketchd in the fields at all seasons with a pencil I catch nature in every dress she puts on so when I begin to ryhme & polish up I have little to do in studying discuss how I am like the boy that gets his book alphabet by heart & then can say his lesson with his eyes as well shut as open—dont be under apprehensions of an offence to Lord M. I know my friends too well to offend one so cheaply I know very well the Milton family is my best patrons & I am in no fear but of them continuing to be so—Lord Radstock's letter was all I did—I only professed my innocence in the Matter— What a fool the Editor of the morning post must be he has left a line out of Townsends sonnet[1] & spoilt the whole get it reprinted in some other paper—I will give you a specimen of poetic madness—

[There follows :]
Address to the Clouds.[2]
This is just a bit of eye salve for my cursed prose—I shall frequently sprinkle such in my letters in future.

Dear Taylor
I this morning got Hiltons sketch of your humble St his hardship[3] John Clare dont let him find frame & glass in the bargain pay him at my account—& as to the picture I will well thresh him for it in ryhme so caution him on my threatnings— the fact is I mean to write him a jingling letter ere long to 'W. Hilton R.A.' ask him wether he woud as leave stand pillory an hour as stand in my ryhmes I think myself the disgrace is only equal & if he is in my opinion I will surely search in my new vol of poems to torment him so tell him bluntly he has forcd poor J.C. from his flail & spade to strut on canvas in the town of humour & I will take him from his 'water nymphs' to lye

on the hobs of our dirty cotteges to be read by every greazy
thumbed wench & chubby clown in spite of his 'Rats &c &c'
so tell the gentleman his doom—nor are you out of the mess
for I have already dressd you out in a letter to Captain Sherwill
I expect you know it ere now you know you do I think it the
best ryhming humour I have yet wrote in that way I was
pleased wi the verse on your worthy self let you find it as you
will I expect to see you & Hilton down next week, so look to't
if any more delays postpone it O.G. expects too remember—
good bye & kind respects to all friends

J. CLARE

To Taylor

Addressed: Messrs. Taylor & Hessey, 93 Fleet Street, London.
[sent]

June 10

MY DEAR TAYLOR

I am sorry to hear you have been unwell but hope you will
weather the storm & make your appearance soon my visit was
not far but good company entices me to make long stays you
know me well & woud know me better if I was nigher london
I have seen the critique in the Quarterly & a deal softer it is
then I expected as for what he says of booksellers care not I
dont—I am glad you was pleased with the verse on Sherwill as
it pleased me I think your taste & mine had I education woud
be as like 'as pin to pin' your selection of my poems gave me
plenty of consciet of your abilities I asure ye—& if I have any
fault it bears to the flattering side more for that—I 'smell the
rat' in the Fancy[1] and shoud have wishd his autograph much—
Poor Keats as a brother wanderer in the rough road of life &
as one whose eye picks now & then a wild flower to cheer his
solitary way who looks with his wild vain & crackd braind
friend to the rude break neck hill where sits the illustrious
inspirer—Fame—who looks with me—as carless of her
anointed few—but who as he turns away cannot help but heave
a sigh I judge colors by complexion & for his feeling his love
for nature & his genius I heartily love him—I like the extracts

51

from his poems & wait their publication anxiously—you will
think me diligent when I tell you to expect my poems soon
they will come directly from me I think next week but the
presise day you shall know of before hand wait till then to
answer me either you or Hessey will be expected to give me
imediate notice of their arrival as you know the feelings of
mad braind ryhmers for the safty of his children—but if you
come down next week I think they will be ready for taking up
with you if you will take the trouble.

I dont think D. right yet therefore the best is the best & you
shall have them direct from me the only copies so take care
of em I often see D. but we are not so familiar as usal poor
fellow he had too much consiet of me he vallued me more as a
poet then I deserved & when his expectations fell he met like
all others dissapointment he is now in your hands use him
well he is like me a stranger to the world & therefore like
mine his conjectures for the most part are wrong founded The
Song 'Here we meet too soon to part' is published dedicated
to Marquis Exeter by Hayden Corri[2] The opinion of the town
is a mean performance—The next book forgive my pride I
shoud like in 8vo well printed with a head & vignette cottage
it is only vanitys conjecteral & left to your judgment as usual
                              God bless you

'The Fancy' is R—ds I think remember me to him & Hessey
to Hilton Dewint Mrs D & little girl

To Hessey

[sent]

June 29 1820

MY DEAR HESSEY

I heard my old friend T. was out by D. & have expected him
every day but am glad you have informd me tho it is a dissapointment tho I think his intended visit in Autumn will be
best as he will then find me busy with the muses as they always
pay their visits more frequent at that season—I shall be glad
when he returns & the first thing you may tell is that I expect
he will get about arranging my pieces for the press if not I shall

set him down as an idle lazy lown like his humble servant—I
am very sorry for poor Keats the symptons of his illness I think
very alarming as we have people in the same way here often
who creep on for a little while—but it generaly proves death
has struck at the root—for they mostly go off—my only master
whom I livd with when a boy at the blue bell went off the same
way exactly—be sure tell Keats to take care of cold & from
extreme fatigue this hot weather—I shoud like to see the fiz of
the man before he drops off & hope he will last till next winter
when I shall hazard myself to Town unaccompanied & then I
shall have no put off on these kind of matters I am as anxious
to see Keats poems as you are to send em as to my opinion it is
not worth twopence if truth in speaking as one thinks giving
blunt opinions without flattery (as I woud not strive to please
the best friend I have with flummery) be of any value you shall
certainly have that—O.G. comes to town soon dont know
anything respecting his enquireys about my new poems—two
kings on a throne—you reccolect—I wish to keep vanity an
utter stranger to such matters—T. was the first & I expect
him to keep so he is a kind of screne between me and the world
—a sort of hiding place for me in the hour of danger—if I
forget a first friend—& let a new friend elbow him out of his
old station let the stings of a guilty conscience by my reward—
& that will be plenty—I intend making my will but think I shall
defer it till winter—I mean to leave Taylor the trouble of
writing my Life merely to stop the mouths of others—& for
that purpose shall collect a great many facts which I shall send
when death brings in his bill—this is the only cause of writing
the will—

Your £5 arivd. safe & I thank you for your thoughts in such
matter—but if married men dont understand economy who does
—had it been T. I might have been supprisd more—this will
serve me while the rest is due as the Marquises Quarter is due
next Saturday at least I shall make it so as I told the steward I
should come every 3 months—instead of regular Quarters—
I think I know the gentleman who called on you he is a London
bookseller 'Widncll' he came to see me Saturday fortnight I
think; very little was said on my part—you guess matters of
course—but in spite of that he was a hearty chap & we got

warm over a pot of beer when he askd me what sort of men was T. & H. I said they was Booksellers but d—d good fellows —at least to me—that finishd the pot & we parted as friendly as usual when he civily invited me to call on him when in london —which I shall not fail of doing—Your M.S.S. will come by Ds parcel this day week if nought happens—I am anxious for you to see them & bother D. pretty well I assure ye to get them copied—I have the foolishness to think some of em will do this is a cursd broken foolish letter but yours catchd me ryhming at full rate so the dropping from ryhm to prose was a breakneck disadvantage still in spite of all cross hopplings to the contrary

I am & ever shall be
Yours & T's faithful St
as warm as ever—Farewell

I had forget to tell you Dr Skrimshire* has set me on my legs I am as well as ever—& have strength to stand John Barleycorns knock down blow as well as ever—tho I fear he will turn a skulking masterly foe at the end—this hot weather I think suits me give my best respects to all friends—I forgot to say I fetch home 'Patty of the Vale' next saturday & that she has got a daughter—but for credits sake to all but our particular friends this is a secret—does L.R. & Mr E. know that matter?

To Taylor

Addressed: Messrs. Taylor & Hessey, 93 Fleet St., London.
[sent]

Helpstone June 1820

MY DEAR TAYLOR

I am sorry to keep you so long in suspence as I suspect you to think my 'Children of the brain' poping in everyday the fact is having an interview with Drury & hinting to him as how my new poems was for starting To London he looked sorrowful I thought I believe we had excluded him out of the list he

---

* Fenwick Skrimshire, author of books on medicine, chemistry, and natural history, attended Clare intermittently, until he certified him 'insane' in 1841, with his masterly analysis: 'Following years addicted to poetical prosings.'

expressed a great desire to have a copy I said if it was any way
nessesary it should be so his reasons stand good as to the proof
coming down we could not do without one & (you know Im
easily turnd either one way or the other) I took em to him but
have made him promise to release em a fortnight at most and
start em on their travels which way they will come I cant say
he likes em much & says they are far better than he expected
to see and moreover then that he vows they are far better then
any he has seen of mine yet if you think so I shall not be a little
proud I assure you—I like R–ds 'To Shellfield' exceedingly
& think him a good racer for the laurel in the ryhme of don
juan 'Shrewsbury'* is sweet I wish he had done more in that
way as to his play I understand it not 2 or 3 of his sonnets I
think fine in fact after what I had seen of his poetry this struck
me he only wants a good subject short irregular Pieces is his
fort I think his 'Shrewsbury' I admire exceedingly I did not
think him the poet he is I assure you dont tell him tho—you are
to recieve Earl Spencers half anuity due now or nearly £5
send it down wi the fund money in a Check on Eatons & Cayleys
Bank Stamford send it as soon as you can too as I am quite out
dont think me extravagant for I feel myself to the contrary—I
have a strong wish you should begin to print directly as soon
as your new cargo comes I have been thinking a small vol:
uniform with the first would be best wi Cot for frontpiece & no
head nor need there be any Introduction I think if there was
people would quiz us a short advertisment the shortest possible
would be sufficient—I keep aloof from you know—what—two
kings on one throne will not suit—still I am obliged to be there
or there abouts—you guess my situation—I am plain enough to
be understood I think now lets cleen up the Quarterly I have
read so you might have savd the trouble sending it—Elisha had a
knack to catch the matter† of his master for what purpose is
well known Critics have a knack in catching at the coat lap of
the poor crackbraind poet not for his inspiration of jingles thats
impossible here you guess

God bless you

JOHN CLARE

* John Hamilton Reynolds's nostalgic 'On Revisiting Shrewsbury' was in *The Fancy*.
† *Not* 'mantle', in manuscript.

P.S. as to your coming I have done thinking about it—it is
5 miles from Wansford 2 from Glinton & 3 from M. Deeping—

J.C.

To Hessey

Addressed: Messrs. Taylor & Hessey, 93 Fleet Street, London.
[*sent*]

Helpstone July 4 1820

MY DEAR HESSEY

On Thursday the M.S.S. starts to London I have some new
ones but shall trouble you wi' them in letters as I finish them
I heard from Lord R. last week & answerd his Lordship this
morning—weres my old friend Sherwill—I began on our friend
Keats new Vol*—find the same fine flowers spread if I can
express myself in the wilderness of poetry—for he launches on
the sea without compass—& mounts pegassus without saddle or
bridle as usual & if those cursd critics coud be shood out of the
fashion wi their rule & compass & cease from making readers
believe a Sonnet cannot be a Sonnet unless it be precisly 14
lines & a long poem as such unless one first sits down to wire-
draw out regular argument & then plod after it in a regular
manner the same as a Taylor cuts out a coat for the carcass—
I say then he may push off first rate—but he is a child of nature
warm and wild Campbell & Rogers must be fine very fine
Because they are the critics own children nursd in the critics
garden & prund by the fine polishing knives of the critics
they must be good no soul dare say otherwise—it woud be
out of the fashion—don't ye think a critic like a gardener uses
his pruning knife very often to keep it in action & find as he
calls it a job—an old proverb is among us 'a gardener woud
cut his fathers head off were he a tree' so woud the other if his
father was a book—to keep his hand in—I have skimd over
Keats & noticed the following as striking

---

* *Lamia, Isabella, and other Poems*, published in early July 1820: of which Taylor
wrote: 'if it does not sell well, I think nothing will ever sell well again . . . and
. . . I am sure of this, that for poetic Genius there is not his [Keats's] equal living'.
But, already under what Hessey called Dr. Darling's 'copious bleedings', Keats
was too ill to care much for Taylor's high praise. Clare's he never knew.

Often times
She askd her brothers with an eye all pale
Striving to be itself

Isabel

Season of mists & mellow fruitfulness

Then in a wailful choir the small knats mourn

Autumn

& joy whose hand is ever at his lips
Bidding adieu

Mel:

No stir of air was there
Not so much life as on a summers day
Robs not one light seed from the featherd grass
But where the dead leaf fell there did it rest

Hyp:

A stream went voiceless by

Hyp:

Let the maid
Blush keenly as with some warm kiss surprised

Hyp:

& poplars & lawn shading palms & beach
In which the zepher breaths its loudest song

Hyp:

I think this volume not so warm as 'Endymion' why did you not
print some of his Sonnets I like them much—I should like
Endymion bound with his autograph inserted if he pleases &
shall send my copy up purposely the first opertunity—'Chaucer'
I shall send by Drurys care quickly—D. has sent me 3 vols
calld 'Percys Relics' there is some sweet Poetry in them & I
think it the most pleasing book I ever happend on the tales are
familiar from childhood all the stories of my grandmother & her
gossiping neighbours I find versified in these vols—I shall
now make a beginning with 'Ways in a village'* I think a
series of little poems connected by a string as it were in point
of narative woud do better then a canto poem to please critics
I mind no fashions Farewell

JOHN CLARE

* Like the 'Peasant Boy', never printed under its first title, this manuscript, with
others, became *The Village Minstrel.*

Give my remembrances to Taylor Hilton Dewint Reynolds Woodhouse Keats &c &c &c

J.C.

I had forgot to say 'Patty' has got to helpstone & I think will prove a better bargain then I expected—

To Hessey

Addressed: Messrs. Taylor and Hessey, 93 Fleet St., London.
[*sent*]

[July 1820]

My Dear Hessey.

I have seen the third Edition I am cursed mad about it the Judgement of T. is a button hole lower in my opinion[1]—it is good—but too subject to be tainted by medlars *false delicasy* damn it I hate it beyond everything those frumpt up misses brought up in those seminaries of mysterious wickedness (Boarding Schools) what will please em? why we well know— but while their heart and soul loves to extravagance (what we dare not mention) false delicasy's seriousness muscles up the mouth and condemns it—what in the name of delicasy doth poor Dolly say to incur such malice as to have her artless lamentations shut out—they blush to read what they go nightly to balls for and love to practice alas false delicasy—I fear thou art worse then dolly say nothing to T.—he is left to do as he likes you know—and if we controul him he will give us up—but I think I shall soon be qualified to be my own editor—pride once cooled[2] grows very fast you perceive—I expect Drury is in London—he will tell you my eagerness of having a new vol I hope you will be as eager and then 'tween us all three we shall get Taylor to work—I hope he will come home from bath a new man and be so far recoverd as to master his puzzling job with pleasure I have a great many more old and new things which I shall muster up for a third vol, if its ever called for— the people round here are very anxious of a New Vols appearence—send me a letter by Drury tell me your opinion, and intentions how you will proceed with the new vol wether the 'head' (vanity agen you percieve) will be engraven—I have

made out *'Scriven'*[3] he is historical Engraver to his present
majesty—as to the cottage for the sake of my young friend I
must insist on thats being inscited[4] so T. must let me have my
wish there—but in these matters false delicasy I think will not
interupt him—I have felt long enough for poor T. I asure you
I know his taste and I know his embaresments I often picture
him in the midst of a circle of 'blue stockings' offering this and
that opinion for emprovement or omision I think to please all
and offend all we should find out 215 pages of blank leaves and
call it 'Clare in fashion'—the hut he may have done just as he
likes on wood or copper as a frontpiece or vignette but tell him
I expect and hope and after all blindly insist it must be done—
T. woud not be offended to find me vext and I think at the
omisions he knows himself in so doing the gold is licked off
the gingerbread—'Dollys mistake' and 'my Mary' is by the
multitude reckoned the two best in the book—I have lost my
tail—by it, but never mind what think you by the new poems
brought by D. just glance over them and tell me I like Keats
last poem the best Hyp:[5]—R's lines on Shrewsbury are passing
sweet I read em over and over if that man (noticing nature
instead of the foibles of the day) is not a future poet I am
mistaken give my best respects to all—dont print nothing
under the hut when engraved let it pass silently and leave
people to guess—you know by now I have been writing [for]
'Powers' I wanted 100 songs but am wore out—I think I shall
take another sheet.

To Hessey

Addressed: Messrs. Taylor and Hessey, 93 Fleet St., London.
                            [*sent*]

                                        July 16. 1820.
DEAR HESSEY.

Send in your letter, *first lines* of the poems sent you in the
first letter of mine, in fact all, as I shall send, which will only
be one or 2 more if not I shall doubtles send you things twice
over—give my love to my old chuckey Taylor when you write
him tell him I am all anxiety to hear from him agen; I think you

will like my last attempts at songs; I have consciet to think I find out the knack of ballad making; I have promisd D.[1] to make a 100, and shall soon compleat it, as I have made 6 or 8 every Day this last week I think I have done 70 or more already, you have a great Sample of them in the Book, and shall have all the best from me, what think at my attempts in the humerous, in 'Alas what a pity etc.'[2] how like you the 'sonnet' and addres to the 'rural Muse',[3]

yours etc. etc.

JOHN CLARE

[There follows:]
The war's of every kind comfort bereft me

To Taylor

Addressed: Messrs Taylor and Hessey, 93 Fleet S^t*, London.*
[sent]

Help A 1820

p.m. 31. Aug. 1820

MY DEAR TAYLOR

I have been out on a Visit to Rev^d Mr Hopkinsons Morton[1] so did not answer your last till now—I had just got seasoned into Harvest Work when the express arrived they sent a horse for me so busy excuses was usless I have been to Grimsthorpe castle & saw many curiosities & several other places & have returnd as idle & listless as ever its no use making resolutions to work you see now—they will not let me keep quiet as I usd to be—they send for me twice or 3 times a day out of the fields & I am still the strangers Poppet Show what can their fancys create to be so anxious & so obstinate of being satisfied I am but a man (& a little one too) like others still as they will come I will still sit in my corner in readiness for them & ryhme & jingle in the teeth of trouble & scrat away at my 'Cremona' striving to make the best use of the world while I am in it—I fancy my W— 'you know you do' will turn out a termagant she is one of the most ignorant & I fear will turn out the most obstinate of women creation—I am cobbling up some pastorals but dont know how I shall succeed I have done 4 or 5 & thought little of them—but a second reading has given me a higher opinion & encouraged me to proceed tis your long-wishd proceeding 'Ways in a Village' you need not write often—do it when you please only in your next tell me how you mean to print the next I must insist on the *Cottage* for the sake of my friend do it in Wood or Copper as a frontpiece or Vignette only 'you know you do' It must be done—he is taking many local spots about the village which may sometime be useful to you & me perhaps & you know friends have vanity & must be a little humourd & encouraged—he is not a Dewint—that I know well—nor is he half an artist—but his drawings tho somthing different in perspective is far from being unfaithful in a general way & must claim a good share of merit by coming from a self-taught pencil—give my respects to Hessey, Hilton, Keats & '*Tothill Fields*'[2] Woodhouse & all others are you coming in the country if you intend calling on me I will wait for you I have a barrel of 'Barley corn' ready so if you are going downward say so in your next but if you are not for tramping I am & mean to be in London the middle of next month I have 11 Cards of address in town & intend to make use of em but reccolect—yours is this time 'head quarters'

farewell

J. CLARE

To Taylor

Addressed: Messrs. Taylor & Hessey, 93 Fleet St., London.
[sent]

Help: 1820 August

MY DEAR TAYLOR

I recieved a letter[1] this morning from London in a very wretched hand—& in a very impertinent manner it cost me 9d. & if I make the additional weight on you we cant grumble at each others losses or gains in the matter—twill be 'tit for tat'—& perhaps you may smell him out tho he is by his writing some mechanic a shoemaker or perhaps a ryhming shoe black—at all events he is a trifle of no consequence—still you can advise me in your next wether I should answer him or wether I need not —as the thing is easily explained

Yours

J. CLARE

To Taylor

[*sent*]

[Autumn 1820]

MY DEAR TAYLOR

You will see agen that I agree in almost every particular of your alterations—my hobby when once begun to go forward— the word 'pounced' is what it is in the original—The Milton Hunt* on a second thought I am loth to leave out but I always disliked the 4 last lines what say you to this proposal—suppose we repeat the 4 last lines of the first verse agen after 'and scampers down his plough' & cut 'The muse &c &c' out I think it would make a good hunting song & free me of being fond of the barbarous sport what think you—The alusion to Milton is what I wish to preserve but do as you please—as my ink runs very much it may lead the printers into errors by seeing letters blotched that was not intended—please to look over them & rectify it—be careful in perusing the Songs & Sonnets as they are my favourites—those songs repaid long corespondence with Hessey in your absence are many of them not in the book nor are several of the Journals sent on your return—I only do this to remind you as you might think the Book contained them their rough sketches are most in the last M.S.S. but the corrected ones in the letters are much better you may print the *hunting song* I say it reads well here it is—

[There follows:]

The Milton hunt again begun . . .

It reads capital: dont it—so be sure & print it I send them back immediatly—I dont intend letting anyone of Stamford see them —Drury may be content to have his share in the publication

* Unpublished.

62

thats plenty for him I wish I could get such a job in being hard
for doing nothing—but my good nature I daresay has made me
my own fool agen in writing the Songs in summer for him which
I fancyd nothing more then a recompence for the suppos'd
injury done him in forcing the agreement out of his hands†
which if he coud he woud have made me believe was an unjust
piece of justice—he is now getting some of them set to music—
& sent me with his last flaming threat of hostilitys (for he sadly
wants me to believe he is sole proprietor of my poems still—
but stop Mr. Conjuror your own words is only great in your
own mouth thinks I—Napoleon may say to the winds I am
emperor of France while the rocks of St Helena daily tells him
he's a liar)—a Mutilated Skeleton of one of the Songs which
made me so d—d mad that I am half sorry I wrote my answer
at the moment—Still if I see my merit at stake I am aright to
cry stop thief—I stopt him however I'll [be] bound for it yet
sooner then eat my first conscent I said if his music man lik'd to
take the words as he found em they was there—if not let them
alone for my Name should never accompany such affectation
& conciet –If I did wrong in writing these songs dont be
offended at me 'chuckey' for I knew little what I was about but
fancyd it a fine thing to have ones name on a music sheet—
I have not had one single farthing for doing them nor dont
know if I ever shall—still if Drury had not proposed it they had
never been written so if I get any merit for them he has the
credit of being the origin of it—& if not I have the credit of
being a fool—I think he'll not write to you now after I ript him
up at such a rate—he was always complaining of injuries & I
thought this request would satisfy him but I am mistaken it
seems so he must (like a bear with a sore head) keep growling
on—he said he shoud stay while the selection was made in the
Vols—but I have found him long ago to be a dealer in falsities
—thats why I feel a desire of having the best Songs in as their
after mutilations of the M.S.S. may not pass as genuine—I

† This was evidently the document signed by Clare in an unguarded moment,
selling the copyright of *Poems Descriptive* to Drury for £20, and for which Taylor's
accounts for 1829 recorded curiously 'Paid Mr. Clare for Copy right per Drury
£20'. Unfortunately, though many of the letters from Drury to Taylor are in the
Robinson-Brooke-Taylor manuscripts at Northampton, it seems likely that some
of the angry crucial ones, both from Drury to Taylor and from Clare to Taylor,
may have been destroyed before the manuscripts left John Taylor's care.

cannot write further as the parcel is ready but shall answer
your promised letter if I see its required which is now at
Deeping I expect

Yours &c &c

JOHN CLARE

To Taylor

Addressed: John Taylor Esq., Fleet St., London.
[*sent*]

[1820]

Now you have the whole mass of rubbish before you its your
liberty to make the best of em you can to select and throw aside
just as you please—I have done entirely with em and were none
or trifling alterations is wanting your proofs in such cases will
be useless sending down.—

To Gilchrist

[*sent*]

Helpstone Sep. 1820

DEAR SIR

I send Mrs. G. the long expected proof Sheet of our new
provincial[1] for an hours amusement, it has cost me three Journeys
for I do assure you I was rather jealous but am now very cool'd
by satisfaction there is but 5 lines that strikes me a little four
of which I suspect are Crabbs Mrs. G. will find them marked as
she reads he is smooth & free to wander on with but the subject
has not novelty enough attached to it to please long if it goes
much further—how long it is I dont know—I will contrive to
get all the proofs for her if I can as they come out but we must
be still—& if she pleases not let them be seen—I intended this
day to call with my novelty in my pocket but as I was always a
football kick'd in misfortunes ways it was to be found I got
into a commonplace hobble before I let[2] Drurys I am & shall be
in a damned flurry of vexation for the present—but ere I relate
it I will give you my first startling adventure for it has been an

64

adventurous day I assure you—as soon as I got to D's this morning my old friend Hankinson [?] came in & invited me to beaver with him at the George the which I accepted in the course of the interview I found out by his father who was with him that his taste is Painting—I fancy I have seen the name to engravings but did not urge my enquiry after I left them I went to Drurys agen & now come the d—d hobble that vexes me after I had been there a few minutes a gentleman came in & asked me how I did I very bluntly answered 'Very well thank you Sir' he stard me very hard & asked the prentice if it was not Clare & told me that he came to hear if my book was out— 'no Sir'—(with my hat on)—was the answer he went out without saying a word more—& he had not gone 2 minutes when the disclosure of the secret came out—d–n it 'twas a thunderbolt to my ignorance & I stood gauping like an idiot to hear the man say it was no worse a person than the marquis— what the marquis will think of me I dont know but I wish very much I had been the length of London out of the matter—but if there is anything to disadvantage the poor devil your humble servant is sure to get overhead & ears in it—still who could dream his Lordship would ever come to D's but tis as it is & I must make up for the blunder the first opportunity—I have been over head & ears in ryhmes till—Mrs G. need not return the proof sheet—Lord R has sent me 'Johnsons Lives' 4 vols & 'Knox Essays'[3] the last pleases me much & the first cannot fail to please everyone I have much more to say but cannot sit to write or think—have not heard a word from Taylor

Your humble Sr

J. CLARE

To Chauncy Hare Townshend

[sent]

Helpston Sept 12 1820

DEAR SIR,

I received your kind letter with gladness this day & shall not have the injustice about me to charge you with forgetfulness any more I heard of your task in preparing a Vol for the press

E 65

by Mr. Hankinson whom I had the pleasure to meet at Mr Drurys lately & I guessed your task was irksome enough by myself as you cannot dislike it more than I do who have been imployed in a similar way & expect to see a proof sheet down every day—I have now the anxiety about me to see C.H.T.'s poems as soon as struck off—you have given transcribing its right name by stiling it the 'drudgery of poetry' & with the exception as you modestly hint of Thompsons couplet it is the same with all The plasters you sent my father have succeeded beyond our expectation & he is able to potter about with one stick & put a few stones in the ruts on the road for amusement —I can assure you your advice is no offence in the least tho I like yourself hate sermonizing in the least so I heartily thank you for it & will reap the benefit it contains if I possibly can— but as blunt I think is best—I will not assure you it is possible— still you have my grateful acknowledgment for the present & future hints for my happiness—all else is a fault with me—you did not drop one hint of your adventures with the lake bards as I understand you have been in the company of the notified Laureat Southey you did not judge what a newsmonger I am or you would have told me amply concerning him—as he is the least known to me of most—I have had a kind letter from 'Bloomfield' & as Mr Hankinson begd me in his last to tell him where Bloomfield lived I wish you would do it for me next time you see or write him he lives at Shefford Bedfordshire 5 miles from Biggleswade on the London Road Montgomery has like- wise honoured me with his notice & put a Sonnet I sent him in the 'Iris' give my best respects to Mr Hankinson your first opportunity—a rival provincial poet has sprung up near me & will soon I conjecture make a noise round the hitherto un- disturbed nativity of my rustic muse—but I wish him success be how it will & with begging excuse for this unconnected stuff as I am very muddy at this time & with wishing every success may attend on the approaching offspring of a valuable friend & brother bard

I remain
With all sincerity
yours kind sir

JOHN CLARE

To Hessey

Addressed: Messrs Taylor & Hessey, 93 Fleet Street, London.
[*sent*]
Helpstone Sep or Oct 1820*

MY DEAR HESSEY

As I know not were Taylor is at this time I send this last effusion to you an intended addition to the second Vol. with no apology than as I feel pleas'd with it my self I am anxious that I should meet your opinion & perusal I had doubtless an additional conciet in view at the time that it would give you pleasure likewise—I know T. is in the country & have heard from him but not were he may be now so excuse the trouble I have given you

Yours &c &c

JOHN CLARE

[There follows]

In life's first year as on a mother's breast . . .†

If you like this *honestly tell me* the first oppertunity, as I will drop similar descriptions in 'Ways of a Village,'—I think vulgar names to the flowers best as I know no others [if] it pleases twill add a fresh spark to my ryhming pride & start me off—if not stop me at once as usless labour is but the best name for idleness—mistakes & blunders will be overlookd as it is done hasty an hours job to-day at most—had a Londoner to see me to-day a Mr. Back‡ of the Inner Temple & feeds my vanity graciously with many praises—best respects to Woodhouse & Tothill Fields remember: & to all friends—have finished the 'Cross Roads'§ 'Rural morning'§ 'Evening'§ 'Rustic Fishing'§ & 'Sunday Walks'§ toward the village job but am little satisfyd till T. calls & passes sentence upon them

J. CLARE

---

* Clare was evidently not sure.   † *The Village Minstrel* (with alterations).
‡ Or Buck.   § *The Village Minstrel.*

To Taylor

Addressed: John Taylor Esq, at Miss Taylors, Market St.,
Leicester.
[sent]

Helpstone Oct 3 1820

MY DEAR TAYLOR.

I write you immediatly & as you seem to wish a long letter
I have taken a leaf out of my ryhming ledger to pleasure you
and a long letter you shall have I am determined if I end with
the same spirit I begin with tho its not often the case for I am
very short winded & if ever I mount my old rawbone hack of a
pegasus determined for a long journey we are sure to be both
of us d–d–ly cut up ere we end it & often cursedly sick ere
the half way is accomplished—the fact is if we begin long
things we always make bad finishes as the prancing hunter
scarce kept in his reins at the beginning sickens by toil and
scarcly hastens from the spur in the close—first I shall answer
your kind letter where I see any answers are nessesary I think
with you about the 2 lines & cannot see anything justly con-
demning them to oblivion I mean 'Ease & plenty' &c The
'dawning of genius' pleases me but I am so conceded in your
taste that I seldom fancy anything displeases of your alteration
in fact it makes me a bad judge of any body beside as I never
can yield in the least to any of them—what I can remember of
the Quarterly (as I cant find it just now to refer to) it is a long
way off of an error in so much that I believe it correct & which
I have more then once told D, who fights very shy with the
circumstance—he never saw a M.S. of the setting sun that I'll
be answerable for as this proof is convincing to sense & reason
—hark ye—I was a few shillings indebted to Thompson D's
predesessor & thinking he would do me some service for his
own interest in hopes of the possibility of discharging the bill
which then had been hopeless I sent him three prospectuses as
specimens for his customers & a short note wishing him to do
me a kindness by giving me time to discharge the bill & using
his interest in my new adventurous station of an author all
which as I learned by the bearer he treated with contempt but

now to the proof if I had sent 3 printed copies of the setting sun
what was the nessesity of sending a M.S. I never was fond of
copying nor Ill be answerable when there was such good reasons
to shun it woud I take the trouble I had but 2 copies in writing
in that time Hensons & my own the first of which you have—
do you want anyother proof or is this sufficient I can say the
M.S. story is a lie tho a friend has said it which I woud not
wish to injure any further any thing of information you want
in matters I am in power to dechyher* be free with—my word
is my bond mind & they shall rest in my bosom & go no further
then satisfaction desires—I say it just to place you on a level with
D. & I was determined to accomplish it—I did not like the
slight mention of the London Publishers in the review & have
hinted it home more then once I have many things on that head
which I shall tell you of in London or at Helpstone I am very
happy for Hiltons news as he is a man I value not only for his
genius but his plain blunt & honest manners which suits me to
a tittle—I hope poor Keats will return to England as he coud
wish—I shall feel honoured with his correspondence I assure
you nor shall his advice be thrown away if I can help it tho
you are well aware of my stubborness I am glad you like my
Pastoral & as I think I have better you have clapt a spur to old
Peggy which starts her off agen at full trott you shall have all as
soon as I can set too to copy them—The 'Vignette' suits & the
'nob' of 'Sir John'† tickles him I assure you 12 months is a
long time but the materials is not yet ready or it woud seem
longer nor do I know if they are ready by then—I shall never
dream of John Taylor acting roguishly as Nature never woud
belye herself by putting such an honest looking face on a rogues
shoulders tho the 'great & good' are so charitable to give them
advice for a twelvmonths longer 'as such things are' I doubt
not, but not among Hessey & Taylor mind; my opinion is
stubborn & so it ought to be thank you for the mile stone
before its put down as then you are aware I shall not have
the oppertunity you shall see some of my friends poems‡ when
I get them I shall write him today & bluntly ask him for them

* 'Decipher'?
† Scriven's engraving of William Hilton's portrait for *The Village Minstrel*.
‡ Chauncy Hare Townshend's?

he has not got the knack of song writing as the attempts he
[has] shown me are very weak & dry—you never mention the
proof sheet poet so shall not trouble you with it as my opinion
tells me its not worth it—I dont hint a word to E. D as I told
you of the matter. I shall expect you in November but mind yet
the barrel will not hold in till then I feel no inclination to see
London when you are from it so 'good speed & guerdon to ye
Johnny' till we meet agen as you liked my last sonnet you shall
have another & a specimen of rural courtship from a new
pastoral 'Close of Eve'* & then if my memorys wore out its
good bye & god bless you

[There follows:]

TO THE IVY†

Dark creeping Ivy with thy berries brown . . .

[Sonnet]

P.S. I made a cursed blunder last week at Drurys shop which
had nearly slipd the letter—the Marquis of Exeter came in &
very condescendingly asked me how I did—I not knowing him
said very bluntly 'middling thank ye Sir' he next asked me
when my poems would come out as that he said causd him to
call 'sometime ere the spring sir I daresay' was my answer he
lookd hard in my face & went out—& when I was informed who
it was I was most confoundedly vex'd & all the way home at
every stile I got too sat & repeated it over to myself how I
acted which every repetition made more ridiculous but I have
now nearly overset it—D tells me there is nothing the matter so
I rest upon it—& now I think of it you must not forget to speak
very kindly of the Marquis Earl Fitzwilliam Lord Milton &
earl Spencer & as you can say a little about each in the narrative
way as I was noticd by them the classification will not be
conspicuous [?] & the anecdotes will I think be entertaining—
as to an introduction one there must be so never try to shuffle
off the task & if you begin it in as happy a vein as the other the
longer you make it the better—I'll furnish you with trifles if
you think additions to the former narrative nessessary—put
in G.'s verses from the London Mag: in introduction & name

---

* It is difficult to decide which poem this is. He may have changed the title later.
† *The Village Minstrel.*

him: as better 'make a friend then miss one' you smell it—
the 3rd Vol I think will do without 'old chuckeys' assistance
but I cant feel myself safe in the second—so farewell for the
present—

                                                    J. CLARE

To Hessey

Addressed: Messrs. Taylor and Hessey, 93 Fleet St., London.
                    [*sent*]
                                        Nov. 28 1820

DEAR HESSEY.
   Having seen an advertisment in the 'New Times' respecting
my new Vol of Poems anouncing them to be in the press and as
I have no knowledge of the matter I feel dissatisfied with
Taylors proceeding[1] and tho I alow his judgement to be
correct in such matters yet he must know without my seeing
the proofs he will not posses that universal taste to please me
always and as such a proceeding is not as I expected it woud be
I woud have stopt it had it not been too late and shall be carfull
to hinder such neglect in future—he must excuse me if my
opinion is wrong founded for I believe if it is as I imagine—
that nothing but neglect woud cause his ommision of sending
the proofs nothing is more satisfying to an author then the
perusal of his writings as they slowly proceed from the press to
see that all pleases him—I cant believe T. woud do it without
my knowledge but the advertisment runs thus
                        'In the press'
'A New Volume of Poems By John Clare a Northamptonshire
Peasant.' I request an answer if you please, and beg to see the
proofs if it be not intruding excuse me I am blunt but more
honest then manouvring flatterers my heart is as warm as ever
in reccolection of Taylors kind exertions on my behalf which
never shall be hid or forgotten—
                                        Yours
                                        J. CLARE

                            71

To Hessey

[sent]

Helpstone
Dec. 1. 1820

MY DEAR HESSEY

I got your kind letter this day I am cursed mad at myself for my last blunder but you then see I woud not believe anything wrong in Taylor & I hope you will burn the stuff & say nothing about it to him—& before I answer your enquireys I shall say somthing conserning myself Sunday last I fancy I had good news the Bishop of Bristol wrote Mr Mossop wishing to know somthing about 'Clare the Helpstone poet' as he calld me in his letter as the Society of Christ's Colledge Cambridge (to which our living belongs) intends to do something in the way of acknowledging the merits of your humble Servant! I told him Taylor & Lord R. was at the head of my affairs & that the Bishop had better write any of them if he pleasd & in particular I gave him Taylor's adress & he said he woud refer him to write there so I expect ere long you will have a Letter from the Bishop if you have forward it to T immediately now supposing as they cannot make a parson of me they should grant what woud be far better an equal income with our Vicars salary £50 there'll be for ye!! I hear nothing of T but expect & expect every hour till I am weary with expecting if he comes he will find Helpstone a rum shop & have a very rum tale to tell you I daresay—I am glad you like the wild flowers the last verse is such a favourite of mine that it is the only one I can repeat of any of my poems & my selfish consiet is constantly repeating it twas first pointed out by a stranger on reading the M.S. who begd to transcribe it—no London this year for me your 'cold drizzling half-wintry weather' has got me so low livd & mopish that your noisey town woud instantly craze me

Are you St Caroline or 'George 4th' I am as far as my politics reaches 'King & Country' no Inovations on Religion & government say I—this night is the grand illumination for our City in honour of St Caroline the woman that is to personate her majesty is a deformed object who is to be dressd in white & all the rest are to have 'white favours' The windows are to be illuminated but as the grand characteristic of an Englishman is liberty of conscience I will for once sustain it—I am persuaded to light up in consequence of keeping the peace & my windows unbroken—but they have their whims & Jack will have his & I am now soon as your letter is done making preparations of defence a large oaken bludgeon & if the devil heads the mob let him head it so he passes my door peacably & if his devilship throws one stone at my window mind ye hostilitys begin & if his hide is not cudgel proof I'll feel for it & for once let him know I am as rebellious against his opinion as he was in old times against a superior adversary

Lord R askd my opinion of the present matters & I bluntly told him that 'if the King of England was a madman I shoud love him as a brother of the soil' in preference to a foreigner who be as she be shows little interest or feeling for England when she lavishes such honours on the [generality?] of another which Nelson has long characterized as a set of 'whores scoundrels poets & fiddlers' poor St Caroline she has seen much trouble & perplexity God forgive her—I am glad the head is going on with & hope Scriven will do Milton* justice as he was my choice you know—when they are done perhaps you coud spare me one or two for a friend—& now I must hurt you to tell Taylor soon as the book is out he shoud send Lord Fitzwilliam & Milton Earl Spencer & the Marquis a book each with a letter as he can do such things far better than I so dont forget it—Lord R is at Brighton he sends me 5 or 6 newspapers every week & I have had 2 letters from him this 8 [?] week & 1 from Mrs E—my Wife is well & the Child gets on bravely I myself am in as low ebb as melancholly can reduce me & as idle as need be sulking in the corner from day to day & scribbling by fits—I am about 'Martinmass Eve'† but am stalld with it— I have written 'the Cress gatherer'‡—I send your addition to 'Reccolections'§

[There follows:]
            & left free to every whim . . .
[and]

* Milton Park, seat of Earl Fitzwilliam.   † Unpublished.   ‡ *The Village Minstrel.*   § 'Recollections after a Ramble', *The Village Minstrel.* See p. 100 seq.

SONNET TO AUTUMN*

Come pensive autumn with thy clouds & storms . . .

I had some time back an invitation to write for the 'Ladies Museum' & promisd the Editor I woud but alterd my mind & gave it up as it dont suit my taste to please boarding school Misses & such like paper Vanities—give my best respects to all
& believe me dear Hessey your faithful friend
& grateful St

J. CLARE

To Taylor

[*sent*]

[1820]

MY DEAR TAYLOR

I have sent you every line I had in my possesion & have for once swept the house clean of ryhmes & have no doubt sickend your curiosity from enquiring for the like ere after for they are worthless stuff still you may jump on some odd things that may suit & those I knew you had I cut out to defray the expense of carriage put all the picces in the last Quarto in your new Vols† which you think good—I shall dash a few more lines in the 'Widow'‡ but that I can do as it goes thro the press the first pastoral I have never yet retouched (Love's Soliloquy)§ I have read it since & find several natural lines well expressd & some affected these I will chop out as they are printed did you take a copy when Drury sent it thinking you did I saved myself the trouble if you have not I will brush it up & send it—dont spare anything for the 4th Vol—I'll be bound to have stuff enough by then—2 or 3 years you know will be soon enough for us after these 2 Vols comes as twins into the world—I have been looking over that hasty scribbled thing the 'Peasant Boy' & find some of the best rural descriptions I have yet written such as the Feast & the Statute & some touches on Love & Scenery I feel little pleasure after a second reading of one's ryhmes in general but the thing is quite decievd me & I think it

---

* *The Village Minstrel*   † *The Village Minstrel.*   ‡ Unpublished.
§ Unpublished.

will take when your Pencil has just gone over it here & there
as its printing. 'Michaelmas Eve' comes unfinished I dont feel
satisfyd with it & therefore cant get on if you think it worth
while ending I will do it I wish Hilton had been in one of these
'Michaelmass holidays with me this year twoud have made as
rare 10 minutes employ for his pencil poor Kate in the dumps
the old man snoring over his pipe & pot & the Boy talking over
the hardships of his bad last years place was the three finest
characters contrasted that I have ever witnessd I was one of
the assembly & these three figures gave me the hint for the
poem & every incident in it is truth & drawn from the life &
therefore I shall feel pleasd with your judgment on it I think
a concluding verse or two will be able to compleat it be as it may
The Statute* also as begun afresh you must gi' me a hint
about [7 lines scored out heavily by Clare]
I have written about the Woodman as you find the Sketch
in these papers as one character for it but I must avoid satire
as much as possible I like the 'all ten' measure best of any now
& shall keep on wi't doubtless they will next say in so doing
I imitate Crabb as they guessd by the same means I imitated
Burns (last winter) 'Tales' I lik'd here & there a touch
but there is a d–d many affectations among them which seems
to be the favourite play of the parson poet—in our 4 Vol I mean
to have a good race with him & have consciet enough to have
little fears in breaking his wind—when I read anything that
gives me a hint I throw the book down & turn to it no more
till mine's finished if thats imitating whats to be said of Milton
Dryden Pope &c &c the Boast of English literature—whats he
know of the distresses of the poor musing over a snug coal fire
in his parsonage box—if I had an enemy I coud wish to torture
I woud not wish him hung nor yet at the devil my worst wish
shoud be a weeks confinement in some vicarage to hear an old
parson & his lecture on the wants & wickedness of the poor &
consult a remedy or a company of marketing farmers thrumming over politics in an alehouse or a visionary methodist
arguing on points of religion either is bad enough & I know
not which is the best—
We are nearly blockd up in our huts wi' snow but I hope the

* 'Helpstone Statute', *Collected Poems* (1935).

weather is going I get on 'like a house afire' with my
'Cremoni'* & begin to be stil'd a first rate scraper among my
rustic companions tho in fact I dont play one tune in 20 by
notes she makes a rare noise & thats plenty—a professional at
Stamford tells me she's a valuable instrument & her equal is not
easy to be met with in our parts so when I go into quarrelsome
company I take my own scraper for fear the other shoud be
broken I have by times no end of tittle tattle to tell you but its
not all at my tongue's end now & as its Sunday I must prepare
for the parson by going to Church for he mostly seeks me up
—& if he brings me any good tiding from the Bishop of Bristol
he will be welcome company—I will fill your last ruld quarto
with as much of my little life as I can & get it done doubtless
to bring up with me in summer as I then intend to storm the
hospitality of Fleet St

—Yours &c

J. CLARE

To Taylor

Addressed: Messrs Taylor & Hessey 93 Fleet Street London.
[*sent*]

Helpstone Dec. 14 1820

MY DEAR TAYLOR

Your Letter met me this morning very early & pleasd
enough to see it I assure you—The fact is if I cannot hear from
John Taylor now & then I cannot ryhme I dont know the reason
but so it is—I get on cursd bad with ways in a village I find the
thing too surcumscribed & narrow for ones thinking always
dinging at rural things wont do & what I have done I can get
no ones opinion off thats worth an ha'penny—now was I to
send them you woud you think the carriage to London & back
too expensive say a word in your next & Ill do as you may wish
but to return to yours your idleness in the country is nothing
wonderfull & your confession of being the same John Taylor
towards John Clare as you began is no more than what he ever
expected your not calling O.G. will make him think somthing

* Whether the fiddle given to Clare by Hessey *was* a Cremona we are not sure.

76

as I have not calld on him this 3 months or longer both of us
fighting so shy will surely make him believe its intended tho
in fact my neglect is that I am quite weary of gossiping tho he is
the most entertaining one for companys sake that I find in this
quarter being the only literary man in our dark little wood I am
glad you like the 'Sonnet to the Ivy' & 'Wild flower Nosgay'
twill urge me to further exertions I am sorry the word 'omit'
shoud have baffled your judgment—& beg to tell you that you
will not mind no such thing in future as I never did insert
them & am mad that D did not rub his 'omits' out as they were
inserted for the purpose he talks of I am glad Keats has got
over his Voyage I heard of his 'Review' in the Edinburgh as
being favourable but have not seen it tho I believe O.G. likes
it—I am glad you will do without me as the very people you
speak of wishing to see me is the only obstacles that dis-
apoints my visiting London they I believe are and have been
great friends to me but the d–d fuss sickens ones vanity had I
ever so much of it—I shall come up two or three days in summer if times goes well but shall come under cover & not let
such & such hear of my being there   I dont wonder at your
being dissapointed at the deciet of the written lye but I hate
controversy & as it is let it go on while a better and more
peacable opportunity offers to contradict it as it where by a
hint for I woud not have told you if you had intended otherwise
—it was your own fault in not writing to me while you was
writing the introduction as I woud have given you every particular about it & everything else but you will soon find room
enough to do it when I am dead & gone as I will leave a written
memorial of my life such as it has been for you; only to do me
justice if I can get another year or 2 over my head tho I am at
'quakebrig'* about it I assure you be as it will you have
enough to contradict that—Scriven is another of those wonders
I have great curiosity to see whenever I come at London that
job you will certainly have to contrive—This cold morning has
produced a Sonnet for you such as it is

The small wind wispers thro the leafless hedge† . . .

* Wright's Dialect Dictionary has no reference to this word, but its meaning is
vivid enough.
† *The Village Minstrel.*

77

I expect you will send the proofs by Ds parcel as usual as expence will be saved & as I can come if not them with nearly as little trouble as by any other means as gardners goes 3 times a week to Stamford in winter & I expect I shall soon have one at least I am in hopes how gets the 'Cottage' on is it done —let me have 1 head & 2 copies of the hut soon as they are ready as I want to send one of each to Mrs G. to get in her favour again after my long neglect & silence as I almost feel an embaresment to renew my visits you no doubt have felt this disagreable & comical sympathy—Thats all the reasons why I want a head & the cottage as the novelty of the offering woud put aside all discussions on the past at the moment so think of me & send me them as soon as you can—you I think like the Songs—has D. sent you copys of his I believe there is between 70 & 80 in all so you will have good choice if he has not I can send you the rough copys any time—when I write anything that pleases me I shall always send it up in spite of postage so you have the caution I coud say much more but as my sheet is at its journeys end I must bid you for the present farwell

JOHN CLARE

To Taylor

Addressed: Messrs. Taylor and Hessey, 93. Fleet St., London.
[sent]

Help: Dec. 18. 1820.

MY DEAR TAYLOR.

With some suspense I opend your last in mourning thinking by the seal you had taken a tour to the other world and written me from thence—but respecting your request—wearied vanity dare not say what she woud willingly say if no reason was attach'd to the matter what that reason is you well know and I hope you will never loose sight of John Clare when such correspondents become burthensome Lord R. I own as a friend and as one in the first order but what induced him to write you in such a manner[1] I know not as my last to him was a plain proof of my satisfaction after Hesseys Letter whose simplisity of manner woud not fail to convince any one that I harbour the

highest opinions of T. and H. Lord R. well knows I now come
to certain points in your letter which I dont fail to reive[2] clear
off—as to his saying 'you ought not to be in possesion of my
M.S.S. without first signing an agreement' that opinion must
be his Lordships own and a very new one too as I understood
him the very same thing was long ago proposed by yourself
and to this I returnd an answer of the utmost satisfaction that
in giving me half and half yourselves (The publishers) which
if I mistake not his Lordship hinted as being Southeys way such
manouvring has been practisd that I know not what I might say
but I dont remember giving the least hint of an agreement
proposd—but your note to Lord R. tho perfectly appropriate
on your part will not pass in its progress without (I Fear)
being a hole in my next subscription list which Lord R. long
ago told me he should resume with his wonted ardour and
moreover that he had influenced Lord Liverpool to take my
part in the next Vol: whose words I cannot turn too but something in this manner 'Your Lordship will inform me when
Clares next poems makes their appearence as I shall be willing
to do him what service I can' Liverpool—These things you
will look too I hope as for myself interest urges me I must and
therefore I must keep the peace with his Lordship—you know
long ago my opinions and I must own the matters you complain
of are very troublesome—as to your opinion in thinking he
wishes you to throw it up I cant fancy so but as to 'doing
justice' the highest vanity cannot concieve the extent of that
bubble there I readily see with the same spectacles as T. & H.
& all who has ever had a specimen of the person would as
readily give the like reply as to his Lordship's opinion that
'had not Lord R stepped forth in support of the work—a second
Edition woud not yet have appeared—' this urgs me to give 'it
readily the lie which (when my merit is put aside for puffing
to come strutting in and say I am the mountebank that got
Clare a name with the public) I woud contradict in the face of
any man let his titles be what they may—as to your yielding to
any ones controul is and has been all along at your own option
you know it—and you are as free to use it at this present
moment as you ever was in respect to the poems—your
request of an agreement I will agree to let my friend Wood-

house draw it up as he thinks proper in the way you proposed half and half and he had better put both in some regular way as Drury sometimes complains of your not complying as you pro-posd well so doing will stop all mouths and save me a deal of answering the both of calumny and gossiping enquiry if agree-able to you it is to me to put all together published and un-published in the same agreement on the same principle—'That J.C. is to recieve one half of the profits arising from the sale of the poems already published and from any that he may publish after and that no other persons than T.H.D. has any right to the copy right what ever etc. etc. etc. you see by this I am ready to do by consent what D. put on one by force which does not argue that I doubt the sincerity of T. and H. I doubt not your acting towards me well afterwards as I shall reckon nothing of the Bond myself but appear as free as ever I have had tempta-tions enough already from booksellers if I had wishd to go astray—as I wishd to say more I must take another sheet—and as I may not forget it I wish you to send me a little paper of letter and other size as soon as you can for I am out and has been a long time and giving a penny a sheet for it here is more than I can expense with

P.S. Dont misguide your judgement by fancying good pieces in the old M.S.S. from the praises these late [critics]—

To Taylor

Addressed: Messrs. Taylor and Hessey, 93 Fleet St, London.
[sent]

Helpstone Dec 21 1820

MY DEAR TAYLOR,

On Saturday the 'Ways of a Village' comes to London all the pieces that are conected none else for the remainder are so far from it they are of little use to you as they will give me a puzzling to make them out if they lie long—My last scrawl was written in such haste that it was wrong dated & the letter I quoted from being such a bad scrawl even worse then mine*

* Lord Radstock's.

that I made a blunder in the quotation tho it is as ridiculous
as ever: & twas ridiculous in me to quote it as a proof of my
ignorance in the custem but I was so damd mad with such
encroaching meddlers that I scarcely knew what I wrote or
read 'Dear Emma has been making much exertions for you in
going to Fleet St that deserves from you more then you will
probably ever have it in your power to repay—Do not let this
dishearten you' I punctually write from the letter & this is
it Lord have mercy on me & free me from such sallies of vanity
as soon as possible or convenient is the prayer of John Clare—
& I hope he will hear me when I come to London I shall bring a
specimen of the precious honey drops of vanity for an hours
amusement—for my part last winter I hardly dreamd such
beings had existence in your wonderfull Exebition of absurditys
in London I have been mustering up the songs one copybook
is lost but that copy has been selected for your Quarto & when
I consider: There is few but what you have got that is worth
any notice if you turn to the letters to Mr Hessey & yourself
you will find what I mean however I will make all out I have
bye me good bad & indiferent & then you do as you please
have a good case* over the sonnets & think you will find first
& last a selection far superior to the first book I shoud not be
crampd for room if I was you but heedless of the price (as the
Sales nearly safe) put all in thats good of poems tales ballads
sonnets & songs—here I am upon unlawful ground prating
were I have no business but you know me my advice is harmless
after all my pratings you are left to do as you please—often
write me at least when you find amusement in so doing for I
can assure you I myself feel a great liking always to trouble
you with my scrawl very often—this moment I am interrupted
with a parcel of News Papers from my old friend his Lordship
but no letter—tis impossible to feel otherwise than gratful for
the many trifling troubles he takes in my behalf weak as some
actions may appear such trifles as these (whatever the simple
design may be) warms & binds him closer in my esteem &
affections & I really think I shall dye with his praises in my
mouth do as he may do afterwards—I always told you to act
as an Editor you may get above such insinuating bother I must

* cast? dial. 'look'.

knock under for my own advantage I find it far easier to have an hours work of flattery then I usd to do an hours threshing in a barn & tho I have not yet been swore at Highgate I have judgement enough to chuse the most easy method in such things—if E.L.E. & L.R. had found me out first & edited my poems what monsters woud they have made can it be possible to judge I think praises of self & selfs noble friend & selfs incomparable poems undoubtedly shovd into the bargain woud have left little room for me & mine to grow up in the esteem of the public but shoud end into a dark corner they woud have servd as a foundation for their own buildings & dwindled away like the tree surrounded with Ivy while the names & praises of patron and poetess flourished in every page—when you get the 'Ways &c' tell me as soon as possible how you like them or I woud not send them had it not been to get on with the rest or leave them altogether—my dear Taylor with the warmest affection I remain your

humblest

JOHN CLARE

To Taylor

Addressed: Messrs. Taylor and Hessey, 93 Fleet St, London.
[*sent*]

Helpston Dec. 30. 1820

MY DEAR TAYLOR.

Having sent off the New Poems a week to day (Saturday) I begin to see fear lest they should be lost I have no clear copys by me and therefore it woud be a loss at least in my conscit by this time you have them if safe and if not you will know of the miscarriage if you have not got them write me directly and I will seek about them but if you have them you need say nothing

I have had 2 invitations from Mrs E to come to London who says she will procure an inside passage for me in the Stamford or Deeping coaches but I must refuse this polite generous and uncommon civility—alas what a pity I also met with John Christian Burkhardt[1] Es^q at M^r G's last Sunday who gave me

another invitation to accompany him which was a giant offer
to resist for he is a very touchy fellow and an exquisite hand at
punch making he says he saw my head at your house and reckons
the painting the finest he has seen latly

I have begun the 'Statute' a second time as a piece by itself
and have several others for the ways in village now on the file
so I shall have plenty for it without taking the old ones.

Have you heard Mr Townsends Poems[2] are publishing by
'T Boys' I wonder what made him choose this picture dressing
publisher and I wonder what he has made of Jerusalem his
longest poem as its name is unnovel after 'Milman'[3] tho I
think any way better than dramatic for such a subject Have you
got my address to Lord R fearing you may not I here send it—
for publishing!!!

[There follows:]

TO LORD RADSTOCK

Tis sweet to reccolect lifes past controuls[4]

I shall send all the rough M.S.S. in a week or two and then
you may do as you like with them tho there is nothing in them
worth publishing.

yours

JOHN CLARE

To Taylor

Addressed: Messrs Taylor & Hessey, 93 Fleet Street, London.
[sent]

2 Jan 1821.

DEAR TAYLOR

I recieved all safe this day & in very high spirits it had made
me I asure you

I have been to Mr. G. & as to the morning headache you are
a good prophet but when a man has had experience in merry
making he knows how to judge for a croney

I like your idea of two vols exceeding well & the Title you
can make no better do as you will so dont attempt a fresh
touching The Cottage you mean to reserve for the fourth Vol

who the d–l do you think will unstring their purses for Clares
4th Vol of Poems I shall have the ague in even thinking to
venture again after my 3 children are christend by the critics
even if they be pleasd to give them a good name I think you
better scrat it on wood for the title of the 3 Vol but do as seem-
eth the best friend John for thou hast been a lucky god-father
for my first child & I leave all the rest to thy own management
The Wish* is earlyish I think about 15 Just when I had got
the knack of writing smoothly with little sense the line from
Pomfret I got from a second hand vol of Miscellanies by
'Werge'† a man then (when his book was printed) residing at
Stamford The authors I mention I had never seen then further
than the title page & Templeman is bad as I have since heard

The £10 is safe & snug in my pocket thats all I shall say on
that You said nought about getting the last Quarto perhaps my
letter hadnt reached you I shall send all the rest up next
Saturday or Tuesday at farthest I am writing 'Winter'‡ a half
salve as it were but as true as the gospel & why is not a man to
tell truth & shame the devil in these devilish comical times—
when thats finished I shall have 'Days gone bye'§ & then the
'Loves of Jockey & Jinney'‖ I have somthing I think that will
struggle and hobble out of me better than I have yet done only
tell me my faults in long poems of the Ways in a village you
last got & I shall know how to escape shipwreck for the future
with your Compass I cannot feel satisfied without leading
strings yet tho I think I want them less then before

Give my respects to Keats & tell him I am a half mad melancholly dog in this moozy misty country he has latly cast behind
him but I feel somthing better at least I fancy which I believe
to tell truth is the whole of my complaint which I am so fussy
over bytimes

Give my best wishes to all my friends of 'a happy new year'
to 'em Tothill I understand by O.G. desired to be remembered
to J.C. & by your letter I return many thanks for his notice &
good memory

J. CLARE

* Unpublished. Not 'A Wish', sonnet in *The Village Minstrel*.
† *A Collection of Original Poems, Essays, and Epistles* by John Werge: printed
by subscription, 1753.
‡ *The Village Minstrel*.   § Unpublished.   ‖ *The Shepherd's Calendar*.

To Hessey

Addressed: Messrs Taylor and Hessey, 93 Fleet St, London.
[*sent*]

p.m. Jan. 1821

DEAR HESSEY

I thought fit to tell you I got the Oysters safe & have tryd to
eat them to be rid of this melancholly humour that attends me
tho I never coud touch them before I fear I shall not match
them while they are good—I am not in the writing kip at this
time I scarcely find words to say anything the information you
got respecting me no doubt has magnified your ideas & 'made
mountains out of molehills' I am not bad in body but in mind
tis an old complaint & 8 or 9 years & every spring & autumn
gives me a touch of it I shall no doubt get one in the sharpest
part of winter as for what you have heard respecting my
uneasiness about Advertisements &c is mere stuff as I am quite
satisfied & never but conjecturd improperly in the latter ere
twas explaind—you have got my last ere now & all is settled I
have been with Drury to a feast 2 days & feel myself much
betterd by it tho the society of farmers respecting books &c is
little preferable to Goths & Vandals their genius lies in eating
& drinking & in that they are nearly fellows I have heard
nothing more respecting 'Christ's Colledge' yet—No London
for me this year unless Taylor thinks it very necessary I am in
no Q for travelling so if he can do without me I hope he will
if not his best plans shall not be dissapointed if he thinks the
book will be any ways betterd by it come I will tho I shoud
not like so and so to know of my being there till the latter end
of my stay if they did there woud be little else done by me but
gossiping 8 or 9 days mark is the extent of my visit be as it
will & if T can do without it I hope he will—tell him the faster
he gets on with business the better when he returns as I shall
have no more excuses for idleness after he has had so much of
it he may now get the book out as soon as the first was if it
pleases him to stick to work—I expect 'Sherrys* Letter' will
appear [3 lines scored out heavily by Clare] I hope he will put

* Sherwill's.

all the Songs he can in & I think the Title of 'Poems & Songs'*
will do but T settles that matter—The 'Vicar' & the 'Wed-
ding'† are my next trials in Poetry you'll not forget Christmas
—you are aware—when T writes I hope he means to tell me
what things pleases him best I hope he may be in London on
Show as I am anxious to prove how the world will favour my
second offering—

Yours &c &c

JOHN CLARE

To Taylor

Addressed: Messrs Taylor and Hessey, 93 Fleet St., London.
[*sent*]

Helpstone Jan 3. 1821

MY DEAR TAYLOR

I thought it woud be more satisfactory to you if the letter
which containd Earl Spencers[1] half annuity was answerd
immediatly to say I have recievd it safe is enough for that
purpose

I did write to his Lordship long ago at the request of Dr
Bell[2] thro whom his Lordships unmerited kindness was com-
municated to me

But I had then recieved none of his benefaction I wrote to
Lord R. some time after midsummer when the first became due
to seek after it & he accordingly did which was sent down I
think at Michaelmas I did not send a note because as I thought
what I had done already made it no less but if you think it not
so I will write immediatly as you first wishd when you made
the Enquirey.

I must now take an oppertunity to answer things I must in
your former letter & make an appology for that blundering sin
which I often commit as I write hastily & never look over the
letters I write if anyone asks me 5 Questions I am quite safe to
forget 3 of em Lord R. often complains of this & a many others
think it willfull but the blunt truth of it is the cause I have above

* 'Ways of a Village' had been dropped as a possible title for the forthcoming
book.
† Unpublished.

mentioned ones mind often being occupyd in ryhming the while
I am writing a letter to one I sit down as nessesary labour to
the other as prompted pleasure the first is like writing a dull
copy at School & the sooner got thro the better is what I
fancy so much for this—

The Prose[3] you speak of is mine entirely such as it is & was
intended to be carried on in a series of Characteristic & Descriptive Pastorals in prose on rural life & manners but for the
want of better judgments then mine I dropt it altogether dont
print it in the books if you think it worth while going on with
tell me so & I will take up my first plan I make no doubt after
the 4th Vol is out such a change as 'Pastorals in Prose' woud
take well—what says John Taylor—he is [has?] only got to
say—to drop it or receive it—as to your putting the introduction in my way I dont know what to say to't wont something in the way do as I gave you a sketch of: when I was in
London I think the latter part woud do well—you must tell me
after a while somthing on this or I cant get on—you never put
in that the last Quarto was come to you safe with the village
poems tell me in your next—do just as you proposd wi the 2
Vols leave the Cott for the 4th your plan cannot be improvd a
second reading of it has pleasd me mightily & I wish no
alteration of what you have just pland if your own judgment
jumps at anything better so it is—I think no body better then
the Editor for returning a compliment in some way or other
to a generous public as his taste was as greatly hazarded after
so warm an introduction—'twas my reputation or downfall—
but just as you please—& I am satisfyd—

Yours &c &c

JOHN CLARE

To Taylor

Addressed: Messrs. Taylor and Hessey, 93 Fleet St, London.
[sent]

Helpstone Jan. 7 1821.

MY DEAR TAYLOR

I just got your letter as I started for Stamford this morning
to recieve my quarters anuity from the Marquis but I shall

never loose the pleasure of answering a letter of those whose
correspondence is always enlivening & welcome I wish I coud
say so by every one—Drurys conscieted ways often provoked
me dont notice his pencil dashes no were if you had been
mistaken & led astray by them my vexation woud have certainly fell home upon him as it did last winter on other matters—
respecting the mistake you had better wait till I am gone and
say nothing of it poor fellow he is humble enough now & I
have had many pleasant Evenings with him at Stamford and
what is past is past I dont like to hurt him so let it pass I
leave plenty behind me to correct the mistake which in any
mans reason I think is already corrected at least in yours
shoud we three ever come together you bring it up & his
arguments will be like children playing with burning paper
'there goes the Parson & there goes the clerk'—but I can
assure you if no John Taylor & Hessey had been in the mess
poor Drury woud have quite lost me after his agreement I have
no confidence in him I now always look up to you as the head
& I only wish to keep up my friendship with him for the early
good he did me for had it not been for him I shoud never have
met with John Taylor & this he often cracks of for it is all that
is left him after his foolish proceedings but I still think twas
ignorance in trusting to others selfish opinions that led him
astray I am glad you like the 'Peasant Boy' for I have read the
rough sketch a second time & think some of the things the
best I have written I sent off all I had bye me yesterday & you
will have them to-night I expect send me your letter I shoud
have had besure ye I shall entirely hate D. at last if he plays
that with me I have often thought he stopped letters directly
to me & have greater cause to strengthen that jealousy put in
despotic & in the 5th Edit: alter it agen to 'cursed' never mind
Lord R.s pencilings in the 'Peasant Boy' what he dont like
he must lump as the dog did his dumpling I woud not have
'there once were lanes, etc.' left out for all the Lord Rs. in
Europe d–n it do as you like I tell you if you like to print
'cursed' too print it—'& a fig for the sultan & sophy'—I wait
anxiously for Tothills poems* if he has got any more like
'Shrewsbury' & 'Tothill Fields' he'll do for the Byron of

* Reynolds's *Garden of Florence.*

Byrons never produced their superiors—I wish him success
heartily my returns to Mr. Hessey warm as the winter alows
me I am in haste for my Journey

so farwell & God bless you

JOHN CLARE

To Taylor

Addressed: Messrs Taylor and Hessey, 93 Fleet St, London.
[sent]

Helpstone Jan 16 1821

MY DEAR TAYLOR

As I wish you to have everything good bad & indiferent that
I can scrat up I copied the two following trifles from Ds M.S.S.
thinking you had not seen them—send the proofs directly to me
as you proposd you say very justly & apropriatly that my case
is like the man with two wives but mind ye when youve culled
out the white hairs Ill stick to the black ones—I forgot to
remind you about putting in '*My Mary*'[1] & '*Ways of the Wake*'[1]
in this 4th Edit also the '*Country Girl*'[1] the ommission of the
2 first cut my muses wings cursedly this you know well & I
doubt not you will remedy it the fittest opportunity your
speaking so warmly of the '*Village Minstrel*' has revived me
wonderfully & I shall proceed next Spring with the string of
rural tales I at first intended—your title will do I fancy D.
says you have all the songs entirely & all the poems he had
by him:—

[There follows:]

WHATS BEAUTYS LOVE[2]

Whats beauty's love a sunny shower . . .

[sonnet]

[and]

BALLAD[3]

Of all the days in Memory's test . . .

[three stanzas]

Doubless you have these if you have not why mention it sometime & I can perhaps seek after others I may fancy you have
not in our next plans I shall avoid this bother & send them up

89

to you direct without allowing others to copy & then keep the
originals & then we shall steer clear from pencil marks &c &
let me remind you not to let Mrs. E. make so free with the
writings but that I daresay youll remember for your own peace
& comfort Lord R. never writes to me nor I to him Mrs E.
has sent 2 letters & I have not answered either yet—still
there is meneuvering in the wind news papers comes again in
abundance—if you think the adress to Lord R will affect the
generallity of my patrons leave it out—twill be quite plenty
to mention him with the rest in the preface—all I say to John
Taylor is *Do as you pleese* were there is no fear of breaking the
peace

Yours &c &c

JOHN CLARE

To Taylor

[*sent*]

Jan 23 1821

MY DEAR TAYLOR

Having betook me seriously to think about my latter end I
send you the fruits of my repentance—in reading 'Gastrels
Institutes'* I found some most beautiful images which I had
never noticed in the Scriptures before and which I never coud
have believed existed in them had I not seen it they are chiefly
from Job on mans Mortallity—Lord R is manouvring uncommonly now he has written to D. and to Lord Milton about
me being ill he fancies flummery pleases me but hes mistaken
for I wish all such bother far enough and am glad Lord M
has learnd to disregard paper kites I pass over tusles without
notice—for I have not heard from him—I wrote Mrs E. and
have given her a thought or two from the bottom of my mind
as naked as possible but I fear shell dream over it and make
two meanings of it and chose the best for herself—Lord R. has
sent for his first letter back—whats this mean—Ill readily send

---

* *The Christian Institutes*, or 'the Sincere Word of God, being a Plain and
Impartial Account of the whole Faith and Duty of a Christian, by Francis Gastrell,
late Lord Bishop of Chester'; it had run into twelve editions by the beginning of
the century.

all if he wants em—O Vanity thou vapouring idol of weak
minds whats thy value? the ilumination of the rainbow and the
painted Clouds of sunset is more lasting than thee thou wordy
war of nothingness and sounding symbol of empty delusion
whoever listens to thee goeth 'into the wilderness to see a reed
shaken by the wind' Thou breath of an euphemism I have lived
to experience thee and am left to sigh with an elder witness of
thy folly 'Vanity of Vanitys all is vanity' When you write me
again I want some instructions respecting making a will as life
is uncertain I intend to leave my parents 5^s a week of the
funded money and patty the rest with an equal share of what
comes from the publications till she remains a widow and then
it drops to the child if I dont make a will she gets all and I shall
be d–d mad at that I asure you so gi's your opinions sometime

farewell
and god bless you

JOHN CLARE

To Taylor

[*sent*]

[Early 1821]

MY DEAR TAYLOR
   I have here faithfully delineated the simple customs of
Labours Harvest holidays of which I have many times been a
spectator & I think I have done them decently for I strove to
avoid indelicacy as much as possible—I need not chide your
delay now that I hear you say you have been looking over all
my letters I more need pity you & praise your patience for I
coud not have undertaken such a task for the world—you
perhaps never was informed that the Rev^d Mr Mounsey[1] of
the Grammar School Stamford was the first man that gave me
encouragement as the first Subscriber & as the first that
heartened me up in my new avocation by giving me hopes &
wishing me success—in my estcem he is worth a thousand of
the contributors who saw the sun rise before they haild my
success who woud doubtless in the storm of disappointment cast

me behind them—Rev^d Mr Mossop the vicar of our parish showd me some notice & deserves remembrance—Rev^d Mr Holland you are well aware of (I had the pleasure of a visit from him a few days back he lives at St. Ives Hunts) The Rev^d Mr Boon of Ufford[2] an utter stranger before sent me £5 with a kind & ingenious letter he is a good friend—my old friend Captain Sherwill you will not forget Townsend too has been very good to me & is worthy notice—to mention Gilchrists name will be sufficient unless you have a mind to print the invitation for the address to the first book sent to him shall not appear in the second at any rate nor in any other thats sanctioned with my good will—you might mention ʻA Ladyʼ[3] as being very kind to me & leave guess the rest the anonymous ʻA.B.ʼ[4] if you like may be noticed his was the first letter I recievd & Sherwills the second memory looks warm on these for ever—here is all as I know of except the nobility which you know well—my warmth for Mr Hamiltonʼs[5] poetry is coold a little on looking into it more leisurely there is too much ado about lilies faireys & roseys but still I like him his garden of florence[5] has many beautys his romance of youth[5] has not its name for nothing for its romantic enough but there is good things in it how much the outline is like mine one coud hardly have concievd such a similarity coud exist in different minds— there is a good deal of Reynolds[5] manner of expression about the poetry as I think & some things are as good as his especially the dedication which is as exactly in the Shrewsbury manner for tenderness in recollection &c that had I seen it elsewhere I should have swore it had been his & laid a wager on the bargain—let the man be who he will heʼs a poet & as far above many as white breadʼs before brown—That sombre sadness of memory that preaching to trees to waterfalls & flowers is just what delights me such is the general breathings of the volume which I shouldnt mind being the author of myself were I man sufficient to wear such a title—so much for Mr Hamilton & I heartily wish him success for he deserves it—I have many more things to say coud I reccolect them

Yours &c &c

JOHN CLARE

To Taylor

Addressed: Messrs. Taylor and Hessey, 93 Fleet St, London.
[*sent*]

Feb 7 1821

MY DEAR TAYLOR

I sent off the parcel of proofs yesterday I carefully sealed them up & hope you will get them safe you will see I approve of everything or nearly which you have done I thought it right to inform you by letter that I had started them lest they may lie upon the road—your critisism on 'Woodcroft'* is just as I valued the thing myself for I think I had easy do better some fitter opportunity I think your ending of the Minstrel closes capital & now fancy in its present dress that it will make a good appearance dont alter your mind in adding the verses already omitted for you will certainly spoil it your alterations of the last lines of each verse cannot be better so I left them untouched— think of the gap in the marks X X X X & tell me your thoughts of the verse I propose for it—if you cant see a defect in its present state tell me so & I readily abide by it get on with the publishing as fast as you can & send me more proofs as soon as possible—I am sorry to hear of you being ill but death shall have nothing to do with you till Ive made use of you—let him dip elsewhere in the Catalogue & welcome he will find food in plenty to keep him from starving that will be little miss'd & not grudg'd at all by your humble St or very few else I dare say you know very well were the allusion directs you—I am now taking a great mess of pills & phisic more by force than other wise—I am now in consiet I shall not dye yet yours &c

J. CLARE

---

* *Madrigals and Chronicles* (newly found poems written by John Clare; edited with Preface and Commentary by Edmund Blunden) (1924).

To Taylor

Addressed: Messrs. Taylor and Hessey, 93 Fleet St, London.
[*sent*]

Helpstone Feb 8 1821

MY DEAR TAYLOR

I am forced to trouble you with another letter but of what worth the information may be I am not able to determine I saw Drury tother day (Wednesday) & he said woud not 'Village Minstrels' do for a general title of the 2 Vols & then 'Village Minstrel' merely at the head of the long poem woud not be so much noticed—I rather liked it and thought I would let you know—you do as you please with it D seems hipt with not having the proofs sent his way I woud not satisfy him a word about the matter only by saying I liked the new method of sending them vastly well for I hate a betrayer of private confidence even in an enemy much more a friend—D. likes 'Village Minstrel' for the long poem uncommon well but has the same opinion of it as you fear still he says if the general title be adopted 'Village Minstrels' the fear of plagiarism will be reduced to a trifle as 'Village Minstrel' will only stand at the head of the long poem— weigh this in your ballance & you will readily see its merits & defects—I have been getting on with my 'Memoirs' & shall have it for you inspection by summer—I did not copy Lord Rs letter because I thought it would not be 'upright & downright honesty' Dxxxx 'you know you do' is develish stunt & sullen at our reserve I went last week & have got a sickening for a while—I think I manage things d–d well by not managing them worse than I have done —too many fingers in a pye will not do 'Chuckey' & you know the meddling fingers of some such peddlers very well—I shant say a word to him I think about the proofs unless he smells it out—I shall then say I only have one now & then that wants much alteration which I am obliged to send back as soon as finished—the fact is I have took a minds vow that no eye shall see them out of my house while I posses them & curse me if I dont keep it—be as reserved as I may

Yours &c &c

JOHN CLARE

To Taylor

Addressed: Messrs Taylor and Hessey, 93 Fleet St, London.
[*sent*]

Feb 13 1821

MY DEAR TAYLOR

Before I turn to your letter I will tell you how to direct the
next parcel for its more speedy arival do it thus 'To John Clare
Helpstone left at the Bull Inn M. Deeping and forwarded to
Mr Butlers Market place imediatly' This will at least prevent
a Fortnights delay for the future

In respect of travelling into the unknown hereafter I hope
that mine may be a long way off and yours longer to stay and
write my life and Edit. as a collected book of the poetry so that
I shall have no dread on my mind of being scandalized with a
bad character and so as to leave no Enemey (for I have many
skulking ones that pretend friends help) a corner to spout his
venom in—hope your statement of your illness may decieve
you for you must not dye a Bachelor if you dislike the business
of feeding Monkeys and riding on ass back in Paradise as they
say all Bachelor and Maids will be forced too in the next world
so hark ye chuckey seek out in time—now to business I have
had my dose of 'Village Minstrelsy' after your information no
worse a singer and no better phisic to sicken a repetition could
be given *woud not sell* is plenty to abandon anything of that
nature so I am content but 'Minstrel Villager' & 'Village Muse'
are very poor & very bad—the 'Peasant Boy' is but middling
while your 'Village Minstrel still sticks in my memory as best
of all—& out of these 2 you chuse for yourself—as for my past
I should chuse the last—I cannot think engrafting the name of
the long poem on the title good—suppose it pass on its own
head & in the contents alone then 'Peasant Boy' or 'Village
Minstrel will not be so noticable—'every hut will stand on its
own bottom' says the proverb—& you know theres such scores
of Titles running 'So & So with other Poems that people
think expectations is only raised to be cheated which 19 times
out of 20 is the very case your alterations of swopping I cannot
but approve when you refer to such authorities else ill bound
fort[1] you like with me swopping best—I thought the verse

'Nature looked etc. woud do as I proposd & knew you would
see in a wink if it did—your alterations in the rest are good—
your 'endangerd pail etc is too fancily expressed

Tormenting maidens neath their kicking cow
Who often murmurd at the elfin crew
& from the endangerd pail with angry vow
Oft rose their sport—to spoil with switch of murdering
    bough

yours woud have passd with me but it was too exaggerated—
This of mine will do uncommon well—excuse my consciet—
I am glad you have urged me to it—but you see I have made use
of your ideas which I coud not better—send the indelicate verse
in your next and Ill do my utmost to suit you which I can do
e[asily] I fancy: but those spotless puritys of '[virgin?]
snows' is hell and purgatory to me because to suit them is
impossible as to this you never had a taste as well as myself
& have been under as like awkward predicaments all provincialisms & everything else required shall be readily answerd when
wishd—*long* 'That on nights pausing can etc.' I think it
sounds well and far better than the old word 'strong' so adopt
it.—*Stone rocked waggon* etc. will do better then I coud have
utterd it had I tryd at it a month so take that likewise—tis a
good thought—I am rather sorry to loose this 'Grey girded
eve and rosey wreathed morn' but a line too much will not do
and *morn of rosey hue* being far from bad—take that also—& get
on as fast as you can—& dont be nice on trifles I shall not
disagree about altering a word or so if wanted as nessesary or
if time be precious—Tho I wish that had been less then 10
lines for I thought it good particularly the line aluded too—but
do as you have done for you cant do better we must as you
justly observe have it as free from fault as possible—write
agen when you want to know anything I always like to hear
of you

                  yours &c &c
                    JOHN CLARE

To Taylor

Addressed: Messrs Taylor and Hessey, 93 Fleet St, London.
[*sent*]

15 Feb 1821.

MY DEAR TAYLOR

I always forget something & bye a second reading of your last I find the enquirey wether its 'Peggy' Bond or 'Band' tho its not of much consequence I like to be particular as to trifles in such matters the old song alluded to is 'Peggy ' *Band*' there is a song of modern date thats call'd 'Peggy Bond' but tis nothing like the old one neither in words or music for the tune of the old one is Capital as my father used to sing it but I cannot say much for the words for you know the best of our old English ballads thats preserved by the memorys of our rustics (what ever they might have been) are so mutilated that they scarcly rise to mediocrity while their melodys are beautiful & the more I hear them the more I wish Id skill enough in music to prick them down—The Marquis of Exeter call'd on me yesterday & enquired very condescendingly & kindly after the new Vols & told me to be sure to let him know when they came out—this is something good in the wind I hope—but I could not make my d–d stupidity to beg pardon for the blunder I commited at Stamford in not knowing his lordship my senses always leave me when I get before these great men but twas uncommon kind of his Lordship to come over to helpstone was it not & it makes me feel more gratful than ever—you must speak morts on his goodness in the introduction 'chuckey' for you know he's bin my greatest friend yet if money has any conscence for friendship but what I value his Lordships generosity was not sought for by a soul he saw the book & the honourable Mr Pierpoint[1] came over to introduce me to his Lordship before he was an utter stranger to me & knew no more of me or the Village then your self did in—circumstancs occurd—you now see more light on my Patron what a contrast between Lord R & this gentle nobleman aye chuckey—I know this notice will make your feelings echo with mine & then what I feel you can express for I cannot so give him his due in the

introduction for you can & no man better—a Londoner calld
on me this day & is just gone he promises me 'Lord Byrons
Works' & Rogers 'Pleasures of Memory' he says he belongs
to the 'London Institution' & appears a gentleman—he fussd
me up by saying that in all parts where hes been latly expectations is strongly excited by the announcement of the futur
poems in the press he asked me some queries, on provincial
words & said he was pleasd with them tho he did not understand them without refering to the Gloss: & thought them the
most prominent beauty in the poems he left & kindly left his
generosity likewise in nothing but—promises

Yours

JOHN CLARE

P.S. If you have printed Bond it signifys not a straw only
notice in 'Errata'

To Taylor

Addressed: Messrs Taylor and Hessey, 93 Fleet St.
[*sent*]

p.m. 17. Feb. 1821

MY DEAR TAYLOR

I have got the verse from Stamford & altered it I think just
such as you can wish no better to be done—at least all indelicacy
is lost or the indelicate will be damn puzzled to attribute that
to it—here it is

[There follows:]

Along the road were coupl'd maid & swain
& Dick & Dolly now for gifts did sue
He'd gi'n her ribbons & he deemed agen
Some kind return as nothing but his due
He told her things a ploughman rarely knew
Bout breaking hearts & pains—a mighty spell
Her Sunday cloes might damage wi the dew
She quite forgot them while he talked so well
& listend to his tales till darkness round em fell

I am pleasd with it by throwing such disguise over it to think how it will wrack the prudes to find fault there is somthing in it but they'll know not were to get at it—tis quite delicate now

The Gentleman of the General Post Office[1] I told you of once has this morning performed his promise in sending me some paper & a fine lump he has sent me I asure you about 3 times the quantity of yours by bulk so I shall not want for paper in haste now as I have got over the difficulties of altering I shall not trouble you further with letters till the other proofs come or nessesity requires it I shall be glad when the Vols gets out for I shall not settle till they are

I have never wrote a ryhme since the last I sent you & I feel as awkard for a thought as if I had never wrote one but a year's rest will do me no harm next winter I mean to start a long poem as some sort of Continuation of the Peasant Boy if it succeeds—Drury sent last night a most passionate resolve of coming hostilities against your silence & reserve—I have this morning answered him as far as I thought right on my part by saying I have no reasons for being in ill humour with London so he did as he pleasd- -I shoud not heat irons any longer to burn ones own fingers in the end—between you & me his quarrels seem after what his agreement did will begin with the farce of 'raising the wind' & end in 'Much Ado about nothing' & if he flames much your contradiction to copy from the quarterly is at your finger ends—I cannot put faith in such lies —so look to't you have my permission to say that I contradict it as a falsity when in London this will make him appeal to me at once which I shall as bluntly contradict now—only mind I shall have nothing further to do in these wars of Pens ink & paper as far as honesty is conserned Ill stick to the text

I am

Yours &c &c

JOHN CLARE

To Taylor

Addressed: Messrs Taylor and Hessey, 93 Fleet St, London.
[*sent*]

p.m. 24 Feb. 1821

MY DEAR TAYLOR

I must trouble you with another scrawl—fearing you might
not find the verses alluded to in the 'Reccolections after a
Ramble' as I have the idea I have dressd it up a second time
as nigh the 2 verses as memory coud assist me these are they

[There follows:]

. . . *& left free to every whim* . . .

[16 lines: but not used in V.M.]

I think them good at least too good to be lost & as I have a
straight forward communication with you in these Vols I like
to give you every trifle to make them as good as possible—
I used to send alterations & additions of certain passages in
the first Vol but now find they hardly ever reachd you we
have remedyd this & I feel a pleasure in the satisfaction that
everything I may hint will reach you without the addition of
others conciets for my own is plenty—the 2 verses must be put
somewhere before the shower commences perhaps before I
entered the wood or just after I get out of it will do with equal
propriety each way tell me in your next if you adopt them &
if they add to the pieces improvment—Is poor Scott gone—
Drakard the Editor of the 'Stamford News' has been severly
beaten this week in a rather cowardly way by a person coming
in with the excuse of buying a book who while D turnd to look
[for] it cudgeled him with a stick & rid off the stranger had a
footman with him & is someone no doubt that the Paper has
provokingly abused but who it is or for what cause he has
beaten him I know not—perhaps this is news to you if you
dont see Ds Paper for I expect it makes a flaming appeal there
with its usual addition of a lye—Never hear from Lord R &
Mrs E. now not a single line they are about weary & so am I
so god send they may find out a new 'child of nature' to foster
& flatter whose name is rather fresher than mine & who has

not yet known the world to give it its proper value—for
he's such likes darling wonders no longer then while he knows
not that flattery must be fed at his own expence—

Yours sincerely

JOHN CLARE

[On front of sheet:]
I dont like the title of 'Impromptu on the Sight of Spring'*
do you: the first word is comical tho I adopted it—still if you
like it keep it by all means what you like I'll not interupt

J.C.

To Taylor

Addressed: John Taylor Esq., 93 *Fleet St, London.*

[sent]

Taylor's date: March 1821

MY DEAR TAYLOR

I thank you heartily for your honest liberallity in wishing to
purchase the Elms[1] for me & shall certainly never forget it—
but you shall not buy them—let them dye like the rest of us—
I have seen O.G. having started on tuesday on urgent invitations for that purpose & according to custom staid 2 days in
the town & made myself confoundedly drunk the last night
I rolld to Drurys who can certainly say plenty to degrade me
if he pleases for I was beastly in for it—I hate Stamford but am
dragged into it like a Bear & fidler to a wake—people that
advise me to keep at employment soberly at home are the first
that tempt me to break from it—I have seen the fourth Edition
—I am agen bothered with visitors by dozens—I was once
proud of being seen—but I now am always glad to hide from
them—my vanity is wearied with satisfactional dissapointments & it rests easy—I find all my former pleasures in my old
companions & skulk amongst them like a deer thats been
hunted with the hounds I fear if I shoud go off they'll say I dyd
by drunkenness—but they may be d–d 'vain pomp & glory of
the world I hate ye'—now to business, your alterations I have

---

* 'On the Sight of Spring': *The Village Minstrel.*

101

adopted entirely—your omissions I shall say little against—only I think those except one in the Woodman which you omit are the best of it—but dont be ruled by me if you are I shoud be vext if I knew it they read well without em—so dont insert em besure ye—Patty keeps the Address to an Infant Daughter by her as I first wrote it she wishd to hear of the objectional verse & thought it a compliment so little does she know of poetry—I am very glad you left the verse out—for I have found out by experience which is a good adviser that I posses a more valuable article in her than I at first expected & believe her from my soul an honest woman her calumniators were all of that sort of lyars that wish to make others as disgraceful as the world knows themselves to be—this sort is very plentiful here —Patt & myself now begin to know each other & live happily & I deem it a fortunate era in my life that I met with her—she thanks you kindly for blotting out the injury on her character in the above poem & is proud she has got such friends I assure you—the cut of her face always delighted me more than any other & had I never seen her my attempts at poetry woud never have been resumed after my removal to Casterton—I like Hessey's opinion of the 'Woodlarks'[2] &c uncommon & have crossd it out to be omitted accordingly—I am at a loss for reading—what sort is 'Hazlitts Lectures of the Living Poets'[3] of if its entertaining you might let me have it to read if not say nought about it I seek only amusement—I shall lay by for another day—& if I've nothing more to say goodbye & God bless you both

J. CLARE

If you dont like the 2 Verses in 'Sunday' cut them out tv·ill do without em very well—youre now going on at a good rate—I shall be glad when these Vols get off our hands & I daresay yourself wont be sorry—You get over your job uncommon well —at least to my consiet & thats plenty—I want a vol of my poems to give as a present—I dont mean to run any more lengths with Drury if possible—so send me one of the 4th Edit if you please next time you send the parcel—all the last sheet is early poems except 'Absence'[4] & as I shall set 'early' on every poem of that sort you may make some mention were

you insert them or any way you please as you know best—I
think if you insert all 'Sunday' it woud be a more varied picture
as it is—there is a sameness [in?] the verse you omit & the 2
Verses you mark are the most near nature in the whole poem—
the 'Woodman' too its omitted verses are too good to loose
but I can make use of them in something to come so never
mind—Patty was taken dangerously & suddenly ill last night—
she is no better yet & the alarm has made me very uneasy—I
coud not have thought I shoud have felt so anxious for her
safety

To Taylor

[sent]
Taylor's date: about March 7 1821

MY DEAR TAYLOR

I shall write little this time as theres little nessesity for it you
will see I approve of most of your alterations as usual—No 5
you left out in the letter so I could not say but be what it will
do as you would with my approval the Poem you wish to omit
I agree too & think it right as there is plenty to pick out of the
2 verses in the Ramble your reasons for omitting them is
convinced me of my mistake in thinking them good so omit
them & welcome—you know I urge no thing—I only suggest—
& if you dont select them with the same judgement as you woud
was they your own productions you do your self an injury by
being cramp'd with opinions was I to know that was the case
I would suggest no more your taste is preferable to any I have
witnessd & on that I rely—mines not worth twopence—& a
critics is too severe for me—a man of feeling that looks on
faults with indulgence & never willfuly passes by a blossom he
may chance to find on his journey is a man to my mind & such
a one (no flattery mind from me) I reckon John Taylor—
'Woodseers' is insects which I daresay you know very well
wether it be the proper name I dont know tis what we call
them & that you know is sufficient for us—they lye in little
white rolls of spittle on the backs of leaves & flowers how they
come I dont know but they are always seen plentiful in moist

weather—& are one of the shepherds weather glasses when the head of the insect is seen turnd upward it is said to token fine weather when downward on the contrary wet may be expected —which no doubte is as good signs as Moore's Almanack profeses—I think they turn to grasshoppers[1] I am almost certain for I have watched them minutely—Drury calld on me at 7 oclock last night I thought he was crazd but I found he had been to Spalding & made Helpstone in his way—he seemd uneasy I knew very well at what but said nothing he asked me if I had got any proofs latly I said I had but had just started them I did not wish him to see them so I told the fib—give him a Rowland for an Oliver if hes too much of it—I never said a word about knowing of his sending you a letter I shall never know about nothing—he talks about coming to London but I think he'll not face you if he does come—dont be botherd with anybody serve him up as the rest if he deserves it—I hate such paper headed consiet about folks—I know friends to whom Im indebted & shall stick there he makes me d–d mad with his meddling that I have given him up to your mercy entirely— he merely helpd me to you thats all the good hes done me & hes reaping daily benefit for it what woud he have—'surely' as you say 'the Author & Editor are men enough to decide on such things without him'—this moment I am interupted by an invitation from Mr Gilchrist in a short note—no I shall not go this time I am in no kip for travelling & am sick of Stamford I have done it over & over & 20 times over—things you know get weari-some at least I know wives of bad fortune does—Mr G. tells me of Scotts[2] death but I know all about it & am as sorry for it as he can be tho I knew nothing more of the man then by his actions which tells me he had more honesty and honour then his enemies Lockhart is a d–d knave & a coward & my insig-nificant self would tell him so to his teeth—but Mr G. tells me to stick to a cudgel when I quarrel—I also hear that Bowles is at him again—Bowles will whine him out at last if he dont mind[3]—I like your alteration of the bucket much in 'Rosey Jane'[4] & am glad your friends urged you to it for I never liked it myself as it stood

yours &c &c
JOHN CLARE

To Hessey

Addressed: Messrs Taylor and Hessey, 93 Fleet St, London.
[*sent*]

17 March 1821

My Dear Hessey

I resieved your letter with the proofs this day—& its contents
was so reviving that I coudnt let it pass unanswered—'Criticism
may do her worst'—& be d–d when shes done it—to escape
the hell of party-political critisism is impossible—so I am
prepared—I am glad your opinion of my advancement is so
favourable—I think much of it and feel its value—I heard of
O.G's being ill but that was all for I have not been at his house
this two months or more—I am very weary of gossoping—I am
glad Woodhouse is better—Taylor should certainly take the air
& more exercise then he does [four lines scored out] your red
cheeks & the garden rose is quite poetical & a good allusion to
its subject—I should have wishd your letter had filld the sheet
at least—but its end is come Now for mine—Taylor said
nothing of 'Jockey & Jinney' he leaves it for another time—
but I am waiting to continue it so spur him up when he comes
back—I have nearly finished another its 'a tale of other days'
I call it 'The Vicar' The man whom I copy has been gone
nearly a century—long before hunting parsons had existance—
his character floats in the memory of the village—& from that
my rescorces are gleaned—I think I have made a good thing
of it—but that stands for nothing still it satisfys me & always
urges me on to the end when I fancy that—his monument is a
little round free stone by the side of the alter it records no name
or date its Latin & the substance of it is thus 'At the day of
resurrection I hope it will be known who I am' his salary was
£35 yearly & his charitys was great considering his income
if he saw a bare footed beggar in the street he woud take him
home & give him is shoes very often the only pair he possesd
waiting in the house till his shoemaker set him at liberty with
new ones—& his last sixpence has often been thrust into the
hands of a widow or orphan—his heart was so open to the
miseries of mankind that his friends often deemed it nessesary

105

to borrow the greater part of his sallery when it was due—
to keep it for his maintenance & let him have it as he wanted
for that purpose—such as these shall never dye—if they must
—'the pillowd firmament is rotteness & earths base built on
stubble'

       my dear Hessey with the sincerest feelings of friendship
            yours unalterably in this alterable world

JOHN CLARE

P.S. The proof of 'Last of March'* is not yet come Taylor
says Im to have it if it did not—so I thought it right to tell you

To Taylor

Addressed: Messrs Taylor & Hessey, 93 Fleet St, London.
[*sent*]

[March 1821]

MY DEAR TAYLOR

     I sent off the proofs yesterday but cannot rest easy without
sending you a letter to tell you of their Starting as there is too
many to be lost—I went over to Deeping myself yesterday with
them as the man said they woud start at 8 aclock to London so
if they speed you have them ere now—your alterations in
'Solitude'[1] are capital & this poem is now one of the best in the
Vols:—your omissions in the 'Woodman'[1] are very good & the
poem reads now uncommonly well so be sure dont take them
in again—your omission of the Verse in Sunday[1] is after a second
thought very appropriate & very just—your wishing to make
one verse of the 2 is right—so be sure send me a copy of the 2
verses & the way you woud have them done your assistance
in such things I find very nessesary & in fact will not do without it—so in future when you want any alterations you'll
know how to get them—your omissions in the other poems are
capital I saw their defects & wondered I never saw them before
you crossd them out—There is a favourite little thing of mine
which you have not yet inserted—'Give me life's ease when my
leaf's turning yellow'[1] you no doubt intend it

     I am very fearful your turning your mind to take the original

* The Village Minstrel.

readings as you hinted in your last letter will be no improvement they cannot read better than they do in your alterations
sent to me & had I been informed sooner I shoud certainly
raised my little voice to disuade you from it but take your
opinion & you cannot go wrong—you cross'd '*gulsh'd*' I think
the word expressive but doubt its a provincialism it means
tearing or thrusting up with great force take it or leave it as
you please—I see plainly there will be sufficient for a fourth
Vol: left behind with a little additions & if these 2 sells well
I've a notion the sooner we have at them the better you no
doubt know the old Song 'Strike iron while its hot & its sure to
weld'—I hear nothing of Townsends Poems yet: they are
devilish long in coming out—I long to see 'Jerusalem'—I have
read parts of Milmans[2] a second time & think the choruses &
Hymn at the conclusion very exelent indeed & very little
way off sublimity in some places but I may be mistaken—
Miriam & Javan are interesting characters—Salones (when
wounded) meeting with her sister puts me in mind of Shakespeare on the whole I think it a very fine poem in dialogue but
no drama—what conscieted little pages Murray puts out—in
this book I have now its calld a new Edition so it may in the
title page—& at the end its 'London John Murray' the fellows
consiets unbearable this is Lord R's fine publisher—peoples to
be noticed put little that praises one so much & then finds out
another that deserves surpassing praises if any one woud be
rulable & suffer to be led by the hand of such like they might be
dragd from 93 Fleet St to Albemarle[3] &c &c &c till they found
themselves at last with Mr. Pitts at Seven Dials[4] or Evans in
Smithfield[4] singing their pennorths of [penances] on the sup-
pression of vice in brown & blue paper with the benevolent &
enlightening Authors of 'Cottagers Friend'[5] & 'Black Giles'[6]—
the friends round here begin to be d—d teazing I shall shake em
off ere long whatever the consequence but I shall talk to you
when I get to London about it—Peaceful ones are very well &
very good—aspiring ones are revolution & perplexity—'You
know you do' were 'the shoe pinches'—but I'll be king of my
little matter in spite of all—trust me for that you know who I
mean without naming them—so farewell

JOHN CLARE

To Taylor

Addressed: Messrs Taylor & Hessey, 93 Fleet Street, London.
[sent]

March 24 1821

MY DEAR TAYLOR

Having had either a visit or a hoax from the Muses I lost no
time in sending it to you which if you like it twill urge me to
dip deep & frequently in their bath of inspiration from which I
have long been an indolent & idle wanderer—wether it be
poetry or fustian, inspiration or bombast common sense or
nonsense your judgment will soon decide & as the paying the
post is the only serious consequence belonging to it be what it
will—I shall rest very quietly for your opinion—having the
free opertunity of exempting myself from that expence & the
independence to make use of it—The poem is 'To Time' a
Sonnet

TO TIME
*In fancys eye what an extended span . . .**

—I had a letter from Drury last night enquiring wether I had
anything to send up to London as his brother James is down but
as I dont intend to go Stamford in haste I declind sending thro
by him as I at first intended—Patt is a great deal betterd since
I told you of her being ill—I find its only the natural progress of
things—you understand me—by G—I may rant & ryhme if its
to be thus but 'such things are' & such things will be in spite
of—Economy or what you will—yours to this worlds end with
the hopes of begining the others as warmly & friendly together
is the wish & ever shall be of

JOHN CLARE

I forgot to say I thought Keats Epitaph[1] very superior to any
I had seen in that line I shoud certainly think like you if seen in
the place describd that no common dust slept there

---

* 'The Village Minstrel'.

To Taylor

Addressed: Messrs. Taylor & Hessey, 93 Fleet Street, London.
[*sent*]

[March–April 1821]

My dear Taylor

I send you my sorrows for poor Keats* while his memory is
warmly felt—they are just a few beats of the heart—the head
has nothing to do with them—therefore they will stand no
criticism—

TO THE MEMORY OF KEATS
Thy worldly hopes & fears have pass'd away . . .†

If you dont like it dont utterly condemn it I did it as I felt
it at the moment your mellancholy news woud give me pause
for reflection—I wishd I had made an Elegy afterwards of it
as my ideas was crampt they flowd freely & I coud have gone a
great length but words are of little value—be as it will I can do
nothing more now—the moment is gone I cannot call it back
I wish I coud—the apathy of mellancholly has again laid her
cold hand upon my heart pointing with a carless finger to my
own fate that awaits me & alowing but a common feeling for the
fate of others to go before me—viewing such in a course of
natural occurances—but dear Taylor with the affection that one
brother feels at the loss of another do I lament the fate of poor
Keats

I am glad I have got your opinion turned to the Cottage agen
—each vol with a front peice will be uniform & quite bewitching
at least to your humble St. but the head only in the first &
nothing in the next woud be unfair to my twin children leaving
one a favourate & the other neglected—a cheap rough etching
will I think be quite sufficient & have perhaps better effect then
a fine engraving the time I expect in doing it as I mean will be
nothing—but you know best: what a fool I must be to preach
so profoundly knowing about things that I know nothing more

---

* Keats's death in Rome on 23 February 1821, and Taylor's letter to Clare
giving the news, of 26 March, suggests late March or early April 1821 for
the date of the above letter.
† 'The Village Minstrel'.

of then their existance—I take it all for granted & like a child when promised a gingerbread horse feel pleased with the expectation of seeing it—so remember if its not in your child will meet a trying dissapointment—if not in this I shall not live to see it in another so while I am here I want to see all I can—your critsismes on 'Time' are just the thing & your alteration capital—but certainly you paid me no compliment when you asked me wether I understood you—I must either have been drunk or blind had I not—you never desert common sense & therefore common sense never mistakes you—your alterations & omissions in the proofs are by what I see good but as I send this off without em I shall say nothing more about them till they come

I cannot correct the proofs yet but they shall start tomorrow or next day—you must forgive me I am in such a tottering trembling state of nerves & have such sickly sensibility about me that I cannot correct yet—things that Ive once done are quite loathing at these times to repetition—

SONG
Fill the foaming cups again . . .

To Taylor

Addressed: John Taylor Esq, London.
[*sent*]

. April 3 1821

MY DEAR TAYLOR

I waited to send off the sketches of my life[1] by your parcel but as its not yet come I have put you to an additional expence by sending it off alone—as it is written expressly for your eye I have been perhaps punning particular in some places especially about my first meeting with your Cousin Drury were by so doing I thought your opinion might more justly decide on things as they ought to be—when I am no more—what is written is the hulk in which when I speak thus much you will doubtless have no hesitation to believe—I am prompted neither by favour or affection to write a falsity & I hope you know

enough of me not to be jealous of my guiltyness in such matters
—its only to furnish you with particulars—remember that—&
not to stand as I have hobbled it you are the person if you
survive me that must do me justice—to you I give these
Sketches & no one else shall I copy a repetition of them tho
I have often been urged to it—What comforts you have pro-
cured for me I shall never or at least never ought to forget—
for what I posses at this moment boasts its original in you—I
readily agree with Lord R. that without your Introduction the
right hand of my success would have been wanting but as to his
Lordships goodness good as it is it remains at a great distance
behind—& to sum up everything—those silly beggarly flattery
in the Morning Post &c &c &c—I think Ive gaind as much
harm as good by it—& am nothing in debt on that quarter—I
went last Sunday to 'Lolham Brigs' in our Lordship no doubt
you have heard of 'em--they are very ancient & are said to be
built by one 'Lollius Ubiens' [?]² tis the King Street road or
old roman bank on the end of which stands 'Langley bush' the
produce of this walk is a poem 'The last of march'³ which if
you have any curiosity to see shall accompany the next parcel
till then I am

yours &c &c &c

JOHN CLARE

P.S. Remember I am just got from the blue bell & am
damnation drunk & consequently as happy as possibility can
make me—God bless you & if my errors make him my enemy
I hope you have conduct enough to keep him your friend

To Taylor

Addressed: Messrs Taylor and Hessey, 93 Fleet St, London.
[sent]

April 18 1821

MY DEAR TAYLOR

I have just got the proofs & am quite satisfied—I have not
time to say aught about your alterations but believe they will
suit me as usual—but your intention of leaving out the

111

'Pastoral'[1] after you have praised it so much will never do for me chuckey the more good things the better so never stand about a few pages more or what not but in with it I shall have plenty after a while—'Pathetic Narratives' I like much & shall muster up plenty of stores for that matter so spare & save for nothing put all in thats good be sure you—& now I think on't youll have the 'Wild Nosegay'[2] & 'Last of March' in it you like them remember—dont baulk these vols by saving for the next for I shall have plenty by then—so never leave aught out for these circumstances besure you I myself expect to see every poem in that you approve of or at least that has not been objected too afterwards by either of us—& as for my part if you make much of my taste I shall not like it—so remember chuckey & leave out nothing you like—dont you complain of me not writing latly for you have got idle in not making the corrections—the letter you sent is from a stranger of the name of 'J. Holland Sheffield Park Yorkshire'[3] the whole purport of his letter is wishing me to send him a scrap of my writing with my name if writing an answer be too much trouble—as he is so easily satisfied let him be who he will he shall be gratified after a bit—he dwells on the 'Village Minstrel' as something more then common lets hope hell be not dissapointed I have vanity enough to think he coud not if hes a feeling for a poets failing & success—why didnt you open it—you are welcome to open anything that comes to you for me—I am happy you like the 'Cross roads'[4] so much the later often touched me as I heard it told from the simple old grannys of the village & I have preserved all their simplicity I could by putting it in their mouths to lay in ryhmes I thought the 3rd verse of drinking song the best—but you know what store I set by my judgement—for I in general get hold of the worst end—excuse this letter my thoughts are hussled up in half stupifying dreamings Ill write you a better & longer next time for if you feel a pleasure in my silly remarks observations &c take my word you shall be pleasd often—

god bless you

JOHN CLARE

To Taylor

Addressed: Messrs Taylor and Hessey, 93, Fleet St, London.
[sent]

Ap. 24 1821

My dear Taylor

Just to pass time away I am sat down to write somthing—
but what yourself nearly knows as much as I do—however
somthing Ill scribble—I have been idle agen—but I have to
make up for I proffited by your lecture & have kept sober ever
since & I am still determined on the plan in thus proceeding
visitors comes on me every other day or nearly & I had a
sensible Gent yesterday no doubt you know him 'Dr Noehden*
British Museum' he talked civily & unasuming & I felt the loss
of his company after he left me—he has given me an Invitation
when in London to visit him & see the museum which he thinks
will please me—he odd enough said 'he had seen my *pretty
poems* & that curiosity had urged him to seize the first opportunity of seeing the author he was accompanied with two other
gents who did not leave their names I didnt much like pretty
but will alter these things when out a second time twas natural
enough—children say so about playthings—& this first book
is our plaything I consider it nothing more now—the muse is
there in the bud in the next she will be in the blossom If I
mistake not—& these will alter the note a little—a smile shoud
dimple to say them pretty—but admiration shall redden the
cheek with pronouncing they are good—& if not in the next—if
we are left as I hope we shall to wind up the story: in the last
admiration shall let fall her muscles into reverence—like one
reading a monument & with sacred enthusiasm between a smile
& a tear—in pity & suspence pronounce em best of all—the
blossoms shall give way to the crimson berries which shall shine
in every leaf as bright & as lasting as the vanity of a crackd-
braind aspiring hopfull thankless son of the muses coud ever
wish for—I coud have gone on dreeming thus to the end but
have stopt to read it over found it very foolish stuff & desisted

* Dr. Georg Heinrich—or George Henry—Noehden, extra assistant in the
British Museum in 1819, assistant librarian in 1822, died 1826. He was author of
books on Goëthe and German grammar.

—but knowing innosent foolishness will meet with all possible indulgence at its journeys end I leave it as it is—what is written is written—I am going to write to Bloomfield very soon shall I say that you will send him the new poems as soon as published I know he will like to see them—& I think you will like to write him as I always feel entertained with writing to those I esteem so by others—& as to John Taylor liking Bloomfield there is not a doubt—nature has so ordered it that he cannot help but love such people who are made of something more than the shreds & patches of this world—So wether I am to tell him you will send him one—or wether I am to say nothing about it—tell me when you write me agen—remember you neednt hurry or be put out of your time one second only when you do write tell me—I shall write to Montgomery after a bit for he spoke warmly of me—aye as affectionatly as one poet can speak of a brother—you know what that is without being told —I felt it & shall for ever—I forgot to thank you for your invitation but youll excuse me: when you mention it agen I shall tell you wether I mean to come or not—Tho nevertheless I shoud like to see very much indeed J. Taylor & his circle of friends once more & if I knew I had seen my last of them I am sure I shoud be hipt with new melancholy—Its a good method of providence in giving no distance in her pictures painting the present & stopping the eye with darkness from seeing further— it saves 100s of head-aches—it gives 100s of pleasant sensations as we always hope for the best before she draws up her curtain —we may meet often yet—god bless you

JOHN CLARE

To Taylor

Addressed: Messrs Taylor and Hessey, 93 Fleet St, London.
[*sent*]

p.m. May 3 [1821][1]

MY DEAR TAYLOR

Youll no doubt have a double letter to pay for ere I get [to the] end—for I copy out the long dream of 'First Love' or 'Jockey & Jinney' as I am in fear its no Poem so as far as I

have got with it I send for your critisism—if you can understand it thats plenty for me—& on that reccomendation I'll
pursue—'The Tale of Genius'[2] is my next when this is done
with—& in case I can[t] rhyme any longer that youll see by
this specimen & tell me

[There follows two sections of]
        'FIRST LOVE' OR 'JOCKEY & JINNEY'
[the first 90 lines, a halt, another 68 further lines][3]

tell me if I shall make aught out of this tale quickly as I stop
from proceeding purposely—your proofs are d–d long I begin
to be impatient—forgive me—when will come the last—not
this time I doubt—when they are done with I can go on again
rapidly I think—& not till then so toss em off as soon as you
can—I should have wrote on tuesday but was busy in dreaming
over Jockey & Jenney & burying a young robin which a cat
had wounded my hand gets crampt & what is worse my head
is empty so farwell

                                        JOHN CLARE

P.S. lets hear from you soon

To Taylor

[*sent*]

                                        [June 1821]
MY DEAR TAYLOR
    I have just got the proofs (Saturday) I shall start them agen
on Monday—I always like to tell you as I get them—you have
not got 'last of March' in yet—you will do maybe—I will write
for the 'London'[1] if you like & shall feel spurd to do it by
having your approbation—The 'New Monthly'[2] in my eye has
sunk into insignificance—it perhaps may be sufficient to say
that all your alterations suit me well & with your proposd
ommisions do as you please I feel very satisfyd with them
myself—do as you like with the lines on Lord R.—but I think
the dedication now to anyone woud be almost presumptious—
there is a debt owing to Earl Fitzwilliam Earl Spencer & the
Marquis tho the last is certainly my greatest patron at least in

my own bosom & you can do him justice with the rest in the Preface—thats the best way as I think: time will tell us more & then we can dedicate you know were we think best so we'll do without dedications this time unless your further reflections on the subject convinces you that your first notions are right—if so I'll readily agree to any thing you propose—

I am anxious of getting my book out & not only that let me tell you but am as anxious of seeing you do justice to Keats by bringing him out agen which I hope you will loose no time to do —excuse my conscieted meddling advice—else I think the sooner you publish a Vol of his remains with an account of his Life &c the better while the ashes of genius is warm the public look with a tender anxiety for what it leaves behind—to let this get cold woud in my opinion do him an injury—the ill treatment he has met will now be productive of more advantages— though the warm heart that once felt it is cold & carless to praise or to censure now—still he left those hopes behind him— which his friends cherish in remembrance that justice woud be done him—is the cold hearted butchers of annonymous Critics to cut up everthing that escapes their bribery or thinks contrary to them is polotics to rule genius—if it is—honesty & worth may turn swindlers & liberty be thrown to the dogs & worried out of existance—& that she has been long ago—I have been reading his 'Eve of St Agnes' agen—were Madeline is describd undressing herself it is beautiful & luscious to describe how much so—

> —*her vespers done*
> *Of all its weatherd pearls her hair she frees*
> *Unclasps her* warmed jewels *one by one*
> *Loosens her* fragrant boddice: *by degrees*
> *Her rich attire creeps* rustling to her knees
> Half hidden like a mermaid in sea weed
> *Pensive awhile she* dreams awake, *& sees*
> *In fancy fair St Agnes in her bed*
> *But dares not look behind or all the charm is fled.*

Look for such a description throughout Barry Cornwalls endless amusements—& were will you find it—you may as well look for the graces of simplicity at a night throughout the

painted ranks & files of Drury Lane or Covent Garden & you
will meet with equal success—I shoud have taken a large sheet
—but my child is very bad[3]—& I was not in mood for scribbling

God bless you

JOHN CLARE

P.S. I look for your promise of a letter remember soon—I
had nearly forget to thank you for your kindness in sending me
the 'London' & the promise of continuing it—but youll excuse
all omissions for my d–d thick head makes a many that are
not intentional

The man you direct the parcels to is become tricky & shifty
—as there is few more to come when you send the rest direct
to the 'Bull Inn' as usual & send a letter to inform me of their
arival & I will fetch them myself—

I have a d–d bad opinion of the Sonnets in these vols &
think most of em poor stuff—lets hope my judgments good for
nought—what think you—you never sed

To Taylor

Addressed: Messrs Taylor and Hessey, 93 Fleet St, London.
[sent]

9 June 1821

MY DEAR TAYLOR

Having made some mistake in the parcel sent off this morning
by the grocers cart I correct it by this letter sent after it as
speedily as possible instead of 'dusty or deaf miller' correct it
to 'Dusty miller' as I am informed the deaf miller is another
drama which I never saw acted myself the rest is all right—I
made another d–d blunder respecting Scrivens fine engraving
in saying I fancyd it not done justly about the mouth after the
painting it showd that I must be meddling with every thing I
hope you have not took it in your head to fancy so from my
conscietcd ignorance for its nothing else & I have been cursedly
terrified in thinking you might think about having it touchd
over again from my blunder this will caution you & I have

found fault with my thick head for starting it ever since twas the effect of colour in the Sketch that cheat me & if you make any alteration it will be spoild altogether

I have nearly compleated the 'Vicar' & fancy it one of the best things I ever did tis one of those tales from your hint of 'Pathetic Naratives' it rather resembles Goldsmith but when I set about a thing I care not who has done it before me— yours &c,

JOHN CLARE

P.S. Reccolect Expectation is at its height & Dissapointment is grinning at her elbow I am not 'uneasy' at your delay but am by times very flutterd with impatience when vanity tickles me 'you know you do'

[There follows:]

TO AN INFANT SISTER IN HEAVEN
Bessey,—I call thee by that earthly name . . .

To Hessey

Addressed: Messrs Taylor and Hessey, 93 Fleet St, London.
[sent]

Helpstone June 26. 1821.

MY DEAR HESSEY

I got the £10 safe this morning & have forced myself into taking the trouble to tell you so: for writing seems irksome at present—I am foolish but cant help it patty is getting well as fast as possible—I cant but confess whenever my thoughts turn to the book but I feel an anxious vexation at the delay—but I care nothing about it at present I'll try at what you hint but think such things too serious for magazines—& much freshness will be taken off from their coming out in a Volume—but I can do nothing now—I am proud of my company in the next magazine as I am affectionately fond of the man as a poet I know nothing further perhaps Taylor will do the thing at his next setting too & perhaps that will be by the end of the week—I hope so I can do nothing till the books out I often strive to get weak thoughts out of my head by ryhming but the latter turns

out to be as weak as the former give me Reynolds's address in
your next letter as I have taken it into my head to send him
a copy myself from here; when they are published—I intend
to try at Songs agen when the fit comes on me but God knows
when that will be; I dont—I [am] forced to find schemes to fill
up my sheet with out much scribbling youll excuse me

yours &c &c &c

JOHN CLARE

P.S. when you have done with the parcel of rough M.S.S.
I last sent you return them as there is much unfinished stuff
that may be usefull—so dont destroy them if this caution comes
in time to prevent it—you need not send them till you have
compleatly done with them as Im in no hurry it just jumpd in
my head & I mentiond it thats all—

To Hessey

Addressed: Messrs Taylor & Hessey, 93 Fleet Street, London.
[sent]

July 8. [1821]

MY DEAR HESSEY

I got your parcel on Saturday about 12 & started immediatly for Burghley & have seen his Lordship who recieved me
very kindly indeed & pleasantly askd me several questions—I
told his Lordship about the introduction he seemd pleas'd with
your sending them down before publication—I daresay he woud
have as favourable opinions respecting a proof picture if youll
send him one Ill send it to you purposly so tell me if you will—
he gave me £1 & told me to call agen at the servants hall to
dinner some time when he returnd—for I coud eat nothing that
day—here ends the introduction you do as you like with the
cottage I say no more about it as I understand nothing of such
things—but think the book will look blank without it after the
advertisment—if Dewint comes this way he can do it well to
be sure & I shall be glad of his call & if he can manage eggs
& bacon & drink middling ale he shant starve while with us so
you may give him this coarse welcome ere he starts—Ill show

him 'Lolham brigs' & 'Langley bush' if hes time enough with
him when he comes—I am glad Earl Spencer thinks of me so
kindly & attentively its no common thing in his station—& I
thank Taylor for his answering his Lordship—Ive had no time
to read the magazine yet—The £5 is safe at hand—the
appearance of the vols is very good—T. seems to have omitted
some for want of room—he has cut up the 'cress gatherer' but
has made a good thing of it indeed—I mean to write the
'Workhouse' some time & what he has cut out here will do
for that—my fine fancyd thing of the 'Vicar' wont do after a
second revival—I shall remodel it over again at my next set
too which will not be long just as soon as you have done with
the thin Quarto send it back to be filld up with the other rough
things & then if I guess right you shall have a sample by next
Christmas as good & better as the two Vols & enew to make
two more such—I think the Sonnet to poor Keats with Taylors
touches is now one of the best I was suprisd to find it read to
well—Ive more to say but my head aches after Burghley ale so
fare well

JOHN CLARE

To Taylor

Addressed: Messrs Taylor and Hessey, 93 Fleet St.
[sent]

July 10 1821

MY DEAR TAYLOR

Are you off the sick list? If not I'll turn it off to Hessey
So here beginneth the epistle behold I have read the magazine[1]
& think it a brave start very brave indeed you have got a lot of
lads of rare promise at labour in your vineyard so the Lady of
prose (if there be any) & the lady of verse be with you & speed
you & fill your silk purse (a cockney purse by the bye) full of
glittering sovereigns ere your labours close is the prayer of a
well wisher to your undertaking—you rogue you, the pruning
hook has been over me agen I see in the Vols but vain as I am
of my abilities I must own your lopping off have bravely
amended them the 'Rural Evening'[2] & 'Cress gatherer'[3] in

particular are now as compleat as anything in the Vols. but the
'Pastoral' & 'death of Dobbin'[4] are left out to save the public
6ᵈ expense—but why do I rant & rattle on at this rate—friend
I believe you are a caterer of profound wisdom in these matters
you know what sort of a dish will suit the publics appetite
better then I—at all events you'll say 'I ought to do'—you
know you will—I am just getting to rights again at least I am
not so foolish as I was a while back things wear off in time
Pattys quite better & a little time to come bids fair to make up
the losses of times past—I've a pitcher of ale at my elbow &
I've now taken it up to drink Taylor & Hessey's good health so
here's a hearty 'God be wi' ye' to you both I hope your father's
mending & yourself not far behind it—Mother went to Lord
Miltons to deliver the Copy & brought home a very bright
young sovereign

When the book is finished you had better send Earl Fitzwilliam one yourself as you wrote to him before time I'd lay
my fine sovereign upon it that succeeds

Send Marquis Exeter one too pray you & dont forget

Also Earl Spencer & I think that will do well & dont forget
that neither

The pivot on which my hopefull maschine turns is vanity
& these are the alphas & omegas that keep it in motion—I have
a deal more to say but when I have gotten to the end of my
doings as the boy remarked of his gingerbread what can I do
further. write to me soon as this is my last letter till then so
fare thee well

JOHN CLARE

To Taylor

Addressed: Messrs Taylor and Hessey, 93 Fleet St.
[*sent*]

July 12 1821

DEAR TAYLOR

I meant to have said in my last letter that the 5 first sonnets
are early as well as the 'Excursion to Burghley Park' 'Help-

stone Green'* 'To the Violet'* 'The Woodcutters night
Song'* 'To the Butterflye'* 'To Health'* 'May Day'* &
'William & Robin'* & that I wish to have it known as such
some how or other: in the Introduction will do if not too late
this is all that I write for this time so farewell

JOHN CLARE

The 'Argument' is well done & a brave set off it is to Lubins
History I forgot to tell you that Dr Bell of Stamford was the
man that got Lord Spencers salary for me by writing to him
before I was known in the world

To Taylor

[sent]

[1821]

MY DEAR TAYLOR

I can hardly say so—you—you—I know not what to call
you Wednesday is past—& Wednesday week has sent it man-
tuesday to tell of its approach—& yet not a proof I fear they
are miscarried I am almost sure they are & feel very unsettled
about it—if they are not I dont care a straw—but I wish the
proof work was done with—3 journeys to Deeping have been
the consequence of your early notice & had I not been with
Townsend I should have wrote to you 10 times before this his
poems are out† & I have them from the author—I see nothing
—to make me jealous or wish for—but he is a great friend of
mine & I shall be a kind Critic—There is one in the measure of
Peter Corcoran's 'Shrewsbury' but its all flat & cold after
Peters as might be expected—there is none of these lines
Chuckey—

> *Manhood is a sorry thing & mine is plunged deep*
> *In faults that bid me weep*

.　　.　　.　　.

---

* *The Village Minstrel.*
† *Poems,* by Chauncy Hare Townshend (1821), were dedicated to Southey.
This, as well as the reference to proofs, dates the above letter.

The fields were full of starlike flowers & overgrown with joy
The trees around my playground were a very statly [stately]
   sight
But some spirit is gone over them to wither & destroy
Who would not be a boy

It peter woud write more from his feelings then fancy that is
less of 'King Tims'* &c &c & more of Shrewsburys he woud
soon be on the top list of modern poets—I myself woud sooner
be the author of this one poem then the half of what Southey
Wordsworth &c have written it thrills me into an ague of
sensibility every time I read it—for gods sake dont tell me more
of proofs coming for the dissapointment is the worst of perplexity I have got on a great way with the tale of 'Jockey &
Jenny' & shoud have sent it to you soon but the job is put all
rhyming out of my head agen—

   I was disatisfied with the tail of this letter so I cut it off
but have no dossity† to copy it over again so take it as it is
                                                  Yours
                                         J. CLARE

To Taylor

Addressed: Messrs Taylor and Hessey, 93 Fleet St.
               [sent]
                                      11 August 1821

MY DEAR TAYLOR

   I have not had dossity enough about me to answer your last
till now—but you'll excuse me I have had the horrors agen
upon me by once agen seeing devoted Mary[1] & have written the
last doggerel that shall ever sully her name & her remembrance
any more tis reflection of the past & not of the present that
torments me here are the verses

[There follows:]

FAREWELL TO MARY[1]
Where is the heart thou once hast won . . .
                                      [3 verses]

* 'King Tims the First', a punning drama on American immigrants. See *The
Fancy.*
  † Energy: *Baker's Glossary of Northamptonshire. Words and Phrases.*

Say how you like this crazy reverie I've expected the Magazine but its not yet come I know by the News that the criticism[2] is not in—so that needs no apology I wish you woud send it directly as next week if all goes well I expect being at Whittlebury[3] forest 53 miles from Helpstone—you shall have the 'Vicar'[4] as soon as I can sit down to collect the scraps in right order just as I have finished it off—'Jockey & Jinney' is not yet proceeded with a single line further then the copy you have got & whose fault is that you neglecting idle rogue you: had you sent your criticism[5] sooner it would have been finished long ago but I'll try agen soon & then you shall have the remainder —you'll have very few more love things from me & that you'll not regret for I'm weary of whining over eyes like Sunbeams lips of rubies & rosey cheeks a liley bosoms with this hopeless weakening clog at ones foot & a proof of its faded realitys at ones elbow—but this is weakness & vanity for there are faces in existance that might make me a liar before this letter i'm now scribbling is finished so no more of that—I have the first no of the 'London' & shoud like the rest up to your engagement in it these I will buy of you as I will then bind them up yearly so remember me I've done nothing for the London next month unless the Farewell to Mary will do—you'll see I'll try agen— I shall write you from Whittlebury so farewell till then & God bless you

JOHN CLARE

Write soon as you can

I have ideas of writing my Literary Life & continuing it on till I live do you approve of the matter if you do tell me

J.C.

To Taylor

[*sent*]

Helpstone Aug 1821
p.m. 18 Aug. 1821

MY DEAR TAYLOR

This letter is written to tell you that after Thursday next you need send no proofs of your progress (which by the bye

seems a foot-foundered & bad traveller) as I shall be gone so
if it be not got ready before you may publish it without my
seeing it as I dont fear in the least but it will suit me—I have
put on the black waiscoat you gave me for this last week &
shoud have done so with the cold but it is too dandyish for this
country—but its not to mourn for the injurd queen—I hated
her while living & I have no inclination to regret her death—
I hated her not a[s] a woman or as a queen but as the vilest
hypocrite that ever existed—commonsense gives me her
spectacles to look upon everything I'm of no party but I never
saw such farcical humbug carried on in my life before & I never
wish to see it agen for its launchd me head over ears in politics
for this last twelvemonth & made me very violent when John
Barleycorn inspird me—[3 lines heavily scored out] everyone
has his share of humbug & I have mine The black waiscoat is
for the last twin children which I fancy are still born[1] & gone
home agen so I am driving away at knocking up stuff for another
as hard as I can & I send you with these a specimen of my new
beginning you do as you like with it—We have got Mathews[2]
coming here next friday (to Stamford Theatre) I dont know
wether I can resist stopping to see him but wether I do or do
not you will hear from me directly after I get to Whittlebury the person I'm going to see is a Mr Bunney[3] an Artist &
Poet!! a pupil of the late Wests[4] he has a poem by him of 10
Cantos which I'll tell you of soon as I've seen it

[There follows:]

SONNET
England with pride I name thee . . .

Yours sincerely

JOHN CLARE

To Taylor

Addressed: Messrs Taylor and Hessey, 93 Fleet St, London.
[*sent*]

6 September 1821

MY DEAR TAYLOR

I merely send this letter to hitch of[f] the Sonnet as I am begun to scribble agen vehemently I've a long piece in hand 'Wanderings in June'* were I indulge reflection perhaps too much but you shall see after a bit when its finishd here is the sonnet

[There follows:]

A REFLECTION IN SUMMER†
One well may wonder oer the change of scene . . .

I am agen recruiting from my complaints & shall wait till the book is publishd ere I start so when it is you may let me know & send me what copies you think fit—you will then hear no more of me for a time unless I do anything to my mind & send it for your opinion

Do you fancy that Dewint will call at Helpston if he did I shoud be sorry to be out of the way but I dont believe either him or yourself ever once meant it so I shall always reckon on that head when you talk of it hereafter—I am sought after very much agen now 3 days scarcly pass but sombody calls—some rather entertaining people & some d–d knowing fools—surely the vanity woud have kill'd me 4 years ago if I had known then how I shoud have been hunted up—& extolld by personal flattery—but let me wait another year or two & the peep show will be over—& my vanity if I have any will end in its proper mortification to know that obscurity is happiness & that John Clare the thresher in the onset & neglected ryhmer in the end are the only two comfortable periods of his life—I sent you 'the Vicar' long ago did you get it

God bless you & farewell

JOHN CLARE

* *Shepherd's Calendar.*
† Unpublished.

To Gilchrist

[1822]

DEAR SIR

I write to let Mrs G. know the reason why 'Jockey & Jenny' were omitted 12 pages & rather more was deemed too long for insertion[1] by Messrs T. & H. so my promise remains at first as of writing it out which as soon as I get the copy from London shall be done—another peice is promised insertion in the next 'The Last of Autumn'[2] you have not found Helpstone yet let's hope new attacks of illness has not prevented you from taking long journeys I have expected every day on your coming—Lord R. has sent me a parcel of books—Feltham's 'Miserys of Human Life'[3] an odd sort of vol—The Cabinet[4] The Guardian[5] Lewes Melodys[6] an odd medley by the bye & if Mrs G. has not seen some of them they are at her service. The last is bad but I think its a novelty if first sight can make it so—The Centaur in one of the Last Mags is Hoods he asks my opinion of it but I dont understand the subject.

Yours &c. &c.

JOHN CLARE

To Taylor

Addressed: Messers Taylor & Hessey, 93 Fleet St, London.
[sent]

January 24, 1822

MY DEAR TAYLOR

I have just nothing to do & to pass time away I scribble this with not a single thought to begin with nor one perhaps worth reading ere I [get to?] the end—I wait impatient for the end of the month to see the Dream[1] in print—you must not decieve me as you have often done by saying so & so is to be in the Mag. & then nothing of it when it comes. I think of writing a love tale in the measure of Spenser but have not exactly pitchd on a subject unless I call it 'The Deserter.' I have been to Milton & spent 3 days with Mr. Artis[2] the Antiquary very pleasantly he has discovered a multitude of fresh things & a fine roman bath is one of the latest discoverys the painted plaster on the walls was very fresh & fine when I saw it & the flues of the furnaces was a proof without the least suposition of its being a bath he has also found the roman road that lead to the river & the pavement is as firm as when first laid down—next summer when the water is low he intends to try for the iron bridge which is said to be sunk in the river—his plan of the Roman City is nearly compleated—he has a great many drawings of curious things & I think his book when published will be very entertaining—he is going to take a plaster bust of my head somtime for myself—his own he has taken himself & I think very like he seems to me quite a clever man & everything but a poet— lets have the Mag: this time as soon as its possible as I am all anxiety to see how the thing will read in print I shall not settle to ryhme a couplet till I see it—I dont know how to account for it, but the good & bad parts of a poem are very rarely distinguished by me while[2] its in print—the M.S.S. book is been out a fortnight or nearly so if its missed you its lost—but I harbour no other opinion than that of your having it safe & that you have said 'this will do' & 'this wont do' long ere now—I think very much of 'Jockey & Jenney' now its gone & fancy it one of the best Ive written reflection dwells long upon things that are favourites & when thats the case with me I always remark it that I am seldom mistaken—excuse this scribbling—

Yours &c &c &c

JOHN CLARE

I have broke my brass seal could you get me one engravd with 'J.C.' on a bone heft mine was a wooden one & its come off & left me at a loss—I gave s2 for it to Drury & its turnd out very dear get me one done if you please as it will be a little better engravd than I get them here & no doubt the expence will be less.

To Taylor

Addressed: Messrs Taylor & Hessey, 93 Fleet St, London.
[sent]

January 31st 1822

MY DEAR TAYLOR

I have had some reflection on the following subjects before I put them to you & tho rather preposterous I think not impossible—what the D–l this mean you'll say or think & well you may—this it is that 'Bachelors Hall' is on the wreck or nearly so when the inclosure was they mortgaged the property for £200 to a Jew a second Iago who employs a lawyer at Deeping to lend money of the name of Baker as big a rogue as himself & they both go hand in hand like a brace of bloodhounds bent on destruction & as sure of their game as death when once in the scent & thus it is that the Billings being my oldest & now only friends in the village I cannot see these rogues pursue their prey uninterupted—nothing is a greater hell to me than to see an old friend wrongd by intentional villany by meditated fraud—hell overtake them but I make one desperate struggle in help of an harmless man—this is my Design—I'll publish a Vol: of Poems under a feignd name were I will try my uttermost to excell—they shall be all out of my way here are some of them: 'A Vision of Hell', 'Shadows of Fate,' or 'Life death & Eternity,'* but this is all idea for not one word is yet begun & the bloodhounds is on the heels of their victim—a long paper has been sent them from this Baker about 'Kings Bench' & 'John Doe & Richard Roe' & a damd set of mystic bother as obscure as the workings of hell to which they belong—the Cottage is a beautifull spot of 6 or 7 Acres there are crowds for it if it be sold but if I coud get hold of the mortgage it woud be mine & still doing a kindness to a friend I shoud like to make sure of it as 'Poets Hall' instead of its old name of 'Bachelors' which must soon be extinct if I dont succeed—Ill do this way if you like Ill sell you my writings for five years for that sum which cant be dear—however be as it will give me your free opinion

---

* This, in *The Shepherd's Calendar*, was the only one that was finished and published.

for I know its a bargain—since I wrote thus far he has been to
Lord Milton who has got the before mentioned paper to do
somthing—still I shoud like it as in handhold & if you seem to
think it worth while Ill write to Lord M. to say Ill pay off the
mortgage—but do as you list I myself hate to be troubld or to
be troublesome—but my feelings are rousd to madness at such
acts of violence & my imagination cannot withold an attempting
struggle to save a sinking fellow creature & more especially a
friend—tho it be like the shadow by ones side mocking our
motions in idle deception & empty nothingness—I have at last
picht upon a subject for a 'novel' it is 'Cares & Comforts' or
'Notes from the Memoirs of Uncle Barnaby & Family as
written by himself.'* I shall write it in Chapters & confine
myself to no mechanical plot but go on just as things jumps at
the moment—The Misterey 'a dramatic Pastoral' I shall
quickly proceed with. I am all madness for writing but how long
its to last I don't know—I want £3 to set straight this year
& hope you will send it as soon as you can find time.

Yours &c &c &c &c

JOHN CLARE

To Gilchrist

[sent]

Jany 31. 1822

DEAR SIR

I return Mr Ts 'Restoration' &c &c I have read about a
couple of pages & thats all so can give but little opinion about
it but I am so far satisfied that such subjects have but little
entertainment for me—I have not been to Stamford latly I
know not when I shall venture to come agen as I am so cussedly
apt to making mistakes & the last was a large one which you
have no doubt heard of ere this I am sorry to say I have not
yet copyed some poems out for Mrs G.—tho the promise is not
quite lost sight of I have done very little new latley save a
trifle or two—a new poet has started at Peterboro name

* Unfinished. Peterborough manuscripts.

Wilkinson The poem published is 'St John!!'*—an old lady at
M— was asked her opinion of it in my hearing who said she
coud not understand it—but her friends had told her it was
written in the Saxon language—as the young man was a
lawyers Clerk & rather learned in such matters—the fact is that
the old lady could find no sense of it for the words are measured
out in english stuff but what the ideas belong too I cannot
tell I am as much puzzled as the old lady I shoud be quite as
apt to overshoot the mark if I tryd to explain them—my best
respects to Mrs G.

& remain &c. &c.

JOHN CLARE

To Taylor

Addressed: Messrs Taylor & Hessey, 93 Fleet St, London.
[*sent*]

February 8 [1822]

MY DEAR TAYLOR

I write this to tell you that the bother of Lawyers & Jews is
all setteld Lord Milton has lent the 'Old Bachelor' £20 to pay
off the interest & that's all that's needed at present so you need
say nor send nothing about it but pass it over in silence as
nothing had been the matter.

I think 'Bradgate Park'† in the present No a good article I can
see in a moment The Dream will do tis the best I've done yet
'unhoped sight' is hard mouthd & dosnt read smooth enough
but it will do—I am at ease agen & 'a vision of hell' & 'Shadows
of Fate' are all laid aside nor do I think I shall go on with the
Novel for these things were began as intended helps to my old
friends & as they are satisfyd I'm the same—I rather feel hipt
at the Village minstrels success the Old Vol had gone thro 2
editions ere this & I think a notice in the London agen of a New
Vol of Poems preparing is nessesary as a stimulant to revive the
flatness of these for I am jealous of their ill success at least I feel
somthing that tells me they don't go off like the others & I

* Wilkinson's poem has not reached the British Museum, nor been preserved
locally.   †By J. H. Reynolds.

prevent that feeling as much as ever I can from damping my further exertions but I cannot help it doing so at some times— still I'm determind in the teeth of vexation to surmount dissapointment by unwearied struggles—under these feelings the dream was written & that is the reason of their explanation—& under the same somthing else shall quickly be with you but I cannot say when nor what—lets have your promise of a notice of the new M.S. poems you have got when leisure suits as it will do me great good—I took this large sheet to insert my new thing 'to Spring' but its not finishd & perhaps if I give it you as it is I never may sit down to it afterwards—I mustn't do no more terrible things yet they stir me up to such a pitch that leaves a disrelish for my old accustomd wanderings after nature—Ill have hold of a love tale that shall have awkard situations in it to give my spirits a rouse & to try ones best— I fear I shall get nothing ready for you this month at least I fear so now but may have 50 subjects ready to-morrow, the Muse is a fickle Hussey with me she sometimes stilts me up to madness & then leaves me as a beggar by the wayside with no more life then whats mortal & that nearly extinguishd by mellancholy forbodings—I wish I livd nearer you at least I wish London woud creep within 20 miles of Helpstone I don't wish Helpstone to shift its station I live here among the ignorant like a lost man in fact like one whom the rest seems careless of having anything to do with—they hardly dare talk in my company for fear I shoud mention them in my writings & I find more pleasure in wandering the fields then in mixing among my silent neighbours who are insensible of everything but toiling & talking of it & that to no purpose.

Yours &c, &c,

JOHN CLARE

P.S. lets have the seal as soon as you can as I am in want of one.

To Taylor

[sent]

[February 21 1822][1]

MY DEAR TAYLOR

I have but just got the letter which seems to have met with delay as the parcel accompanyd it—your verse is a devilish puzzle—I may alter but I cannot mend grammer in learning is like tyranny in government—confound the bitch I'll never be her slave & have a vast good mind not to alter the verse in question—by g— I've try'd an hour & cannot do a syllable so do your best & let it pass the last way woud please me the best—what say you to this

> *And fairest daughter of the year*
> *Thrice welcome here anew*
> *Tho gentle storms tis thine to fear*
> *The worst has bade adieu*

d–d lame but I can do no better & have had work enough to do this—

Do you mistake my imitation of W.W. as a serious attempt in his manner—twas written in ridicule of his affectations of simplicity—& I had thoughts of imitating the styles of all the living poets as I got hold of them to read them nor has the thought left me yet—Southey & Crabb I fancy I can do to a tittle the ones affection in mouthing over big words & the others tedious prosing over trifles often border on the ridiculous tho they are both great men & geniuses as I venerate & esteem. I thank you for the contents of the parcels vide heads & cottages I shall send to Burghley & Milton immediately & give one to Artis when he comes whom I expect this day—The Seal is a very handsome one & I shall try it for the first time on this letter—The Cast from my face is taken & I expect he is going on as fast as possible—I told him my intention & he said he woud make you one purposely—twas a hard job for the eyes as I opend them too soon ere the oil was off which made them bloodshot & smart to a tedious degree tho I think now I coud sit for a hundred for a trifle—I can scarcely believe it will be like for I was in terror when the plaster was laid on & lost the look that is common with me—I have written no sonnets lately—I am sick of the short winded pevishness that hovers round this 14 line article in poetry²—I have been idle a long time & never coud muster a thought for anything prose or verse lately—The next attempt for your Magazine is 'April.'³ I will contrive a short thing for March if possible I harbour your notions respecting the novel & am almost ready to give it up —you mentioned sending a note but you have not done it— have you any hopes of my getting in the Edinburgh next quarter⁴—I have tho I dont know when—& why I have I shant say this time—you need never be without a short piece (at times when my hussey is idle) for the magazine from the great Quarto for I am certain there are good ballads and songs left there yet—& such as I shoud be vastly sorry to let die still born—I cannot refer to them but if you look whenever you want a short piece you'll find those I mean—In the meantime I'll exert my utmost to serve you & if my next attempt is not a masterpiece in its way its failing shall not be indifference or neglect.

Yours &c &c

JOHN CLARE

'Aprils' not begun yet so dont expect it ere it comes tho I think I shall soon finish when once begun, the swallow come & the cuckoo sings.

To Edmund Tyrell Artis*

[sent]

Helpstone March 9 1822

DEAR ARTIS

I have taken the first oppertunity to send the Magazine which you may keep till Thursday & on Friday I must send it to Stamford:

You may inform Mr Henderson† that Cunningham's Poems

---

* See Biographical Memoranda.
† Head gardener at Milton Park and botanist. See later letters to him.

are not yet publishd as I promisd to send him them to read—
Taylor is coming into the County but were I cannot tell at
present but I expect a call from [him?] ere long

Yours &c &c

JOHN CLARE

To Hessey

[*sent*]

Mar. 16 1822

MY DEAR HESSEY

I got the Mag safe but have not been able to tell you so &
am as little able to write as ever—I have been very poorly in
fact very bad all this month but I hope ere long to be myself
agen—I have not yet lookd over the Mag: but with the
encouragement in your letter I shall quickly begin at least as
soon as I loose this confounded lethargy of low spirits that
presses on me to such a degree that at times makes me feel as if
my senses had a mind to leave me Spring or Fall such feelings it
seems are doomed to be my companions but it shall not over-
power me as formerly with such weak & terrible dread & fears
of dropping off when death comes he will come & while life's
mine I'll make the best of it & have the courage to treat such
things as trifles—I take a great deal of Exercise & try to write
nothing which I do as the best way to mend & get better next
month I hope to have somthing for you good or bad this
month you must excuse me tho I shoud feel happy to be able
to get somthing for it & if opportunity dont come too late I will
make use of it—give my respects to Taylor & I remain

Yours etc etc

JOHN CLARE

To Hessey

Addressed: Messrs Taylor and Hessey, 93 Fleet St, London.

Tuesday Apl. 2. 1822

[*sent*]

MY DEAR HESSEY

I shoud not have written thus soon had you not appeared to feel more embaresment & consern for the ommission of my last then was nessesary: to me it was no dissappointment I was almost persuaded it woud not do in that state[1] twas an attempt out of season at least with me—Get Taylor to copy it out for me if he pleases with remarks as soon as Leisure permits him as I have no Copy by me his opinion will soon set me at rights I wish I had him near me & I shoud do—I am not a lot better than I was for writing. The blue devils are my constant Companions & I feel very ill so much so as almost to feel alarmed at times: flutterings run from my head to my knees as if something was alive in my veins what it is I cant tell but I must be better after a bit—dont forget to thank Allan Cunningham for his kindness to me of 'Sir M. Maxwell'[2] I will read it over & give my real opinion (such as it is) when I next write—I thought of writing a 'May Mornings Walk' as a description of the next month but the Muses have I fancy forsaken me altogether I know not if I shoud succeed best in writing a 'Farewell to the Muses' or 'The Muses Farewell' as suited to the moment—I had & still have thoughts of continuing the 'Village Minstrel' 'the Golden Days of Boyhood are related & I think the dark shadows that encompass the man with all the doubts fears & sorrows that life posseses woud make me at home still & produce a better thing than the first—Taylor's opinion shall decide it if he will give it shortly if not it will be begun bad or good & when once begun the end will never be lost sight of till finished —Drury is left Stamford or leaving altogether & someone has taken his shop so I hear for I have not been there latley—'The Edinburgh' nor 'Quarterly' has no hold of me yet I expect have they? but you woud have said if they had my remembrances to Taylor

Yours &c &c &c

JOHN CLARE

To Taylor

[*sent*]

Milton April 20 1822
Franked Wentworth Fitzwilliam

A SHADOW
OF LIFE DEATH & ETERNITY.

[There follows:]
*A shadow moving by one's side.**

DEAR TAYLOR
   I have scribld the above thinking it may do for the London
if it will not the chance of conveying it has made matters of
little consequence be as it will—& that was one encouragement
to think of sending it
                              Yours &c &c
                                        JOHN CLARE

To Hessey

Addressed: Messrs Taylor and Hessey, 93 Fleet St, London.
[*sent*]

[p.m. 11 May 1822]

MY DEAR HESSEY
   I have alterd the thing but wether better or worse I know
not its not worth a deal of trouble be as it will
   I expect 'Wanderings in June'[1] will be in this next month
wont it? I am trying 'Walks in May' but dont know how I
shall get on—what think you of my friend Bloomfields 'May-
day'[2] I've not yet seen it but a friend of mine at Milton says its
'A Mayday of Messrs Baldwin Craddock & Joy[3] & I am not
without my suspicions as to that being the case by what I keep
hearing of it I am in no kip for writing so excuse me
                              Yours &c &c &c
                                        JOHN CLARE
[There follows a second version of:]
A SHADOW
OF LIFE DEATH & ETERNITY[4]
A shadow moving by one's side ...   [3 stanzas]

* *The Shepherd's Calendar.*
137

To his Family

[sent]

London. May 1822.

DEAR FRIENDS

I have just written this to say I am safely arrived in London*
& at present with Mr. Taylor & Hessey—my promise will be
performed but I cannot name the precise time nor is it nessesary.

My journey up ended very bad indeed we went 20 miles &
upwards in the most dreadfull thunder storm I ever witnessed
& the rain was very heavy & lashing but as I am safe thats
satisfaction enough my respects to all & a kiss for Anna

Yours &c, &c

JOHN CLARE

To his Family

[sent]

Fleet St. 93.
[May–June] 1822.

DEAR FRIENDS

I have at last performed my promise they are both of the
same price & both my choise but thats no reason why they
should please Patty & Sophy two very difficult creatures on that
point as I have before experienced—but if they don't suit I
make no more attempts to please let them remember that—one
is 6½ yards & the other 6 yards the first is of course intended for
the largest but Patty may chuse which she pleases or at least
they may divide their choise between them—Ive done all I can
& all I intended—

I hope everything goes on well remember to take care of the
Doves I think it odd that no letter comes I have expected one
3 or 4 days

I have got an invitation to go to Bristol & I shall accept it if
nothing requires me at home but if you wish me to desist I will
return to Helpstone very shortly sometime next week at the

* Clare visited London, for the second time, the third week in May, 1822.

138

furthest on what day I cannot tell so dont expect till I come

The parcel started this morning Tuesday I have directed it for Deeping as usual

A second thought tells me you need not write for as I am weary already* you may be sure of my coming home next week & Bristol shall be left for another excursion

Yours &c &c &c

JOHN CLARE

I shall send some thing else ere I return if my money holds out

To Henry Francis Cary†

[*sent*]

Helpstone Aug 23 1822

REVD SIR

I have long thought of writing to you . . . Lord R. in a mysterious hint some weeks back told me you wondered I did not this has set me at liberty . . . [he and his family are all ill]

The two days spent at Chiswick have left pleasant remembrances behind them of friendship & hospitality I beg to give my remembrances to Mrs Carey & family & to your curate Mr —— & his lady . . . [disappointed Cary did not have a Lives of Poets' article in the London Mag.] I shall fill up this letter with 14 lines which I made yesterday morning as I walked out agen for the first time . . .

[There follows:]
Morning awakes sublime: glad earth & skye‡ . . .

I have written some things for a new Vol entitled 'Summer Walks' . . . With the hope of hearing from you in return

Your faithful & obed^t St

JOHN CLARE

* Clare returned to Helpstone from this second London visit a day or two after the birth, on the 16 June, of his daughter Eliza Louisa.

† See Biographical Memoranda.

This letter is from the transcripts of Mr. R. W. King, author of *The Translator of Dante* (1925). See Introduction, concerning the Cary letters.

‡ Sonnet: 'Sunrise': *Collected Poems*.

To Hessey

Addressed: Messrs Taylor and Hessey, 93 Fleet St, London.
[sent]

p.m. 4 Jan. 1823

M<small>Y DEAR</small> H<small>ESSEY</small>

This morning came with its expectations but all are dis-appointed now as I hear the Mag is not come. I shall moreover want the money directly that is as soon as possible & I fear an Addenda[1] to the old sum is absolutely nessesary I hate to be troublesome but I cannot help it I intend to leave the Marquises for half yearly payments as I think it will do me more good for the quarterly sum being odd is often squandered away upon trifles—I have gave Taylor up for good I shall follow his own system

& disdain
To pray to Gods that answer not again.

I have just finished my 'Parish a Satire'[2] & this is the motto: 'I have injurd no one as a nameless character can never be found out but by its truth & likeness' from Pope—here is a specimen—an overseer

Art thou a man thou tyrent oer distress . . .

The Satire consists of a string of characters farmers of the New & Old School a village politician & Steward a Justice of the peace &c &c I have put the fable of the Grasshopper into verse to please my little girl & intended to write a few storys for children but I fancy the first attempt a failure—you shall see soon

I am
Yours sincerely
J<small>OHN</small> C<small>LARE</small>

To Hessey

Addressed: Messrs Taylor & Hessey, 93 Fleet Street, London.
[*sent*]
Taylor's date 17. Jan. 1823;
p.m. not clear

MY DEAR HESSEY

Here I am yet I can hear nothing expecting & expecting & all to no purpose & people that I deal with are expecting likewise as well as myself—this is always a troublesome time with me & I like to get over it as soon as possible so I hope you will lets hear from you quickly—Mr Cowen[1] has been here & sketchd the house & street he said he shoud see you on Monday last & I shoud have wrote by him but he did not stay an half an hour as he was going to London the same day Lord Milton I understand is his patron & sent him to Italy last year to improve himself he will have somthing in the exhibition this year

He is a native of Rotherham in Yorkshire & his first things that attracted Lord M's notice was a publication of some Scenery in the Lakes—tell us how you like his sketch & wether it will do the house seemd to me too tall & thin but the fault was that he left out the new Cots adjoining & took their gable from the width of the old one which tho level on the street side is in the yard a full yard wider—I saw so little of it that I can say nothing—it often happens that as money makes a gentleman Flattery often makes Poets & Painters & Poets & Painters often makes them nothing—I wish I was somthing better than both for the present & leave trying to be better than I am for the future.

I shall expect Saturday & if I am disappointed so it is but I cannot help expecting I am in no spirits to fill the sheet & still

I am

Sincerely yours

JOHN CLARE

To Hessey

Addressed: Messrs Taylor and Hessey, 93 Fleet St, London.
[sent]
Taylor's date and p.m.: 20 Jan 1823

MY DEAR HESSEY

Patty went over to Deeping to-day & got your kind letter for which I heartily thank you I am sorry to be so troublesome but when nessesity urges I cannot help it I shall want £8 more at any rate I can leave the odd shillings of each bill unpaid[1] I shall & must do without drink next year let matters go as hard as they may its not only hurting myself but my family likewise I am well aware of that I have not written a song since I left you & it is months now since I even scribbld a Sonnet but I have finished up an old silly thing 'The Statute or Recruiting Party' which you shall have tho I dont think it worth much— its a wonder Cowen didn't call perhaps things fell out to prevent him he has neer hand bin ere now tells how you like it![2] I coud say what I think about it was it finished—my Father is going to send you & T a few apples they are of a particular sort we call them the 'Golden Russet' The tree is an old favourite with my father & stood his friend many a year in the days of adversity by producing an abundance of fruit which always met with ready sale & paid his rent it has borne less latterly till this last season when it has produced a good quantity—you never tell me how you like my poems you might have said somthing of the last bit in the letter for I am always anxious for your opinions & pleasd when I get them wether for or against it— I shall attempt something of a song or address to someone but they will be only attempts I expect I felt for Taylor's situation[3] & coud preach up that consolation which I shall want myself when such things come about & come they must—give him my respects

I am
Yours sincerely
JOHN CLARE

To Taylor

Addressed: Messrs Taylor and Hessey, 93 Fleet St, London.
                    [sent]
                                    Feb. 28. 1823

If this is worth publishing* (& may be it may) any month
when you have a corner to spare I shoud like to see it in however
tell us how you like it in your next letter—I have got in this
dancing measure which runs so easy that I can hardly get out of
it several of my summer walks & 'Helpstone Heath' which I am
now writing are in the same but I must een give up awhile now
so you'll have no more at present from
                    Yours sincerely
                                    JOHN CLARE

To Hessey

Addressed: Messrs. Taylor and Hessey, 93 Fleet St.
                    [sent]
                                    [February–March 1823]

MY DEAR HESSEY

I now send you The Apples and beg your acceptance of them
their peculiar Flavour makes them esteemd here but how your
cockney pallets are I know not yet I hope you will find them
good—The passages in a Criticism in the last London of
Beddoes Brides Tradegy[1] highly delighted me it promises me
to be the best modern Tradegy I have met with the calm placid
manner of the verse breaks into no fustian but runs smooth deep
and sometimes sublime and beautiful surely its a stamp for
immortality and I wish him well unenvious and heartily I could
point out what I like and what I do not like but its needless I met
with a poetical song tother day 'The Foundlings Lamentation'
told by a neighbour some of the things struck me so much as to
copy them she traced its origin to a 'penny book' from which
she had gotten it by heart years afore and if it is not as pathetic
as 'Old Poullem's Mare' Im mistaken thats all—The Plot is of

* The poem, not now with the manuscript of this letter, cannot be identified.

143

a child found by a traveller and it tells its own story a winter's night long.

[There follows:]
How many a smiling babe hath dyd.[2]

I have written them down just as I heard them and the simplicity and tenderness struck me uncommonly but I may be out. Give my respects to Taylor.

Yours etc. etc. etc.

JOHN CLAR]

To Hessey

[*sent*]

p.m. 1823
[April 1823]

DEAR HESSEY

I am glad you liked the apples as it turns out as I expected I am glad also to see the Second Edition[1] so forward The Cottage is a very pretty picture & it is like too but there are some trifling mistakes owing to the cold frosty morning on which he sketched it that woud not allow him to attend to trifles I am pleasd to see antiquity as I have done nothing latly only made an attempt to continue the Village minstrel with an ardent apostrophe to the spirit of infancy & I intend to proceed with a general description of its lost joys & enter abruptly upon the subject pursued—should you like a specimen be as it will you shall have it—

[There follows:]
Live on thou spirit of departed years . . .[2]

[3 stanzas]

Will it do to go on tell me will you & tell me about Green's packet[3] I am anxious to hear but you take no notice in the world about it men of Business and poets are the worst correspondents that can come together—I am very sorry Taylor is ill but I am very poorly myself & have had a regular sickness every morning as soon as I got up for this 3 weeks on Friday I took a vomit & am a great deal better—you like my Valentine you say therefore I shall expect to see it in—I shall be glad of a few copies of the 'Minstrell' when out & I woud like to make your London friends a present of a Copy Cunningham & Reynolds & Hood I will give it so remember & I shoud like to give others too—I have never presented Hilton with a copy of my works yet & he is one of the best fellows I am acquainted with but I'm determind I will do—Taylor promised me Cunningham's 8vo Maxwell[4] I shoud like it—& I shoud like if it was not too presumptuous to ask it if Taylor woud give a copy of the Opium Eater he is a great favourite of mine—if you will give an opinion of my poetry you shall have the 'Parish' but if you will not I am determined I will send no more for your Criticism at present.

My dear Hessey believe me ever
Yours &c
JOHN CLARE

To Taylor

Addressed: John Taylor Esq, 13 *Waterloo Place, Pall Mall, London.*
[*sent*]

May 8
watermarked 1823

MY DEAR TAYLOR

I wrote to Hessey a long while back when in a very bad & restless state respecting coming up to London but he never so much as noticed that letter—an old post horse when he has done all he can is laid bye perhaps that is my case but I woud not willingly think so however there is one comfort left me I am still in the land of the living & as experience is a wise teacher I may if I recover get more knowledge among the mysterys of men [2 lines heavily scored out]

I recievd a letter from Rev[d] Mr Brooks[1] written as he says at your request I cannot answer him at present but his views on religion are the same as mine he appears to me an enlightend & what is far better a good man & I heartily thank him for his

kindness tho I fear I shall neither be the one or the other for
doubts & unbelief perplex me continually & now I think
seriously about an hereafter I am more troubld in my thoughts
then I was before & I much fear that I shall never feel a suffi-
ciency of faith to make me happy[2] the sincerity & enthusiastic
manners of the methodists in devotion puts my glimmering
conscience to shame—there is a preacher of the name of Black-
ley comes in our circuit whose voice is just like your own I never
heard such a similarity in my life I mean he preaches just in the
tone & manner which you read in it struck me the moment I
heard him & seemd as if you was addressing me he is a favourite
of mine but the people dont think much of him his persuasive
tenderness of speech is not deep enough for them they like
shouting & ranting far better—he has been a printer & is a good
scholar having a knowledge of several languages & likes to
talk about books of which he has a general knowledge I felt an
affection for the man the moment I saw & heard him—Dr
Skrimshire has been 4 or 5 times I dont know which but I am
almost sure it is no more than 4 I have now done with him &
perhaps it woud be as well settld as to Mr Walker[3] he was
sent by Lady Milton at first & he pretends that he sent in his
bill to her & started on my account when Dr Skrimshire came I
have reflected on this & believe he had no business tho I have
no desire to make a disturbance but he shall dress me no more
for it looks like quackery & I woud as lien have been without
him as with him for I think he has managd the matter with Lady
M so as to injure me for she woud doubtless wonder why her
assistance was not needed any longer if I get well I shall sift
the matter & serve him accordingly

I wish now to hear that the book is going on its high time to
start & I am satisfied there is enough & more than enough for a
Vol I shall wish to hear from you about it I have been written to
about a little Vol of descriptive Poems for children in plain
language without provincialisms I have not been able to answer
it yet nor shall I agree further then that I am willing to attempt
one but not to have my name to it in case it be sanctioned by
the public & then to be sure I shoud own it for when one longs
to be simple one is apt to be silly & thats what I fear but its far
out of my power at present to produce either exelence or

folly—a poor fellow a farmers son who thinks himself a poet &
in that uncomfortable self-opinion has publishd a Vol: has
written to me to use my interest for him & to tell him wether
it woud be of use to send a copy to the editor of your Magazine
& they are such lifeless things that I coud scarcely have patience
with the mans egotism & self-consiet he may do as he pleases
with your Editor but he gets no favour from me I have long
been troubled with these sort of gentry & am sick of them—
lets hear how you think of the Calendar for I want it out now
as I feel a little revivd tho I know its not for long continuance
for my head & feelings are as dead in apathy & my insides is as
sore & out of order nearly as bad as at first—what the complaint is God knows I do not I know one thing that is I am
very anxious to get better because I know when a family looses
its father the provider is gone & I have a little consern about
my fame because I think I can do better than I have done if I
am sufferd to resume a little longer

Yours &c &c &c

JOHN CLARE

To Hessey

Addressed: Messrs Taylor and Hessey, 93 Fleet Street, London.
[*sent*]

p.m. 17. May 1823

MY DEAR HESSEY

I thank you for the books—I have not been well latly but its
nothing further then the old complaints of the nerves—I have
however gone on scribbling at a cursed risky rate & writ a
poem on Spring[1] of a Serious Length & continued the second
part of the Mary poem[2] a long way with neither beginning
middle or end as yet I send you a trifle with this & if it suits
you may insert it in the Mag & if not its at your option to
burn it as soon as you please

[There follows:]

TO AN EARLY FRIEND[2]
Thoust been to me a friend indeed . . .

[6 stanzas]

147

As I hate particularity I shall never give the 'early friend' a name but let it remain a shadow while the person addressd & the readers (if its worth any) take what liberty they please & if they like each think themselves worthy of the caracter & every one who has any claim on the author's gratitude take it to themselves

I am

ever yours &c &c

JOHN CLARE

To Hessey

Addressed: J. A. Hessey Esq., Fleet St, London.
[*sent*]

June 1823

MY DEAR HESSEY

Here is your books but wether injurd or not I cannot say I packed them up as well as I coud—I have broke the tail piece of my Cremona not by fair means perhaps for it was done by substituting a second string for a first as a makeshift I wish it to be mended if possible as it is a limb of the fiddle & a new one in my opinion would have but a shallow claim to that character I have written to Tomas[1] & told him about it & sent the thing in the parcel—my bills are now in these are my dog days I hate arithmetic that proves these sad calculations here is the sum next door in extent to eternity with me £27 . 11 . 3 I must cut a string from the Minstrel so there ends the whole & live by the loss—£7[2] from the sum grins at my Folly on the greasy manteltree at the Bell thats the curse of the Confession

I shoud almost dread to see Taylor now for his small beer sermons woud quite undo me I will resolve next year to be more respectable & more independant & you shall hear no more confessions till then—I am just getting ready to visit Milton so I cannot fill the sheet—I have written a letter to the Marquis but have not sent it till you see it—tis on the subject of a further dedication as I think I have done wrong in not giving him the Minstrel's but time explains all this & it will mine he is now in France

Yours sincerely

JOHN CLARE

To Taylor

Addressed: John Taylor Esq, 13 Waterloo Place, Pall Mall,
            London
            [sent]

                                                    July 1823

MY DEAR TAYLOR

It perhaps woud have been more appropriate to have said
'Sir' considering the long silence between us has gone a long
way to make strangers but the past is always a poetical name to
me & therefore I adhere to it: I write this to tell you that I have
got a letter from the Marquis respecting a dedication to the
visionary Vol. which I wish to publish next winter & which I am
anxious for your opinion about the propriety of such a thing
I mean the pieces in the London with some new ones woud it be
right or woud it be too near you know I told you in London I
shoud bother you the winter after the next remember what you
say is law & I hope you will write me & say somthing here is an
Extract from his Lordship's note 'I am happy to hear that you
intend to amuse the Public with a fourth Vol of Poems. I am
obliged to you for wishing to dedicate it to me & am much
pleasd with your intention of doing so—I beg you will put my
name down for 10 Copies & remain your Obt St Exeter—'
Thats all

I hate dedication hunting worse then fox hunting tho I like
neither 'hope' that jilt & 'gratitude' that worrying hussy
woud not let me be—whats done is done & cannot be undone—
I coud give more reasons for my being tempted to do this but
as they are like blossoms on the fruit tree that come ere the
Spring in danger of being blighted I shall say nothing of them
the last prayer of a malefactor is but a doubtful sort of repentance & the hope that accompanys it but a fit consort for such a
companion—but its time to have done with such mysterys—
I write about the book & earnestly hope you will gratify me
with an answer about it as soon as you can—Poor Gilchrist is
done[1] I could not have thought it woud have affected me so
much when I first heard it I was stupified & woud not believe
it but its too true—God help us its the 'common lot' & the
passage were friendship, loves, hopes, fears, joys, & troubles in

oblivion meet—well it must be so & I have grown to care nothing about it—I have apathy about me that looks on the powers of hells & heavens as mysterious riddles & death as an animal consequence I hope its not heathenism—I hope its not worse but so it is—I expect Mr Allen's[2] book about me is no news to book I consider him a sensible & clever fellow & I expect you think likewise—with the attachment of old remembrances my dear Taylor yours as sincerely as ever

JOHN CLARE

To Taylor

Addressed: John Taylor Esq, 13 *Waterloo Place, London.*
[*sent*]

July 31. 1823

MY DEAR TAYLOR

You will be supprised to see another letter so soon—tho from one who has teasd you with so many—I this morning got a letter from my old friend Captain Sherwill who wishes me to write you to send him the 'Village Minstrel' & I in addition wish you to send him all the 3 vols as a present—he wants me to write my name in them so if this comes in time for the Magazine send me the first publishd Vol: with it to do so & that will serve as a substitute for all 3—They are to be directed to 'Captain Sherwill to the care of Mr Armstrong Caen France' 'They must be sent from London by the Southampton Coach'—I have found out a value for early friends since the loss of poor G. a tender & lasting regret that I did not think I shoud feel—the letter gives a description of the peasants of Switzerland but not so well as I think I coud have done it myself that it did not come up to my romantic notions I am uncommonly taken with your account of the Preacher of Hatten Garden* The explanation of harping & singing in Heaven is poetical & fine & goes a long way to convince me of its propriety if there is much in this way in the Vol you speak of I shoud like to see it & shoud reap satisfaction & benefit from it but dry arguments do more to puzzle then relieve me— I have talked to Hessey about the Poems publishing next

*Edward Irving.

winter for you did not satisfy me with your opinion—if you
think an entire new one dare be ventured on I shoud be proud
enough to hazard one & woud send you up all my M.S.S. in
the rough as they are for the purpose for God knows when I
shall have resolution to smoothen them off in copy I have
'Spring' the longest nearly copyd for you but fresh calamitys
forbid me to finish it off at present my eldest child has fell with
the Meazels which are very brief here it has been desperately
ill this 5 days 3 of which kept hope in suspense with danger so
long that my heart cannot forget aching tho this morning has
found her so much better as to leave her bed & resume some of
her innocent playfulness had I known the troubles that come
with children in spite of the pleasures I woud have had none
The youngest has not yet fallen when she gets over it safe you
will hear from me agen accompanyd with a scrap of ryhme—
dont forget to send the first Vol. of 'Poems' for me to insert the
Captains name in it I shall then leave the rest to you to convey
them in the way you chuse to think properest—I have chosen to
trouble you with it as I think Hessey not quite so sure—for I
think he often forgets things—I am uncommonly pleasd with
'Flora Domestica'* The account of them is poetry— I think
our new Vol might be calld 'The Wilderness' or Pastorals
Summer Walks & Sonnets

I am ever my dear Taylor
Yours sincerely

JOHN CLARE

To Hessey

Addressed: Messrs Taylor and Hessey.
[*sent*]

[Aug 1823]

MY DEAR HESSEY,

I read the Mag! to be bound for't I shall take my time over
the M.S.S. & send all up together as soon as I can but I dont
suppose that woud be yet tho I am anxious to get on as fast as

---

* By Elizabeth Kent, Leigh Hunt's sister-in-law. Taylor had just published her
book, but without her name on the title-page. This accounts for Clare's reference
in the following letter to 'him'.

I can my eldest child has had the meazles & got better the youngest is still to have them—Taylors willingness to publish next winter[1] has made me anxious & busy in copying and poetizing about 10 days will bring you the result I cannot make 2 copies so you must look to them safely when they arrive—& tell me directly I think there is no safer way of sending them then the common one we practice—think about Captain Sherwills job & send a vol back with the Mag: when bound & get it done as soon as you can as I shall want to return it with the M.S.S. parcel & give us your opinion when you get them how they suit you—you must excuse my filling the sheet as I have now got busy with other matter believe me yours etc etc & I hope the threatened music will charm you when its heard

JOHN CLARE

P.S. I have offerd some remarks about the 'Flora etc' but they are for you & not the author unless any hint would furnish him with improvement

To Hessey

Addressed: Messrs Taylor and Hessey, 93 Fleet St, London.
[sent]

watermarked 1820
[1823]

MY DEAR HESSEY

I have waited this while to send up the Mag: for binding & with it a MSS 'on Spring' but I have been prevented from returning it by the illness of my 2 children who are both getting better as I shoud hope but the fate of a neighbour makes me uncommonly uneasy & unable to do anything who lost a son & a daughter both in one day when they thought they was improving it commences with a hoarse cough & ends with an inflamation of the lungs & carrys them off in a moment when death is the least expected as soon as I find them safe I shall write agen—-but what is the reason you dont give your opinion of my latter poems you must have had time now & then to do it if you chuse—'as there is a time for all things'—Do you know

anything of a something publishing upon me (a critique or
Essay for I know not the like) by Murray[1] I can give no
opinion on things I have not seen I can only surmise I believe
Lord R & Mrs E. 2 of my best & very best friends but I must
have consciet enough in me to think they cannot read the world
so well as myself & I must prophesy thus much on its futurity
if its such an one as to please his Lordship it abounds in praise
on my poems which my enemys will readly conjure up into
flatterys! Criticisms overflowing with milk & honey are as vain
as those of the reptile uttering nothing but the venom of gall &
bitterness There never was a land of Canaan discovered as yet
but it raisd a nest of wasps to share in the spoils if its impartial
I shall give it welcome if not god help me I can but turn back
to other days & sigh in vain for times when friends were
needless & when foes were few I have made up my mind to
publish next winter & have written to Lord Exeter respecting
the Dedication whom I expect to hear from every day—I turnd
it over & over a many times in my mind before I ventured for
your silence seems determined & not to be broken but I coud
heartily wish you woud say wether I have done wrong or
right—yesterday fortnight is Helpstone feast I shall want to
settle my accounts as usual before it for that is 'doomsday' is
nigh agen so I wish you woud send me the half yearly rents as
soon as you can—I know were the last poem is wrong but I
cannot correct it now & have no short one to send you still

        I am
           Yours as sincerely as ever
                    J. CLARE

To Hessey

Addressed: Messrs Taylor and Hessey, 93 Fleet St, London.
           [sent]
                    p.m. Aug. 1823

MY DEAR HESSEY
    I got T's letter with the Mag but if you sent one likewise its
lost the parcel is generaly open'd ere it gets to me & I have
often thought of cautioning you to clap a seal upon it for security

I might with more propriety have sent it to T— but I can
answer his with yours & make one serve both—You have spoilt
the first Sonnet of Greens & improvd the second—I am very
pleasd with the title of the new book[1] but will the subjects
support it as it ought to be I fear T indulges too great expectations on my new M.S.S. which he has not yet seen—I look back
& think I have done nothing they are not a great many in
quantity either but plenty if good for our purpose I shall be
the worst off for a tale that most assuredly ought to accompany
every month I coud soon daub pictures anew[2] for the Descriptions there is a thing or two on Spring that I am pleasd
with I know the thought is new & hope it is general & true to
nature tis the description of a boy running races with the moon
—& another hunting the landrail or landrake—I dont think
you know these names but you know the bird its a little thing
heard about the grass & wheat in summer & one of the most
poetical images in rural nature tis like a spirit you may track it
by its noise a whole day & never urge it to take wing—I will
set seriously to work to make the thing as good as I can—but
I think I had better let T. see what I have done (for I like the
Title) & then he will be able to judge how far we can support it
—I wrote to Taylor last Thursday of the ' Wilderness &c ' but I
dont like that title now—I have had a letter from Sherwill he
has been travelling Switzerland & is now at Versailes he wants
my poems & wishes my name to be in them I wrote to T. about
it to let the first Vol come with the Mag: for that purpose but it
came too late I found if you coud send a fly leaf anyhow in a
letter it woud answer the purpose for I shall send up a parcel
shortly of all I have written & I coud return it with them—I
coud wish Taylor woud give the old M.S.S. another hunt over
for I think a few things might be found in them too good to be
lost & as he goes on I wish he woud mark such things with a
pen that want improved & are worth it for some time I shall
send for them to mend some & burn the rest for I shant dye
happy if I leave any disgraceful remains behind me & T— &
you will not live forever to prevent others from publishing what
exists—poor White's[3] 3rd Vol woke my suspicions very
strongly—Artis's Castor[4] is out have you seen it tis nought but
plates—his bust of me has fallen to pieces—I mean to sit for a

cast sometime & send it up to T— as a fulfilment of part of my
promise—for I hate to be worse then my word even in trifles

I shall have a frontpiece in the new Vol but Westalls &
Cortoulds[5] I dont like & their names are too bookish by half
Coudnt our friend Janus[6] create us one of his long legd beauties
that might suit the purpose—I have just thought of another
thing which strikes me as good & which he might & coud do
well vinettes at the heads of the months in easy outline tell T.
& he will think of it I care nothing like stubbornness about it—
but the frontpiece in my mind is a fixture & perhaps Leslie[7]
might do it well

Yours &c &c

To Hessey

Addressed: Messrs Taylor and Hessey, 93 Fleet St, London.
[*sent*]

Sept. 11. 1823.

MY DEAR HESSEY

I hope you will forgive me in putting you to a double charge
for I had nothing ready to make a parcel & I thought delays
might be dangerous—How you will like my letter to Sir M. B.
Clare* I know not but I have done it as well as I coud & I
dont suppose I coud do a better I shoud have written a note to
Messrs Budd & Calkin but I hope you will manage that for
me & give them my respects—Somebody has sent me this
morning a 'Sunday Times' under cover of Earl Grey with a
hard-naturd puff in it have you seen it I shoud suppose it to
be written by a Scot but setting politics aside its not amiss

Lets hear how you like my letter the first oppertunity & if
it will do send it as soon as you think proper to Messrs B. & C.
I think it will myself excuse my saying more for I am very
busy in the harvest & have stolen part of my dinner hour to
write this give my respects to Taylor

Yours &c &c

JOHN CLARE

P.S. The Letter unsealed mind—

* Sir Michael Benignus Clare, M.D., a rich West Indian, sent Clare £5 for
the name's sake.

To Taylor

Addressed: John Taylor Esq., 13 *Waterloo Place, London.*
[*sent*]

p.m. 5. Jan. 1824

My dear Taylor

I recievd the thing safe* & am very pleasd with your early attention to my nessesitys

I am very supprisd that you had not got the M.S. as it was sent to Deeping on Sunday last but I hope you have it now & if you have I hope you will skim it over & tell me directly how you like things as I am waiting for your remarks—I have just finishd a tale on a subject given by you sometime ago you remember the Yorkshire Farmer going in disguise as a labourer you said it woud make a tolerable subject for a Drama be as it will I have made a tale of it & I think not a bad one as gossip tells it

Any other things that you may think woud make tales or any pictures you may have noticd in the months of rural scenery woud be very acceptable to me now you know better then me what will suit & I am certain a man of your taste has not let them pass by without notice

Hessey proposd 'Harvest home' as a 'capital subject' but in my mind it is too barren of incident unless it be connected with a story & I am looking over my mind for one to suit it

When I have done with the 'Shepherds Calendar' I shall make up my mind to publish no more for 8 or 10 years wether the thing be successful or not

& in that interval I intend to try the Drama in pastoral & tragic pictures & I have made it up in my mind to write one hundred Sonnets as a set of pictures on the scenes of objects that appear in the different seasons & as I shall do it soly for amusement I shall take up wi gentle & simple as they come whatever in my eye finds any interests not merely in the view for publication but for attempts

I have not yet got the Mag: & if it be not sent off ere this

---

* The parcel in which Taylor enclosed Clare's half-year's annuity (British Museum correspondence).

arrives I wish you woud send me a blank book ruld & fellow to the former that I may copy the things down in as I write them

Be as soon as you can wi your remarks as I want them to go on with

Yours &c &c &c

JOHN CLARE

To Thomas Inskip[1]*

Addressed: Mr. Thomas Inskip, Watchmaker, Shefford, near Biggleswade, Beds.
[*sent*]
Helpstone near Market Deeping
p.m. 10 August. 1824

DEAR INSKIP

You will have drawn some unpleasant pictures of my carlesness and seeming neglect in not answering your letter ere now but the fact is easily explained I have been in London 3 months for the benefit of better advice than the country affords and I am sorry to acknowledge that I feel very little better I have been in a terrible state of ill-health six months gradually declining and I verily believe that it will upset me at last I was taken in a sort of appoplectic fit and have never had the right use of my facultys since a numbing pain lies constantly about my head and an acking void at the pit of my stomach keeps sinking me away deeper and deeper I returned home last saturday were I found your letter and I have attempted to answer it as soon and as well as I can I shall only be at home for a few weeks to try the air to be sure if it improves my spirits I shall remain if not the next thing for me to try is salt water I woud have call'd on you at Shefford if I had been able but I can get no were by myself I am so ill still I think I feel better since I got home and if I get better I will write you word of my remaining here were I shall be heartily happy to see you but visiting a sick man has no sort of temptation in it as I can do nothing with Sir John Barlycorn now I have often thought of our London Evening and I have often thought of

* See Biographical Memoranda.

writing to you—poor Bloomfield I deeply regret now its too late I had made up my resolution to see him this summer but if he had been alive[2] I shoud have been dissapointed by this coldblooded lethargy of a disease what it is I cannot tell it even affects my senses very much by times—I heard of Bloomfields death and it shockd my feelings poor fellow you say right when you exclaim 'who would be a poet' I sincerely lovd the man and I admire his Genius and readily (nay gladly) acknowledge his superiority as a Poet in my opinion he is the most original poet of the age and the greatest pastoral poet England ever gave birth to I am no Critic but I always feel and judge for myself I shall never forget the pleasures which I felt in first reading his poems little did I think then that I shoud live to become so near an acquaintance with the Enthusiastic Giles and miss the gratification of seeing him at last—I am grievd to hear of his family misfortunes were are the icy hearted pretenders that came forward once as his friends—but it is no use talking this is always the case—neglect is the only touchstone by which true genius is proved look at the every day scribblers I mean those nonsense ginglings calld poems 'as plenteous as black-berrys' published every now and then by subscription and you shall find the list belarded as thickly with my Lord this & my Lady tother as if they were the choicest geniuses nature ever gave birth too while the true poet is left to struggle with adversity and buffet along the stream of life with the old notorious companions of genius Dissapointment and poverty tho they leave a name behind them that posterity falls heir too and Works that shall give delight to miriads on this side eternity well the world is as it is and we cannot help it—I wrote 3 Sonnets to his Memory[3] but I did not feel satisfied with them if I ever get better I mean to write a Monody whose only reccomendation perhaps will be its sincerity—as soon as I am more able I will write to you again in the mean time if you feel inclined to answer this letter I shall feel glad to hear from you—I heard that Bloomfield's Remains was just published as I left London but I was so ill that I could make no inquirys about them I wish them success and

I remain sincerely yours &c &c

JOHN CLARE

To Taylor

Addressed: John Taylor Esq, 13 Waterloo Place, London.
[*sent*]

watermarked 1823
[August 1824][1]

MY DEAR TAYLOR

I got all safe & Dr Arnold* shall recieve his claim on friday
I have felt as bad as ever since I wrote you but now I am
thinking I feel improving again I think the doctors none of them
know the cause of my complaint I feel now a numbness all over
me just as I shoud suppose a person to feel when bitten by a
serpent & I firmly believe I shall never get over it be as it will
I am resignd for the worst my mind is placid & contented &
that is somthing for when I was first took God forgive me I had
hard work to bare up with my malady & often had the thought
of destroying myself & from this change in my feelings I satis-
factorily prove that Religious foundation is truth & that the
Mystery that envelops it is a power above human nature to
comprehend & thank God it is for if a many uneasy discontented minds knew of the bargain they shoud gain by being good
they might still be discontented & I might be one of them
besides there is little merit in undergoing a hardship for a
prize when we know what it is—the labourer goes to work for
his hire & is happy or sullen according to the wages aloud him
—I agree with you that the religious hypocrite is the worst
monster in human nature & some of these when they had grown
so flagrant as to be discoverd behind the mark they had taken to
shelter their wickedness led me at first to think lightly of
religion & sure enough some of the lower classes of dissenters
about us are very decietful & in fact dangerous characters
especially amongst the methodists with whom I have declined
to associate but there are a many sincere good ones to make up

---

* Of Stamford. In Clare's early reminiscences, where he tells of the 'fits'
brought on through his seeing a man fall from the top of a load and break his neck,
he says Dr. Arnold eventually 'stopt' the fits. Arnold attended him, at Taylor's
request, in spring 1824.

& why shoud the wicked deter us from taking care of ourselves
when they ought to appear in our eyes as a warning to make us
turn to the right way—my opinion Taylor of true Religion
amounts to this if a man turns to God with real sincerity of
heart not of canting & creeping to the eyes of the world but
satisfying his own conscience so that it shall not upbraid him
in the last hours of life that touchstone of faith in practice carless of what either for or against him that man in my opinion
is as certain of heaven in the next world as he is of death in
this—because we cannot do wrong without being conscious of
it—& if no dread overweights us at that hour it is the surest
proof of innocence—I feel it impossible for me to copy over [?]
rough things so I have sent you them to do what you can with
them yourself

The marks will lead to were the outslips are to be inserted
I know you have but little respect for afterthoughts but they are
not much it is the way in which I always compose & you will
see most of them nessesary for corrections sake The Pastoral
is my idea of one but if Popes definition be true that everything
in nature is vulger & every monstrous fancy out of it a pastoral
then mine is grossly wrong your judgment is my standby & if
I live I intended to write 11 more in that way & had begun
another 'Love & Flattery' your approval or condemnation if I
am ever able to write agen will settle the matter—I believe
with you that there is quite plenty for a Vol & a respectable one
likewise so consider of it & act just as if it was your own you
have now every poem in your possession that I am worth what
is left are but outlines or shadows & not fit for your eye at
present—this book is the only copy in existence—the sooner
the book is begun the better so I shoud think once but I'm in
every way anxious about anything now—I coud wish if you
thought it proper not without that you woud write to the
Marquis to explain the delay

I have not answered Hessey's last letter I delayd it to have
some doubtfull passages in our dissenter creeds here explaind
but I can see thru the vulgar errors that blinded them & correctly find their original notions myself it was respecting their
ignorant notions of tenets which they stile 'Free Grace'
Election & Predestination' things that are far better kept out

of the way of the ignorant who interpret them to suit their own purposes & make religion grossly ridiculous by such abuses

Yours &c &c &c

JOHN CLARE

To Hessey

[*sent*]

20 August. 1824

MY DEAR HESSEY

I have not written to you a long while I waited partly thro indisposition & partly to get some doubts explaind which I do not want now I feel resignd & quiet & thats enough as to my health I can give you but a bad account tho I have gave up doctoring save the taking of opening pills occasionally I am as stupid as ever & blood comes from me often my insides feels sinking & dead & my memory is worse & worse nearly lost the sensation as if cold water was creeping all about my head is less frequent now tho it comes on now & then in the evening for at that time I am always worse I have found the Ranters that is I have enlisted in their society they are a set of simple sincere & communing Christians with more zeal then knowledge earnest & happy in their devotions O that I coud feel as they do but I cannot their affection for each other their earnest tho simple extempore prayers puts my dark unsettld consience to shame this is how they keep the sabbath at 7 o'clock they meet to pray at 9 they join the Class at half past 10 they hear preaching at half past 2 they meet agen to pray & at 7 in the evening preaching again this passes the Sabbath with the Ranters making an heaven on earth there is a deal of enthusiasm in their prayers & preachings & manners but as it is real & not affected it is not to be found fault with but commended my feelings are so unstrung in their company that I can scarcly refrain from shedding tears & when I went Church I coud scarcly refrain from sleep—I thank God that he has opened my eyes in time & let all scoffers remember the line of Young 'They may live fools but fools they cannot dye'—I shall never forget the horror that I felt in reading this line but enough—I feel desirous Hessey of having Dr. Darlings advice & woud feign get to London if I coud but I am so fearful of the way lest I shoud be taken for the worse & unable to proceed on the journey & I have made such an expensive doctoring at home that perhaps I ought not to come to you to increase it but life is sweet & I feel feign to get better tho I am next to hopless— what shall I do if I thought Dr. D. coud do me no good I woud not come for I cannot enjoy no pleasure & am loath to leave home but if I knew he coud I woud try for it tho double the distance it is I am able to come up outside if the weather suits & if it does not I can wait I cannot reconsile my own mind what to do for I think my disorder incurable because I feel as I have never felt before in my life & further I cannot feel much better if I do its only for a day or two & then I am as bad as ever—give me your advice as to what you think woud be best & I will abide by it you did not send the Mag: this month you might for I can read betimes tho very little & I have not as yet lost my relish for the things of this world tho I feel my situation very awful & often lingering* on the brink of another well we must all come to it at last tho some has more trouble in getting there then another

Yours &c &c

JOHN CLARE

To Cary†

[sent]

Helpstone

Sep 18–24

MY DEAR SIR

. . . [wants advice on a school book for his children] I am ill able to write or do anything else I thought I was getting well but I've not a hope left me now I have employed myself when able since I came home at writing my own life which if I live

---

* The manuscript might read 'languishing', or even 'longing'.

† This letter is from the transcripts of Mr. R. W. King, and quoted by him in *The Translator of Dante.*

to finish it I shoud like to trouble you to read it & give your opinion of it for my own judgment in such matters is very often faulty . . . [praises Cary's Life of Chatterton* and asks him to do one on Bloomfield.]

I am

Yours affectionatly

JOHN CLARE

To Artis

[sent]

[September 1824]

DEAR ARTIS

I have not been able to write to you till now & now I am ill able to scribble over a sheet in my usual way for I believe at one time I was uncommonly fond of it—I have sent you the '*will*' the *London one* to look over you will see the original copy the other scribblings are such things that I reccolected after I got better at intervals & stand for nothing till I have a new will made† take care of it for they have a copy such as it stands on the first leaf with a few remarks but not so many as there is in this give me your opinion of it & if you object [to] it when you see them in London say so & in the mean time I will get one copied which you shall see before it is made—I think self-interest (not mine) is the 'ruling passion' of the London one but you may understand them better than I at least I think you know my will plain enough to see that this is but an odd interpretation of it—I have heard nothing of them yet—I have sent you two specimens of fern if you have not got them I will send the roots by Moor before next weeks out— the dark one grows by 'Wood lane' side in a dyke & the other in 'Oxey wood' I have brought two home ready for you but if you have them its not worth while sending them so I will wait till I hear from you

* *London Magazine,* June 1820.
† The 'new will', he records in his *Journal* for Friday, 1 October 1824, made E. T. Artis one of his executors.

I cannot send Betsey the book this time as I wait till I hear from London it shall come with the ferns—give my respects to Mrs. Artis & her

& believe me

Yours sincerely

JOHN CLARE

I will look out some ms for Mrs Artis as promisd when I get more settled in health & temper for I can do nothing now Excuse a short letter

To Charles Abraham Elton[1]*

[sent]

Milton

Decr 18. 1824

MY DEAR SIR

I have got from home a few days to pass away time & try to improve my present miserys by other amusements than reading &c which has long ceased to be one I have at the same time taking an opportunity[2] of getting a frank for what I can say is scarcely worth the paper tho at one time it might be expected that I thought otherwise by my fondness for scribbling & if I had been well I make no doubt but I shoud have taken so much advantage of your invitation to hear from me as to make you wish you had not . . .[3] get so well as to write any thing or even correct what I have written—I mentioned the Shepherd's Calender to Hessey a long time back but he made no sort of answer in return in fact this is always the way they serve me I know not how they serve you but when I ask any thing about what may concern me or mine they pass it off & talk of other things a great length from the main road—there was nothing in the 'Epistle'[4] &c that I objected to but the two verses mentioning the Casts at Devilles & that was in the expression which I thought rather flat & as spoiling the general tenour of the other verses the rest I would rather have seen as

* See Biographical Memoranda.

they were I recollect the line you mention & thought then that the word *'intensity* of age' very good & happy—I like the 'Solitary wasp' in 'blakesmoor'[5] & thought that Dequinceys article on Goethe[6] exelent. . . .[3]

To Cary*

[*sent*]

Helpstone

Dec. 30. 1824

MY DEAR SIR

I shoud have written long ago if I had been able for I always feel a pleasure in writing to those I esteem but had I been well I should have had little to say worth reading . . . I have not yet finished my life . . . I feel anxious to finish it & I feel also anxious that you shoud see it & I shall be greatly obliged for your opinion of it as I mean if I live to publish it I have gotten 8 chapters done & have carried it up to the 'Poems on Rural Life' &c—I feel it rather awkard to mention names as there are some that I cannot speak well of that is were I feel an objection I cannot flatter over it & I woud not willingly offend anyone. I have made free with myself & exposed my faults and failings without a wish to hide them, neither do I care what is said about me but if you shoud see anything that might be against me in speaking of others I shall be thankful of your advice & also your remarks on the thing altogether for it is written in a confusd stile & there will doubtless be found a deal of trifling in it for I am far from a close reasoner in prose . . . [more of his illness and troubles] we must abide by providence who by the bye appears but an indifferent observer of troubles by times but we are not to play with destiny . . . [mention of L. E. L., Alaric Watts, etc.]

Yours sincerely & affectionatly

JOHN CLARE

* This letter is from the transcripts of R. W. King, and quoted, in part, by him in *The Translator of Dante.*

To James Montgomery*

[*sent*]

Helpstone. Jan. 5. 1825.

MY DEAR SIR

I copied the following verses from a MS on the flye-leaves of an old book entitled the Worlds Best Wealth, a Collection of choice Counsils in Verse & Prose printed for A. Bettesworth at the Red Lion in Paternoster Row 1720 they seem to have been written after the perusal of the book & are in the manner of the Company in which I found them, I think they are as good as a many old poems that have been preserved with more care & under that feeling I was tempted to send them thinking they might find a corner from Oblivion in your entertaining literary paper the 'Iris'[1] but if my judgment has misled me to over-rate their merit you will excuse the freedom I have taken & the trouble I have given you in the perusal—for after all it is but an erring opinion that may have little else than the love of poesy to reccomend it

I am

Yours sincerely

JOHN CLARE

[There follows:]

THE VANITYS OF LIFE.

To Joseph Weston†

Addressed: 12 *Providence Row, Finsbury Square, London.*

[*sent*]

Helpstone

March 7. 1825

DEAR SIR

In answer to yours of the third I am sorry to say that I posses but little of the corespondence of my departed 'brother bard' what I do posses you are welcome too & as to my letters

---

* See Biographical Memoranda.

† Editor of Bloomfield's 'Remains' (1824). The manuscript of this letter is among the Bloomfield papers, British Museum.

to him you may do with them just as you please & make of them
what use you like I deeply regret that ill health prevented our
corespondence & that death prevented us from being better
acquainted I sincerely loved the man & admired his Genius &
had a strong anxiety to make a Journey to spend a day with
him on my second visit to London & I intended to have stopped
at Biggleswade on my return home for that purpose but my
purse got too near the bottom for a Stoppage on the road & as
it was too great a distance to walk home this with other matters
prevented me from seeing him as one of my family was very ill
at the same time & hastened my return—

Whatever cause his friends may have to regret the death of
the Poet—Fame is not one of them for he dyed ripe for immortality & had he written nothing else but 'Richard & Kate'* that
fine picture of Rural Life were sufficient to establish his name as
the English Theocritus & the first of Rural Bards in this
country & as Fashion (that feeble substitute for Fame) had
nothing to do with his exaltation its neglect will have nothing
to affect his memory it is built on a more solid foundation &
time [one line heavily scored out] will bring its own reward to
the 'Farmers Boy'—I beg you will have the kindness to take
care of the M.S. & return it when you have done with it as I
wish to preserve a scrap of his handwriting—The Copy on the
other side is a note which accompanied his present of 'Mayday
with the Muses' I gave the original to Allan Cunningham the
Poet who has a high respect for Bloomfield's genius & whose
request on that account (to posses a scrap of his writing) I was
proud & happy to gratifye—soon after the Poet's death I wrote
in a mellancholy feeling 3 Sonnets to his memory I was not
aware that his 'Remains' woud have had such insertions or I
shoud have sent them to his daughter—I shall fill this sheet
with them for your perusal tho I expect they will come out in
the volume now in the press that will be published this Spring:
with my best wishes that your kindly labours for the memory
of the departed Poet may meet with the success it deserves

I remain
Yours very faithfully
JOHN CLARE

* It was Bloomfield's realism that appealed to Clare. There is nothing of his
own deeper quality in Bloomfield's verse.

To Artis

[sent]

[March or April. 1825]

MY DEAR ARTIS

How are you getting on nay I may be like the Irishman & ask were you are for I dont know were to find you nor know wether you are at London¹ or York as I write at a venture & the purport of this is to beg your kindness to get a frank for the enclosed letter if in case the pensil marks be rubbed out the Direction is to 'Mrs William Wright Clapham Surrey'² How are you getting on with your 'Fossil Plants' & 'Antiquitys' I have found some more fragments of pot in Harrison's close³ near Oxey³ & am now convinced myself that there is some more worth the trial one of the bits had the letter 'V' on it a mark of the potters I suppose I have saved them all for your inspection when you next come to Helpstone—have you been to see Hessey I suspect you have as they have begun printing the New Poems⁴—lets hear from you—a little news of any sort is acceptable here—did you see the poems in Montgomery's 'Iris' I think you heard me talk of it when you was last here.

I am dear Artis
Yours very sincerely

JOHN CLARE

To Hessey

[sent]

April 17 [1825]

FRIEND HESSEY

I have waited a long while for a proof of the book & my patience being exhausted I must write tho I have neither the inclination or wish to be offended—Artis brought down a story that made me perfectly satisfied that letter writing was but waste time & paper a thing is easily written tho it is never to be done & he said that he found on his second application for the M.S.S. which I have written for about twelve times that you did not

mean to send them for what reason I cannot tell—I shall want
them & cannot get on with my present occupation without them
tho I have been unable latly to do anything if I had them—
another thing that surprised me very much was the confession
that Van Dyk[1] made at my plan for the new book by saying that
he had not many of the poems mentioned therein—now this is
very strange that an editor should be employed by Taylor to
get out my poems & that he should still neglect even to make
him aquainted with the M.S.S. this is a very odd way of taking
in a substitute for tho he could not find time to correct them
himself he might certainly have found time to have put them in
his hands—I felt very vext at the time & I am far from satisfied
with the neglecting manner that has been going on latly Van
Dyk said I should have a proof in three days it is now three
weeks & none has yet come if this is to be the plan of proceeding
I would really from my heart that my M.S.S. were returned
altogether & I left to do them myself—I cannot meet with
worse success than I have lately be as it will—my friends have
been long busy with advice & cautions &c but I did not heed it
then tho I find at the wrong end of the story that it would have
been much better as a preventive to an often uneasy mind of
restless anxietys had I taken an earlier heed of what they told
me as to the determined neglect & mysterious manner of the
profession in general I do not wish to hurt the feelings of
anyone nor do I wish they should hurt mine—but when delay
is carried into a system its cause must grow a substitute for a
worse name—I will go on no further but I will just ask you to
give a moments reflection to my situation & see how you would
like it yourself

Yours

JOHN CLARE

These never were returned nor accounted for*

---

* How this comment of Clare's appears on a sent letter is a mystery. The only
solution is that Clare looked over his letters to Taylor and Hessey while in London
in 1828.

To Taylor

Addressed: John Taylor Esq, Waterloo Place, Pall Mall, London.
[sent]

Helpston May 5. –25

DEAR TAYLOR

I delayed to answer your letter till a proof arived to prove that you had not forgotten the promise of sending one & getting on with the book but as nothing of that kind come I must write without it—I had hopes when I recieved your last that your resolves to get on with the poems were in earnest—it is not for the mere gratification of seeing it out that makes me urgent but it is for more substantial reasons which I shall not lengthen the letter to explain—for I am weary of writing or talking about my conserns—Anticipation is a pleasant feeling but it borders on dissapointment which is a very unpleasant one therefore I have waited & hoped for the best & as I hate offensive correspondence I pass over the unpleasant part of ours as well as I can[1] I might be under a mistake & if so the feelings they excited woud be irritating yet I feel now the negligence in getting out the poems woud make any one complain & whatever harm may come from complaining of matters that appear to claim no commendation I am sure no good can come from speaking in their praise—when I feel anything I must speak it I know that my temper is hasty & with that knowledge of myself I always strive to choke it & soften hard opinion with reasonable interpretations—but put yourself in my place for a minute & see how you woud have felt & written yourself & if you feel that you shoud have acted otherwise then I will take it as an example & strive to correct my failings & be as perfect in an imperfect world as I can

I have no desire to seek another publisher neither do I believe any other woud do as well for me as you may do much less better but when obligation is sought or offered it sells the kindness therefore I will go no further on that head & if I did drawing comparisons from others woud not be adding praise if the complaints of authors are to be noticed & why shoud they not have cause for their lamentations as well as Jeremiah—

all I have to say is that if you want to get out of the job of publishing my poems you may tell me so & I will seek another & trust to providence but if you have no desire to turn me adrift the speedy publication of my poems will gladly convince me that I was mistaken & I shall be happy to prove that you are my friend as usual—here with me endeth the matter I shall say nothing further I dont like to write under such feelings & I wish to get out of them as soon as I can

I beg that Miss Taylor will accept my kindest remembrances & I am heartily glad to hear that she recovers so much—as for my part I cannot get rid of my complaint at all it leaves me & returns again as virulent as ever last week I was much worse & this week I am much better agen but I have little hopes it is not lasting I shall be very happy to recieve Mrs W. Wrights kind present of the flowers which she so readily assented to give me & will as gladly send her anything that I posses in return I wish you woud tell her so—I dont think it woud be too late to send a sucker of the White Provence Rose provided it were lapt up in wet moss & not kept on the Journcy the Tiger lily too woud not hurt if sent in the same manner moss keeps the wet like spunge & if this is not to be had fine hay well wetted woud do nearly as well I hope you will tell her as I have been expecting them this 3 weeks I shall send my flowers to her in Henderson's parcel to Milton House for I fear they will be too bulky for any other conveyance & not worth the expense of carriage

I will conclude with the hopes of seeing a proof of the Shepherds Calender in a few days—I told Hessey that I was ready to join the Young Lady[2] in writing the History of Birds but I have heard nothing about it & I have such a fear of my own inability to do anything for such a matter that I cannot enter into it with any spirit as I find that I dont know half the Swimmers & Waders that inhabit the fens & I understand that there are a many of them strangers to the Natural History book makers themselves that have hitherto written about it

I am dear Taylor
Yours sincerely
JOHN CLARE

To Taylor

Addressed: John Taylor Esq, 13 *Waterloo Place, Pall Mall,* London.
[*sent*]

June 19 –25

MY DEAR TAYLOR

I have been puzzling over the matter in your last letter & cannot tell in which opinion to agree exactly but I will say thus much & leave you to deside yourself It appears to me that the insertion of the Descriptive poems woud only make a very vague book among the generallity of readers & ryhmers & woud leave them with an unfavourable opinion of the book at the end & on the other hand the mere insertion of the Naratives or Tales woud not correspond with the title—all I can say is that I think the best woud be to select the best parts of the descriptive pieces as Introductions to the Months & then let the story follow that was judged to be most suitable & in some cases were a Story was not to be had the whole of the Descriptive Poem if good might be inserted only such for instance as 'Spring' for April which I consider one of my best Poems when it has undergone your pruning for it wants a good deal to avoid repetitions—I will leave the rest to your Judgment—the two tales that I had inserted in my former plan of 'Fate of Genius' & 'The Vicar' I consider them as not applicable to the present Title & if you think the same they might be cast out & leave room for others & were the descriptive pieces contain nothing worth extracting then the Story may fill up the month of itself but I woud always get a character of the month were I coud—the insertion of the 'Cottage Evening' for January by itself & the 'Valentine day' for February without the descriptions are very good improvements as I think for there is nothing in the Description for Feby that is worth preserving but I think the one for March is better as there are images in it not noticd before by me or anyone else as I am acquainted with & one of these is the description of the Droves of Wild Geese that are very charactistic companions of this Month but I will leave these things to your reason the 'Sorrows of

Love'[1] will come in for March very well—'Cottage Stories'
woud certainly have been a fair title & I think a better title
than the Calender but it has been made use of by a Poetess here
(at Oakham) name Anna Adcock[2] who a little while back
publishd a Volume of very middling poems under that Title
which was printed in London by I forget whom—there is
another new poet started up here & I was favoured with a
sight of his M.S.S. a little while back his longest poem is
entitled 'Memory's Musings' it reads smooth enough but
there is nothing striking or new in his images or expressions
his name is Kenrick[3] the son of Captain Kenrick of Alwalton
Hall—I hear he is about something of a good length in blank
verse but I am sorry to say I have no expectations to indulge
in—I think I have about nine neighbours Poets who have
printed their trifles by subscription—the first of these was an
oldish man named Messing who wrote 'The Rural Walks' &
another thing which I have forgotten[4] then up started two in a
bunch at Peterbro name Rose[5] & Wilkinson[2] the first was a
schoolmaster he published a version of 'Ossian in Ryhme' &
the others Poem was 'Saint John' the first was like the ravings
of a madman 'full of sound & fury signifying nothing' & the
other was dull & tame in addressing the Lark which 'at
heavens gate sings' & was Miltons at first he made a terrible
blunder addressing it as a male at the beginning & as a female
in the end Artis from this always called him the 'Hermaphra-
dite' after this started a Parish Clerk name Banton[6] who had the
impudence to style his poems 'Visits from the Muses' &
Dedicated it to the 'University of Cambridge' because two or
three boys (the sons of Clergymen round his own village) had
[subscribed] to it—another is Stratton[7] the best in the bunch
whose consiet stopt him from being something better than he
is—his book was dedicated to Lord Russel it contains a curious
medley of pretending love for ryhme & simplicity & a deal
of laughable absurdity is the consequence of the couple There
are 3 or 4 more but I am getting to the end of the sheet with a
digression that is no part of the story so I will end—I shall
be urged to continue the stories for children by your opinion
but they woud have been done already if you had told me
before—I have got only some early fragments beside the

Grasshopper done yet they are 'Flower gathering' 'The
Butterflye's Dream' 'The Moth & the Faireys' & two or three
more that have got no further then the titles—I am very poorly
& Patty is very ill the children are something better that is
they are playing about agen & only drouk[8] in the evening

I am

Yours &c &c

JOHN CLARE

To Hessey

Addressed: Messrs. Taylor and Hessey, 93 Fleet St, London.
[sent]

July. 7. 1825

MY DEAR HESSEY

I recieved your letter of the 30 of June enclosing my sallary
of £15 safe but in my letter to Taylor I told him that I shoud
want £10 more then my half yearly dividend & therefore I was
dissapointed in paying off my accounts as they exceed the
present means so far as to make it useless to begin to settle
them till I get a sufficient supply—so if Taylor thinks it
impolitic to supply my present need I wish that he had said so
for in that case I must make a breach on the principal somewhere or other but if he will let me have the £10 I shall feel
obliged to him as I can get no further at present without such
assistance—the proofs have grown into a standstill again I
doubt. I keep expecting them every day lately & am expecting
on I feel very anxious to see the end of it & have strong hopes
that I shall get paid for the dedication or I shall be curst mad
if I am dissapointed—I shall always be glad to correspond
with you & if the alteration between you & Taylor* had made
any difference in that much less broken it up altogether I shoud
have felt a great dissapointment but when business is out of the
question you must not plead so often busy to get off with short
letters for I like plenty of news & a sheetfull tho I am not in
the situation to demand it for tho I am not busy I am not able

---

* The firm of Taylor and Hessey was dissolved at midsummer 1825, Hessey
retaining the retailing and Taylor the publishing. Taylor also sold the *London
Magazine* to Henry Southern.

to get on with a long letter for I am very dull headed & very ill not far short of being as bad as I was this time last year with you & I am so far from my old assistance that I feel in a delicate situation of telling my complaints on paper too often tho Dr D always kindly bids me write him how I am when ever I feel worse which I have done several times since I wrote him last but I wait & wait to see if I get better & somtimes feeling or fancying I am so I delay it a little further my family are all pretty well just now here comes the blank in my head & I sit gaping to see what I can say further—I can find little or nothing so I must give my remembrances to Mrs Hessey
& remain your debtor for a better letter next time
yours sincerely

JOHN CLARE

To William Hone*

2. August 1825

SIR

I have an old Copy of the 'Reliquiae Wottonianae' on the flye leaves of which is the following verses in M.S. entitled a Defiance to Love & attributed to Sir Henry Wooten by the writer if they are worthy mention in your everyday book[1] they are at your service as I see by your insertion of a Poem of Andrew Marvels[1] that you give room to such 'Reliques'— I myself am very fond of these old votarys of the muses & I may confess my taste to be laughd at by the moderns when I say that I prefer Shakespear to Byron Spencer to Sir Walter Scott Sir John Suckling to Moor[2] & every other of the Elizabethan Bards to the rest of the Moderns—I am also a constant reader of your Every day book & a yearly purchaser of Moors Almanack & I am in the habit of taking your key to unlock every mystery of Saint Abudquenty[?] inserted in the months of the latter in the mysterious garb of abridgment till they become as dark & difficult of explanation as the Hieroglyphics of the Sarcophagus in the Museum & to my disappointment I find you have omitted to say anything of 2 subjects in July viz

* See Biographical Memoranda.

175

4M—Tr of St Mart & 7TH[3]—Thomas à Becket & perhaps I may have further room for complaints tho I hope not & I wish you woud give us an explanation of the above as it is not yet too late for every old fashioned reader of Moors Almanack will be equally dissapointed at your omissions of such things & gratified to see you correct them & fullfill the prospectus with which you started in making your book a 'perpetual Almanack'

Yours &c

F. ROBERTS

[There follows:]

Love & thy vain employs away . . .

To Taylor

Addressed: John Taylor Esq, 13 Waterloo Place, Pall Mall, London.
[*sent*]

Helpston Sept. 15. 1825

MY DEAR TAYLOR

I recieved a letter from friend Hessey last week saying that you had been very ill[1] but I had not such an idea of its severity till my friend Emmerson told me & I have taken the oppertunity to convey this letter by him (for himself & Mrs E. has just been to Helpstone to see me) to offer you my regret for what you have been suffering & to say that I am happy at your recovery for I begin to feel a desolate sort of conviction that all my old friends will go off before me two of them are gone & a third I find was very near departing but I hope I shall see you agen & that you will yet be able to give me another call at Helpstone & seek for fresh Roman bricks & Saxon castles I am in no sort of feeling for letter writing but I coud not let this oppertunity slip of saying that 'auld lang syne' had not left such apathys with me as to make me forget her & her acquaintance tho I am almost weary of myself as well as the world & feel as if I shoud be glad when my time comes to join those that are gone—health is the root of happiness & like the plant called 'Barrenwort'[2] it seldom produces a blossom diseases spread such continual winters about it—I have been much

better these last two months then I have ever been since I was
first taken & the last prescriptions that I had from Dr. Darling
set me up as I had hoped in earnest but this last five or six
days I have been alarmed with fresh syntons of that numbness
& stupidness in the head & tightness of the skull as if it was
hooped round like a barrel but it is only by times a few minutes
& sometimes longer—I feel sorry the book has met with a
fresh stoppage in its progress but I cannot complain further
then feel a regret for the cause & I hope that you will soon be
able to proceed & I doubt not but that we shall both feel glad
when it is done with
  I cannot write further then wishing you to believe me
     My dear Taylor
      Yours sincere friend
       & faithful servant
          JOHN CLARE

  Give my remembrances to Dr. Darling & Hessey & all others
that enquire after me—you will find my friend Emmerson a very
sensible plain unaffected & unpretending man in fact I have
found him just the sort of man that suits me & he has a large
share of my confidence & esteem

To J. Power [?][1]

        Helpstone Sept. 24. 1825.

DEAR SIR

  I hasten to answer your letter of the 22nd to tell you I have
no objections to what you require in publishing my words to
the music which the gentleman has set to them but as I have
always recieved a trifle for such permission for those that have
been already put to music before & as my circumstances make
such acknowledgements however small very acceptable I cannot
give them away for nothing lest I may forfiet by such per-
missions any benefits that may arise in future from such publications & this is the only reason in the present instance why
I require a remuneration for such permission for I am convinced that the setting any Song to good music from a Vol of

M   177

Poems goes a great way to make the book popular & to convince you that no other is my object for asking it then what I have above stated I will leave the remuneration to be just what you think proper to give & as I do not attach a great value to such things a trifle will be thankfully received by

Yours respectfully

JOHN CLARE

To Hessey

Addressed: J. A. Hessey, Esq, 93 Fleet St, London.
[*sent*]

Helpstone Decr 8. 1825

MY DEAR HESSEY

I write to you earlier perhaps then I shoud have done (tho not earlier then I ought to do perhaps) to know if Taylor has returned from the country for I think him very long & am all anxiety to hear of him—I told Mrs E. to get Mr E to call at Waterloo Place to hear if he was returned so that I might write to him but I have heard nothing from her so that I am at a standstill I am uncommonly troubled about getting out the book—& shoud like to hear how he is getting on with it & when he will be ready—if Mrs E makes anything more of her errand for I know she is rather full of officiousness I wish it to be understood that I did not say anything further than what I have above written I do not like to be worried myself & I do not like that others should be worried either where I am the cause so I wish you woud tell me as I may write to him that I may hear from him I have got a great deal to say & a great deal of lumber for his inspection as I shoud like nothing better then what you propose in letting him see all I write—but hitherto his carlessnes has been so excessive that it woud be of no use whatever for the things that I did send up for his opinion I never heard of afterward not even a word of good bad or indifferent—I wish he woud shake off this lethargy he could do me a great service with but little trouble to himself if he chose as I can find nobody's Judgment so agreable to my fancys as his own but 'words are idle' & if I am to send up Magazine articles for his opinion they woud be thrown bye & forgotten so I must jog on with my own taste as well as I can but I dont think I shall trouble the 'European Magazine'[1] much more with my contributions as the pay is but poor & the insertion very uncertain as to the Poetical Almanacks they may all go to Hell next year for me for I can get nothing by them & my contributions are so mutilated that I do not know them again—the Ballad in the 'Souvenir'[2] I will send up to you as I wrote it at least to Taylor & then he may see the *improvements*—I should not have written for such matters at all for I do not like it but nessesity has troubled me so terribly that I thought I woud do somthing to get out of them if I could & many of my friends held out such profitable representations of them that I was tempted to try & the result is that my hopes are broken & I am as deep in nessesity as ever nobody pays half so well for periodical trifles as you & Taylor did & I find its a useless barter for profit but I was glad of trifles for it payed for my medicines of which I take a great many this leads me to my illness I am somthing better since I wrote Dr. Darling whose prescriptions I find now give me instant benefit in a far different & more direct manner then they did when in London for which I cannot account why or werefore the reason—I feel now I owe to Dr Darling my present existance & I am grown into such a stubborn opinion of his skill that I can believe in none other in fact they are very poor creatures here & I make no doubt kill as many or more than they cure & I feel not that they woud have speedily done for me had I not met with a better remedy— Give Taylor & Dr. Darling my kindest remembrances & tell Taylor of my anxious expectings about the 'Shepherds Calender'—My youngest girl is very ill alarmingly so & I am very uneasy in consequence—give my respects to all enquiring friends—I am glad you liked the 'Gipsey Song[1] & the Popularity[1] I have some other things scattered about in different periodicals that I shall aquaint Taylor with bye & bye as I fancy they are among the best I have written

I am
                    Yours very sincerely
                                    JOHN CLARE

To Taylor

Addressed: John Taylor Esq, 13 Waterloo Place, Pall Mall, London.
[*sent*]

Decr 19 –25

MY DEAR TAYLOR

You & I are such strangers now that I hardly know wether I may write to you or not I did write to Hessey a few days back to enquire if you was got home but I got no answer in return & since then Mrs Emmerson has told me that Mr E. has seen you & her account of you has much pleased me tho I do not like that anyone shoud forestall me in my intentions I did neither wish nor authorize him to make any further inquireys then about your being at home that I might write to you & if I knew that any other use was made of my desires I should be mad I like Mr. E. very much but Mrs. E. is too intriguing in her friendships & dwells too much on show & effect to make me feel that it is not one of the first value neither do I admire her opinions & judgments often for they are of the same kind & if I loose by the openness of my opinions I must generally speak as I think—with you I have nothing to find fault with but your delays & seeming neglects for I must confess that they not only injure my temper but hurt my mind very often but I hope that we shall become better correspondents & that your health will be the cause of better despatch in getting out my poems for I often fancy that it is a burthen to you & that notion makes me loath to trouble you with things that I am obliged to trust to the judgment of others who mangle & spoil them very often & the Ballad that I wrote to the 'Souvenir' is so polished & altered that I did not scarcely know it was my own I shall trouble you with a copy of it just as I wrote it I feel a disgust to write for such things but I did it for the sake of making a little money which is so little that I shall not attempt to get it by writing for such things agen if I remain in the same mind I am in now as to the European Magazine They only give 12s 6d a page but the[y] promise better pay after a while—will you correct my things for me for the Magazine I—attempted to

venture in prose there & they tell me such favourable opinions of
it that I shall venture agen it was not written for the Magazine
it was an episode taken from the Life I am now writing of myself
which is not yet done to my mind tho I have taken great pains—
I often think that 'Essays' upon common everyday matters &
things of Life may take I feel very anxious to expose the cant
& humbug of the days fashion & opinions but I am unable now
to do anything for I have been uncommonly ill agen & am
very little better now I feel so very stupid & chill & cannot get
out of the house for exercise—I shall want my sallaries as soon
as I can get them & I almost feel afraid to tell you what I want
besides for I shall need as much more [as] they to get me
descent if not straight with my creditors but if the 'Poems' had
been out I shoud have been able to close without any at least I
think so—I shall feel very anxious to hear from you & to hear
that the proofs are coming for I feel as if I was writing to a
stranger & a patron & am almost in an uneasy suspence as tho
my hopes might fail of success for you have been in my memory
so often that you are almost [never] forgotten excuse this
scrawling letter in lieu of a better & believe me my dear Taylor
Yours very sincerely & affectionatly

JOHN CLARE

To Taylor

Addressed: John Taylor Esq, 13 Waterloo Place, London.
[*sent*]

Helpstone Jan 24. 1826

MY DEAR TAYLOR

I am very much aggitated & alarmed at your long silence &
delay with my earnest applications for the £15 which I am in
wants of directly & must have from somewere or other therefore if I do not hear from you on or by Sunday I must be under
the nessesity of writing to Mr. Emmerson to request him to
lend it me till I am able to do somthing to get it myself—
really I cannot bear my patience for such expectations for
promises of this kind are like lawsuits in Chancery tho I dont
say that you feel that they are so—so keenly as I do because you

have so many things in town to attract your attention while mine has nothing but one point to look at every day till the same repetitions make me half mad with additional dissapointments —I hope you will write to me to say wether or not you will send me the money & I shall then know what I must do—I have recieved a very pleasing letter from Miss Kent & I shall answer it as quickly as possible & give her all the information about birds that I know of for I have abandoned my own intentions of writing about them myself as I think she will be able to make a much better work of them then I shoud—I think I shall not be long before I see London agen for I cannot rest here with such delays & cross purposes that keep continually upsetting me for I cannot hear a word from anybody scarcely— I am all anxiety about the book tho I almost fancy now it will never come out at all the words that have been spent about it are idle ones & proves that promises & performances are not near neighbours by a very wide difference but I will end this letter as I have nothing further to say then an anxious request that you will write to me—I am just going to Milton for a few days were I shall write to Miss Kent

I am

Yours very sincerely

JOHN CLARE

To Taylor

Addressed: John Taylor Esq, 13 *Waterloo Place, Pall Mall, London.*

[*sent*]

Helpstone Feb. 1. 1826

MY DEAR TAYLOR

I recieved the money safe & heartily thank you for sending it—but I am greatly dissapointed at hearing that you are not able to get on with the poems I think if you look among them you will find something that will do as a substitute in the others place 'A Sunday with Shepherds & Herdboys'* that perhaps might make shift for it or 'A Days pastime in Summer'† but

---

* *Collected Poems.*   † Unpublished.

I have no Copys by me to refer to—had I had the M.S.S. by
me last summer I coud have made them much better—if you
cannot find anything that will do I must come up for I feel
anxious to finish the thing either one way or another & as
you are busy I will get Mr. Emmerson to call on you to know
wether my coming up woud be of any use to help you out with
it as I shall come up before the years out to see them be as it
will tho I do not wish to start yet if you coud get on with the
book without me—I feel now that 'Cottage Stories & other
poems' woud have been a much better thing than the one in
hand that is to have taken all the tales in & filled up the book
with small pieces but its too late now for such a plan—I did
fancy the poem I sent to you one of the best I had written or I
shoud not have sent it—surely you will be able to get the book
out by spring for if it does not come out then I shall be obliged
to write a sort of apology to the Marquis as he will think that
I am a liar by writing to him so long for permission to dedicate
a book to him that never appears but I expect such things are
common cases if one knew of them—I shall still keep writing
on with my Percy Green M.S.S. & lay the good & bad in a
lump till I have finished—a poem in 'Hones every day book'
signed 'Marvel' is mine & another in Montgomery's 'Iris' on
the 'Vanitys of Life' The first poem is on 'Death' I dont
reccolect what No. it is in—

I remain

Yours very sincerely

JOHN CLARE

To Taylor

*Addressed: John Taylor Esq, 13 Waterloo Place, Pall Mall,
London.*

[sent]

Feb. 26. 1826.

My dear Taylor

Here is 'September' for you which I hope will suit I had
overlooked the pleasing occupation of nutting untill the Poem
was written therefore I have placed a few lines on the margin
to be inserted at ☞ mark

I hope you like 'August' which I sent you a while back &
'November' shall be with you as soon as possible perhaps in
a few days & as I shall write more at large then I shall end for
the present with being

Yours very sincerely

JOHN CLARE

To Taylor

Addressed: John Taylor Esq, 13 Waterloo Place, London.
[*sent*]

Feb. 28. 1826

MY DEAR TAYLOR

You have now got all that you have desired & if the other
two months are needing corrections or alterations I will gladly
do it so that I can be of any use towards getting out the book
without further stoppage—the 'Tales' I think you can deal with
better then I as they want nothing but pruning those that I
consider the best for the present purpose are 'Jockey & Jenny'
'Valentine's Eve'* the 'Memory of Love'† & the 'Broken
Heart'† & if there is found room for more the 'Soliloquy of
Robin'* will do well for the series but I do only suggest & leave
the matter entirely to yourself to do as you please & am always
ready to help you out as well as I can I hope I have not made
you wait for anything for I have taken more time to be more
correct—& to prevent any further delays in the next Volume if
another shoud come out you had better look out all that is
worth publishing or correction & send copys of them down to me
when I can remodel them & alter them at leisure in fact if I had
had the M.S.S. by me this winter I coud have made desent
things of a many of them that cannot be fit for anything as they
are—I shall now expect to hear from you to know how you like
the things & wether you need me to do anything further to help
you to bring out the book for I think it needless to send down
any proofs of the months I have alterd as you can alter them as
you think of it & when my best is done there is no bettering it
—when the Tales go through the press I shall be glad to see

---

* Unpublished.   † *The Shepherd's Calendar.*

184

them & to do any alterations you may suggest only do the
cutting out yourself—I shall now anxiously await your answer
to hear how you like them & how the book is getting on while
I remain

                    my dear Taylor
                        Yours very sincerely
                                            JOHN CLARE

To Taylor

*Addressed: John Taylor Esq, 13 Waterloo Place, Pall Mall,
        London.*
        [*sent*]
                        Helpstone March. 12. 1826

MY DEAR TAYLOR

  I have waited untill to-day for your sending me the M.S.S.
to correct which you said was to be at Deeping on Tuesday or
Wednesday & I made three journeys to meet them but I have
as yet heard nothing of their arrival it leaves me in an uneasy
uncertainty by the suspense as the work is not going on if you
still intend to send them but if you have altered your mind &
are going on with the book without any further corrections I
shall be as well pleased for I know you can make much better
of the Tales then I can & if you think the two remaining months
want bettering I will do them instantly & all the rest likewise
—I only want to be done with the Poems & to see the book out
as I am now busy with a thing that indulges my anxiety &
raises & depresses my fancys alternatly as I get on with it in
hopes of success & fears of dissapointments I did not wish to
say anything about it till I had done it but as I have said thus
far I will not try to leave it a mystery longer it is nothing more
or less then a Tragedy & the subject is 'Jealousy' or 'Consience' There is little or no plot & therefore nothing to talk of
I intend it for 'Kit Marlow' I shall be glad to hear from you
directly as my mind is very unquiet & life has more causes
than one to torment us—

                    I am my dear Taylor
                        Yours very sincerely
                                            JOHN CLARE
        185

To Taylor

Addressed: John Taylor Esq, 13 Waterloo Place, Pall Mall, London.

[*sent*]

Helpstone March 18. 1826

MY DEAR TAYLOR

I recievd the parcel & thank friend Darley very heartily for the present & not for the book merely but for the kind manner that offers it but I have not had time to look into it much there are two fine Sonnets & a beautiful string of verses called the 'Bees somthing'* that pleased me very much there is a mysterious melody in its ryhmes that sounds very musical on the ear they are all in the 'Enchanted Lyre' I have got no further yet for Mr Watts has sent me a parcel of Books among which is 'Wilsons Poems'† & I am uncommonly pleased with them—I have been looking for 'May' & find about 3 pages more from the lines you mention to the end from which I have only been able to transcribe what follows the rest is very worthless & these are hardly worth inserting but I send them for you to do as you please with & finish the Poem in the best manner that the materials allows you I knew you would doubt my abilitys in writing a Play & effeth‡ well you may for I feel nothing satisfied with what I have done as yet but if I do have courage to go through with it you shall see it the moment I have done— I have none of the copys of those M.S.S. that you cannot find therefore I cannot rewrite them the tale of Robin's Soliloquy I should liked to have inserted in the Calender but if you cannot find them now they must wait for the next—I shall say more of Guy's* Book when I have read more of it

I am my dear Taylor

Yours very sincerely

JOHN CLARE

* 'The Wild Bee's Tale' from *The Labours of Idleness*, by 'Guy Penseval' (Darley) (1826).

† John Wilson, of Elleray, Professor of Moral Philosophy at Edinburgh, who, De Quincey says, divided his time and love 'between literature and the stormiest pleasures of real life', had published *Isle of Palms and other Poems* in 1812. They were republished 1828.

‡ 'In faith', sometimes spelt by Clare 'efeth'. We have not found the tragedy about 'Conscience'.

[There follows:]
& mint & flag leaf swording high . . .[*]

There is the best I can make of it & the all I can get out of
nearly 200 lines quite enough by the bye for the part that is
already printed is long enough I dare say however here is
the best I can do with it & 'October' & 'December' shall be
with you directly tho I shall try to do the best I can with them
& the 'Tales' I will copy out in as plain a hand as I can I hope
I shall not only make better M.S.S. in future for you but better
poetry at least I will try the best I can & I do assure you all
that I write now undergoes severe discipline for if a first copy
consists of a 100 lines its second corrections generally dwindle
down to half the number & I heartily wish I had done so at first
I have been hunting up some samples of my later things to send
you but I am not satisfied with the second reading of them & I
shall correct them before I send them which I have no time to
do just now as I am anxious to see what I can do with those
I have not finished

I am Yours &c &c &c

J. CLARE

To Alaric A. Watts †

Addressed: Courier Office, Manchester.
[*sent*]

Helpstone March 19 1826.

DEAR SIR

I thank you very kindly for your kind present of books tho
I almost feel ashamed to accept them as I think I do not deserve
so many favours from you for the trifles I sent you however I
will make the best return in my power by sending you some
others to insert in what publication you chuse I shall be very
happy to assist your new work of the 'Literary Magnet' if any
contributions of mine will do anything for it & I haste to send
this for that purpose tho I fear it will be too late for this month
as I did not get the parcel while yesterday (Saturday) I really
cannot tell you how to send the 'Literary Magnet' to me unless

* 'May': *The Shepherd's Calendar.* † See Biographical Memoranda.

I can get it down in a Stamford Booksellers parcel from London of which I will tell you hereafter as I shoud very much like to see it & if my contribution comes in time enough to be printed in this months send it to me by Deeping as usual & if not I will contrive another conveyance before the next I have not time to say anything of the books you sent me nor of your own poems but I will tell you in a letter bye and bye how I like them I have but little judgment of poetry further than what pleases me & I am in the habit of stating my likes & dislikes very freely I sometimes may offend without intending it but I shall tell you exactly as I think about them all for I have looked into none of them yet as I am busy in re-writing a portion of my poems over again & as the press waits for me I can lose no time & I am also heartily sick of former delays—I can hardly have the face to state as you desire me what books I like as I do not wish to intrude on the kindness of anyone or else I have long desired to see the poems of Miss Landon which I have not been enable to do as yet Montgomerys too are strangers to me excepting some things in periodicals which only make me desire to become acquainted with the rest the reading of no poem ever left such an impression on my fondness for poetry as his 'Common Lot' did which I met with about 10 years ago in a little volume called the 'Beautys of Poetry'*

> I am dear sir
> Yours sincerely
> JOHN CLARE

To Taylor

Addressed: John Taylor Esq, 13 *Waterloo Place, Pall Mall, London.*

[sent]

Taylor's date: March 27. 26

MY DEAR TAYLOR

I here send you the last month I have only cut out one verse & the one crossed above which you may retain if you like I am

---

* No doubt for its very universal ordinariness Montgomery's 'The Common Lot' found its way into *The Beauties of Poetry Displayed*, observations on the different species of English versifiction, the first edition of which had appeared in 1757.

more pleased with the second reading of this thing then with
any of the others tho it may not be any better for that—I shall
begin to write out the tales tomorrow & shove all I can into a
Sheet I shall like to know which Tales you like best as I may
write them out first & if its of no consequence I will write
what I happen on first

I am Yours &c &c

JOHN CLARE

N.B. I shall not rewrite the 'Sorrows of Love' as you have
corrected it already & as I have had the proof of it I dont think
it nessesary to do it over again I shall like to hear how many
tales the book will hold & which you wish to insert as I will
send them up first I have hunted over the M.S.S. & cannot find
the Tale of 'Valentine Eve' among them but I have a rough copy
that I must make shift with this with Jockey & Jenny & Robin's
Soliloquy I like best of any & shall feel a wish to have them in
this Vol

Yours &c

J.C.

To Taylor

[*sent*]

11 April 1826

. . . the book trade is at a low ebb now but I hope you will not
give up business till my thing is out be as it will for nobody can
do it so well as yourself—I never recieved a farthing for the
songs you speak of nor do I know anything of who published
them or what they made¹ I only know that 3 of them were
cursed bad ones I mean the words & one of the others scarcly
middling I wish they had never been published at all for they
brought me neither credit nor profit—give my respects to
Hessey & to all others that you mentioned in your letter—you
will be supprised to hear perhaps that I have no correspondents
or friends now but yourself I have broken with them all &
neither write nor recieve letters from anyone I thought once
that Mrs Emmerson was everything but I found that the stron-
gest link that held us together was a sheet of paper therefore

when I got into my mellancholy moods & ceasd to write she ceasd likewise & I have never had the mind to take it up again if such friendships are so easily dissolved they are not worth the keeping—I will write to Hessey almost directly for I like him as well as anyone I am acquainted with but I cannot keep a regular correspondence with anyone tho I think I was once as fond of teazing friends with my scribbling as any author existing—I forgot almost to be remembered to your sister though if my memory had not failed me she would have been one of the first I should have enquired after—I have been very busy these last few days in watching the habits & coming of spring birds so as to be able to give Miss Kent an account of such as are not very well known in books—do you publish her Vol of Birds if you do I should like a copy interleaved when its published to make what remarks I may jump on in reading it & to insert all I know about them which I find is not there on purpose to send them to her—our Village is this day in almost as great consternation as I imagine it will be at the day of judgment in consequence of some idle fellows who are found to be Resurrection men or grave robbers who under a pretence of selling a few cheeses contrive to rob the Churchyards at night of their newest inhabitants they have stolen four bodies out of one Churchyard & the empty coffins are now placed in the Church by the Sexton for the inspection of the curious but as nothing can be found on the depredators they are still at large to pursue their avocation—I almost feel the horrors at the matter & think I shall never like cheese any more

I am dear Taylor

Yours very sincerely

JOHN CLARE

To Montgomery[1]

[*sent*]

Helpstone,

May 8, 1826

MY DEAR SIR,

I will lose no time in answering your letter, for I was highly delighted to meet so kind a notice from a poet so distinguished

as yourself: and if it be vanity to acknowledge it, it is, I hope,
a vanity of too honest a nature to be ashamed of—at least I
think so, and always shall. But your question[2] almost makes me
feel ashamed to own to the extent of the falsehood I committed:
and yet I will not double it by adding a repetition of the offence.
I must confess to you that the poem is mine, and that the book
from whence it was pretended to have been transcribed has no
existence (that I know of) but in my invention of the title. And
now that I have confessed to the crime, I will give you the
reason for committing it. I have long had a fondness for the
poetry of the time of Elizabeth, though I have never had any
means of meeting with it, farther than in the confined channels
of Ritson's 'English Songs,' Ellis's 'Specimens,' and Walton's
'Angler;' and the winter before last, though amidst a severe
illness, I set about writing a series of verses, in their manner, as
well as I could, which I intended to pass off under their names,
though some whom I professed to imitate I had never seen.
As I am no judge of my own verses, whether they are good or
bad, I wished to have the opinion of someone on whom I could
rely: and as I was told you were the editor of the 'Iris' I
ventured to send the first thing to you, with many 'doubts and
fears'. I was happily astonished to see its favourable reception.
Since then I have written several others in the same style, some
of which have been published: one in Hone's 'Every-day Book',
on 'Death', under the name of Marvell, and some others in the
'European Magazine:' 'Thoughts in a Churchyard,' the
'Gipsy's Song,' and a 'Farewell to Love.' The first was
intended for Sir Henry Wootten, the next for Tom Davies: the
last for Sir John Harrington. The last thing I did in these
forgeries was an 'Address to Milton,' the poet, under the name
of Davenant.[3] And as your kind opinion was the first and the
last I ever met with from a poet to pursue these vagaries or
shadows of other days, I will venture to transcribe them here
for the 'Iris', should they be deemed as worthy of it as the
first were by your judgment, for my own is nothing: I should
have acknowledged their kind reception sooner had I not
waited for the publication of my new poems, 'The Shepherd's
Calendar,' which was in the press then, where it has been ever
since, as I wish, at its coming, to beg your acceptance of a copy,

with the other volumes already published, as I am emboldened now to think they will be kindly received, and not be deemed intrusive, as one commonly fears while offering such trifles to strangers. I shall also be very glad of the opportunity in proving myself ready to serve you in your present undertaking: and could I light on an old poem that would be worth your attention, 300 or even 1,000 lines would be no objection against my writing it out: but I do assure you I would not make a forgery for such a thing, though I suppose now you would suspect me: for I consider in such company it would be a crime, where blossoms are collected to decorate the 'Fountain of Truth.' But I will end, for I get very sleepy and unintelligible.

I am, my dear Sir,
Yours very sincerely and affectionately
JOHN CLARE

Mr. Montgomery, Sheffield.

To Taylor

Addressed: John Taylor Esq, 13 Waterloo Place, Pall Mall, London.

[sent]

Helpstone May 12th, 1826.

MY DEAR TAYLOR,

I have been anxiously watching for a long time the appearance of a letter or proof with your hand on it but all in vain & I have been wondering & wondering & conjuring up fifty reasons for & against them till I have come to the resolution this morning to sit down & enquire after you as to how you are in health & what you are doing & wether you have got on with my Poems for I am still in hopes that you have not so far forgot my anxietys as to throw them aside again I have hunted all over the M.S.S. & can find nothing more suitable for the book neither tales or anything else there is a long Poem on Spring which will make a desent one when corrected & shortned for another oppertunity should another oppertunity ever occur & the Parish which is the best thing in my own mind that I have ever written & I mean to take some pains in altering & making it better still if I can—you dont know & can scarcly imagine how anxious I am for the appearance of my poems in fact so much so that my mind occupations are utterly at a stand still I can do nothing at writing & even a letter makes me pause twenty times before I get to its end at what I am to say next tho I hope yet that you are doing your best at getting on with it & that it will shortly appear—I recieved last sunday a very kind letter from Montgomery full of heart stirring praises which pleased me mightily for praises from such a man as Montgomery cannot but be pleasing he wrote to me in consequence of my sending him a Poem last year for the 'Iris' to know wether it was mine as I told him when I sent it that I had found it in an old book—to escape the punishment of his neglect if in case he had thought it unworthy notice but he thought otherwise & wishes to know wether it be mine or not as he is making a 'Chronological Collection of Christian Poetry' & wished to insert it if it was really old as I had pretended & as he speaks so much in its favour I have hunted up the Newspaper to send you which comes under a cover with this Letter & I shall be glad to hear what you think of it as I also shall of others that I have long been about which are in too much disorder to make any thing of at present & I have had no inclination to do any thing laterly but I think the above circumstance will start me anew to try my utmost at *mysterys* with which it appears I have made a desent starting I want sadly to get a look over 'Ellises Specimens of English Poetry' I once read it when poor Gilchrist was living but I did not read it with the attention I could wish to do now in fact I know as much about its contents as if I had never seen it—I have not yet written to Hessey for one reason & that not a weak one I have nothing worth saying & have sat down frequently laterly to write to friends & burnt the [sheet] when I have looked it over because it could [say] nothing not even nonsense & I must lap th[is] up the moment I end it or I shall perhaps find it deserving the same fate give my respects to all & believe me

My dear Taylor
yours very sincerely
& affectionately
JOHN CLARE

To Taylor

[sent]

Helpstone July 15. 1826

MY DEAR TAYLOR

I hasten to acknowledge the reciept of the £20 Check & thank you very kindly for sending it down so speedily I will see if I can do without the £5 more & if I can I shall feel very happy in not having to trouble you further but if I cannot I must—I do assure you that I live as near as ever I can & tho I did not tell you I have been out to hard labour most part of this summer on purpose to help out my matters but the price of labour is so low here that it is little better than parish relief to the poor man who where there is a large family is litterally pining I know not what will be the end of these times for half the Farmers here will be broken again this dry summer & I think that low rents & no taxes is the only way to recall a portion of their former prosperity but I am no Politician & know little or nothing about such matters I have not gotten any tale by me of any sort to send you but I am very willing to have the Magazine Poems inserted & like the idea much & if there is not room for all of them you may take which you think best but I must have one opinion in the Pye if youll alow it & that is I shall like to see the 'Superstitions Dream' in for one & I think it would be better to call it there simply *The Dream*[1] you know better when to publish the Vol better than I do & I shall leave it wholly to you but I shall thank you for a copy for the Marquis as soon as you can send me one & I should like it very plainly bound with very little gilt on it he ordered me to send him 10 Copys but I think they should not be sent untill it is Published—I have often tryed at a Dedication for him & cannot get one to my mind I want one simply honest & out of the beaten track of fulsome dedications one very short & very plain & I think if I set it down here in my own way you will soon make one out by it properly in your own I want something in this way I expect I must call him noble—To the Most Noble the Marquis of Exeter these Poems are Dedicated in remembrance of un-merrited kindness by his Lordships faithful servant the Author' or 'John Clare' as you please—I dont like to puff nor I dont like to flatter so if you dont like it put a simple straight forward thing down in your own way—Drury has not sent me his Bill he only hints demand of payment from me & speaks as if he was not far from troubling me for it but I know now he cannot I saw the Bill at his shop some years back & told him then that it was extravagant but I cannot say as to what it was now he took hold of every oppertunity to get me in his books & then made a boast of it I shall tell you a few facts in explanation of what I have said in another letter as to its extravagant 'notchings on' & then you can judge yourself as I wish to reserve all the room here for other things I am very pleased with your idea of 'Visits of the early Muses'[2] as a Title for my *old* Poems & shall keep adding to the number as I feel inclined & l shall not publish any more of them in periodicals now you have past your opinion of them so favourably for I only did it to try the opinion of those which I thought superior to mine but I am greatly at a loss for the want of seeing some of the Best pieces of the old Poets I have a Copy of Spensers Poems & Cowleys Poems lent me by a friend but I wade about them untill Im weary & my mind cannot rest to feel their best spirit & manner but when I see their best selected by others I take it for granted that it is their best & muse over it till a thought strikes me how to proceed—I should have liked to have seen these old poems at the end of my present volume but I like your title so well that I will reserve them all for a future volume as you suggest & shall send you them up from time to time as I write them which will be but very slowly as I feel anxious & almost certain that they are to be my best the Winter is my best time for them for I can sit in my corner in the long evenings when the children are all abed in peace which I cannot do now I am sorry you have troubled yourself so much to procure 'Ellis's Specimens' for I dont suppose you can readily meet with it I sent to the Library at P[eterborough] for to Borrow it but they had it not tho they kindly sent a Vol of Specimens by Cambell instead it is a new work & by Cambell the poet I fancy but I dont like it much as the Specimens dont seem to be selected for their exellence often but for their novelty in not being collected by other editors & this would mislead me—I will get Henderson to have a good hunt in the old Library at Milton the next time I go & perhaps he may succeed in finding something useful there & if he can I can have it & replace it before they return—give my respects to Hessey & all friends & believe me

My dear Taylor

Yours very sincerely

JOHN CLARE

To Taylor

[*sent*]

Helpstone
Dec. 1. 1826.

MY DEAR TAYLOR

I did recieve the parcel safe & I most heartily thank you for all favors especially the Scotch Songs[1] which I longed anxiously to see I have just dipt into it & seen some of witching beauty whose names I never heard of before—The notes Introduction &c &c are in my opinion too long & plentiful they are full of Scotch kith & kin Scotts of Scotland—but I shall trouble you with a whole Foolscap of Gossip very quickly & should now only that I have got a Poem just struck off which I am anxious to have your opinion of as I want to send a good thing for Watts' Souvenir next year[2]—there is another thing with it tell us how you like them—

I hope Dewint will do me the favour of a Frontispiece tell him what I wish when you ask him there is an excellent engraver name Roberts[3] tho not known I have seen some Landscapes of his doing which pleased me mightily—tell Mr. Darley that I shall write to him in a day or two to thank him for this & his other favours & thereby kill two birds with one stone I am pleased & proud of his friendly notice & when I do write I shall write to him freely & openly as to an old friend for as such I prophesy we shall be with my other acquaintances the brotherhood of Poesy has turned out cold indeed but the world is with them & they forget those who are left in solitude —Robin Hood is good but I have seen ballads that pleased me

better in an old book called the Garland of Robin Hood at least
I think so but I shall leave it off a while to pursue my 'Visits'
of which I hope to get up a good sample bye & bye—But do
you know I shall insert some imitations of the Provincial Poets
in Sea Songs Love Ballads[4] &c &c & a specimen of each shall be
quickly with you—Your getting into Paternoster Row supprised me but you know best shall you leave Waterloo Place
I think not its name sounds much better than the other & if
you keep that on your title pages it matters not who sells them
for you but Paternoster Row is a too Bookmongerish sound I
think & I am sure it is a cursed dirty place to yours but I am
saying what I know little about so here is the Poem:

[There follows:]

THE SPANISH REFUGEE
O false love is a bitter thing . . .[4]

[and:]

FREEDOM
When we read in fame's pages . . .[4]

These two trifles are a few minutes ryming from reading in
an old newspaper of the distress of the Spanish Refugees in
London & as I fancy one reads a little pathetic & the tother
goes a descent musical poney canter I feel anxious to have your
opinion of them—

I have a great many things to ask you about but my thoughts
are so busily confused that I cannot think of them now—I forgot
to say that I shall send a copy of my Poems to the Marquis &
that he will want 10 copies as soon as they are published for
good—I shall therefore tell him that a Frontispiece is engraving
for them which delays the publication at present & when the
Poems are out I shall want if you please 4 copies each of my first
Poems & the Minstrel for particular friends to present with the
new ones & among whom is Montgomery who showed me much
kindness in passing judgment on my disguised poem that I sent
him these things ought to be remembered as kindly—so
Hessey has met with another son I have the fortune or rather
misfortune to join chorus in the nursery song for I have got a
new son also[5]—I should like to give Darley one of these new
Vols I have gotten but I dont like to send it because I think he

may not fancy it a compliment to have to pay the carriage of a
6 shilling book would he think you tell me I much want to send
him one—I shall also venture to send Dr. Darling one & I feel
almost in mind to send one to Sir Thomas Lawrence should I
he behaved very kind to me you know but I shall not do it on
my own judgment so we'll talk it over another oppertunity
also—only taking the present to say how sincerely I am

Yours &c &c

JOHN CLARE

P.S. What has become of Miss Kent & her Birds?

To Hessey

Addressed: J. H. Hessey, Esq, 93 Fleet Street, London.
[*sent*]

Helpstone Jan. 21 1827.

MY DEAR HESSEY

I thank you kindly for forwarding me the money for it did
not come before it was wanted I assure you & what I now wish
is that the book was out so that I could take the 10 Copies to
the Marquis as I wish to cover my expences without troubling
my friend Taylor which I cannot unless the book is out directly
for this half year is rent day with me & that takes an extra £5
which my sallaries cannot alow me yet I hope that the dedication will fetch it nay I may be sure of it so I wish you would
tell Taylor to forward the 10 Copies as soon as ever he can &
if they do not come quickly I must write to him for assistance
which I feel very loath to do at the present times for they are
dead letters to the book business I dare say—I intend the first
oppertunity that offers to take a cottage with as much land as
will find me employment the year round for it is very irksome
to be obliged to beg of people to get work of them which is
actually the case for there is so many that they are forced to
employ that those they are not forced to take not being paupers
they will not have therefore if labour will not bring a man
independance it is worse than nothing & he may as well sell
himself for an indian slave as belong to such places This is not

without illustration for it was asserted in the Newspaper about
a fortnight back that a man actually turned thief to get himself
transported because he would not go home to his parish &
that where he lived at would not employ him I need not add
that his hopes were not dissapointed but how he feels himself in
his new situation I cannot tell—I heard of Giffords death but
not of Mrs. Bengers[1] in fact I never saw her in my life so if I
did see her name in the papers my memory passed over it—
I see that Hood is making great ado in newspaper notoriety
yet I thought better of him than ever to expect to find him
flaming among the Colbourns[2] Puffs & Warrens[3] dirty
blacking paragraphs & when I saw him there I could not help
exclaiming in the chorus of the old Song 'O what will this
world come too'—I have been amusing myself latterly in
collecting fragments of old Ballads not with any other view than
amusement & I have found a very simple one & yet I think a
very pretty one it is called 'The Song of all the Birds in the
Air' but I have not yet got the whole of it tho a lady at Milton
that is one of the head servants knows it & Henderson has
promised to copy it from her saying[4] for me & if he does I will
send it to you somtime or other as I fancy it just such a thing
as you would be pleased with merely as a trifle—I have got on
a good way with my 'Visits &c.' but have done nothing at them
latterly I intend that they shall be my best & therefore I spare
no pains in trying to make them so—the post is ready for
starting & I must conclude—give my kindest remembrances
to Mrs. Hessey & to Taylor who I hope is not so seriously
or severely ill but he may get better soon.

> I am my dear Hessey
> yours very sincerely
> JOHN CLARE

To Taylor

Addressed: 13 *Waterloo Place, Pall Mall, London.*
[*sent*]

Helpstone August 20. 1827

MY DEAR TAYLOR

I recieved the Five Pounds safe & take much discredit to myself in not writing to say so before but I have not had much time untill this wet Day—I feel much hurt at the odd Conduct of the Marquis for he still remains as silent as ever & all the money I have gotten for the 30 Copies is £1 . 19 . 6 I have calculated it up & that is the truth & an aggravating truth to me it is I am sorry too that I shoud have been forced to ask you for money but urgent nessesity forced me & I coud not help it & I feel very dissapointed at the bad sale of the new Poems but I cannot help it if the public will not read ryhmes they must still read Colbourns Novels until they are weary for he will never be weary of being a quack & puffer till he gains by it—to tell them what they ought to think of Poetry would be as vain I fear as telling the blind to see the age of Taste is in dotage & grown old in its youth—as to the Accounts I am sorry I have so over-shot them but I am sure I have never been extravagant but on the contrary kept striving & fancying I was illustrating the annals of thrift & keeping within bounds & I hope for your sake that the Poems may turn the tide & sell better for Novels & such rubbish were in as bad repute once as Poetry now & may be again as matters turn out I dare hardly remind you of an old promise much less a new one however I must tell you that I never recievd the 4 copies each of my Poems which you told me you intended sending a long time ago if you did I never recieved them & as I am at a standstill from writing to a Friend or two which I cannot make up my mind to do without accompanying them with the Poems I should feel greatly obliged to your kindness if you would do me this favour— Darleys Play* I make no doubt is a good one & I shall feel

---

* *Sylvia, or the May Queen—a lyrical drama* (1827). Clare had first written to Darley early in 1827 (which letter is unfortunately not included here). By 1827 Darley was almost the only friend left to Taylor of the inspired 'London' days. Writing to Clare (30 March 1827, B. M. correspondence), Taylor called Darley 'the only good that ever came from *The London Magazine*'. He was publishing Darley's text books on algebra and trigonometry.

anxious for its publication & happy at his success for I esteem
him both as an Author a Poet & a Friend tho I almost fear that
the paradoxical truths of Mathematics will do something
towards shattering the visions of Fancy but perhaps they may
sharpen it—I shall write to [him] directly I recieved the letters
from him when I had not the power to reply & worldly vexa-
tions often take the advantage of time to damp the spirit &
obliterate the early feelings of friendship for when I think of
days gone bye & the hearts that are cold some in the world &
some in the dust & every other association connected with
them I am often affected even to tears Give my best respects
to Darley my dear Taylor

Yours very sincerely

JOHN CLARE

To George Darley*

Addressed: 13, *Waterloo Place, Pall Mall, London.*
[sent]

Helpstone Sep 3 1827

MY DEAR DARLEY

I fear you have long condemned me as a neglectful correspondent but the fact is otherwise for I waited for the pleasure in
being able to beg your acceptance of my Poems as a trifle from
a friend to a friend & brother Poet & I should very much like
your opinion of my last Poems no 'fine things' to say of them as
the world does but I want to know my faults & your critical
judgment in such matters will be both pleasure & profit to me
we hear a great deal of opinion about this Poet & tother Poet
even in almost every Newspaper but we have very little of that
advice &c which is the offspring of sincerity—I have sent you
with my new Poems the other 3 Vols not out of vanity mind ye
but as a token of esteem for without flattery (I dont think I've
a bit of it in my blood) I am bound to enlist ye among the
catalogue of my best Friends & tho my judgment may not be
worth a farthing I have the vanity to feel that I shall one day
be found a prophetical critic for once when the world shall

* See Biographical Memoranda.

201

discriminate what I believed from the first that you are one
among the many that shall be elected as true Poets of the 19th
century & I assure you I will do my best yet if I live to make
one of the number with ye tho I have not yet bid so fair for it
in quality as in quantity for you must know that my judgment
some years back was as green as a child's in matters of taste
& now I think it is ripened & good & if I dont yet know what
is Poetry & who are Poets Fashion shall not make me believe
she does in spite of her trumpeting clamour about her L.E.Ls[1]
Hemans's[2] Dartford[3] Morrison[3] &c but I dont wish to be nasty
among these Delacruscan gentry & I am sure I shall be if I
go on for one has no patience with the humbug that teams from
the Literary stews Monthly & Weekly aye & daily & almost
hourly for I expect bye & bye we shall have 'Hourly papers'
chiming over their praises as well as we have 'Daily ones' now
but the Plague of a century is coming to sweep them from the
face of light with other cobweb that such spiders have spun so
proudly in the Temple of the Muses I may not see it but (to use
an expression of your own) 'I am sure I shall feel it in my
grave' when it happens but enough—before I go further I must
tell you that I could not make out what Hill it was where I was
to address you at Staines it was the only word in the letter that
I was foiled with to make out & I am as foiled at it yet so pray
give me your direction as plain as you can The Poem you sent
me I like it is good but in comparison to the manner in which
'The Green of the Day' struck me my likes of this are shadows
to sunbeams there is somthing in the latter that is inimitable [?]
I never see the Bee or hear the Blackbird or Cuckoo but its
instant up & awake in my memory the images are so original
& so happy[4] Taylor tells me you have a new Poem in the Press
& if I have many such passages in it as my mind concieves the
Green of the day to be then a fig for the world & the critics
my boy for you will make your own (as I believe you will some
day) & kick up a worse confusion among our paper tabernacles
then the building of Babel for as has been observed the poet
often makes Critics but critics never make Poets nor mend
them either often while fashion is their idol—I intend for my
own part to strike out on a new road if I can & my greatest
ambition is to write something in the spirit of the old Poets

not those of Dr. Johnson but those half unknowns who as yet
have no settled residence in the Land of Fame but wander about
it like so many Pilgrims who are happy to meet a stranger by
the way to make themselves known or heard once in a century
& I think from these you have made your own model for there
is a 'sweet savour' stirs my imagination when I read your
Poems particularly the descriptive passages the same as when I
read those above mentioned I should like to see a fashion for
those sweet old songsters revive again & then it would be a
fashion worth following—I have gone on & on all about self
till I have not yet thought about turning to your letter to
answer it & as I have got so far I dare not now for fear of
making my letter too long so I will put it off to the next for I
have sat up tonight with a determination to write to you tho
my fancys are exceedingly ruffled with the Harvest as I am
working away at it as hard as a negroe I am my dear Darley
Your affectionate Friend

JOHN CLARE

Write soon remember me to Taylor as I've no time to write

To Peter de Wint*

Addressed: P. Dewint Esqr., Percy Street, 40 *Upper Gower St.,
London.*
[*sent*]
Helpstone Oct 1827.

MY DEAR DEWINT
  You will be supprised perhaps to meet with this but I have
determined on the matter ever since the New Poems were
published & and that is to give you my thanks on paper for
your kindness in drawing the Frontispiece for my new Vol.
& I hope a time is not very distant when I shall be able to thank
you personaly it is a very beautiful thing the figures are well
grouped & the maiden with the face fronting is a beauty but the
bottle in the reapers hand is too big for the company in fact it
appears too big for a bottle at all in my eye but thats perhaps its
own fault & not the bottles I think the engraving is done

* See Biographical Memoranda.
203

uncommonly well & that altogether it possesses attractions that aught to have pushed the book into a good sale but I heard from Taylor a good while back that the contrary was the fact and that comparitively speaking it did not sell at all & turn out in the end as it may we cannot help it I am sure its dress is sufficient to win even the hearts of the Muses tho they scouted the rest but ryhmes is gone or going out of fashion for a season & Mr Colbourns Novels by new unknowns & little great knowns coming in— — bye & bye its to be hoped things will come round agen—I had intended to have accompanied this with a Vol for Miss Dewint but thinking it would be scarcely worth the cost when at the end of its journey I desisted till a better oppertunity offered to send it a cheaper way & I ought to have said at first what I have left unexplaind till now which is the reason for my not thanking you sooner & that was occasioned by my waiting in hopes of getting a frank but the Milton family have been out all the summer & have not yet returned so you must excuse the postage—how is friend Hilton he has been in a rare way with his painting latterly if accounts be true & it seems that the scriptures have showered on him some fat benedictions for his conversion from the heathens which are as good perhaps as fat livings to the clergy tho efeth they may not be so certain of durability—I have seen mighty praises of his Picture for a Church at Liverpool in our papers & I expect bye & bye that the next news is of his being a Sir William of the Academy well I heartily wish him more luck then he has met with & more luck then that give him my kindest remembrances as also to Mrs. Dewint & your daughter & as I have nothing in the way of news to fill up the sheet I will leave it and save you the trouble of reading my scribbling trifling further then that I beg to remain

my dear Dewint
Yours very sincerely

JOHN CLARE

To Taylor

[*sent*]

Helpstone
November 17th 1827

MY DEAR TAYLOR

I expect you will be supprised when you open this to see from whence it comes so scarce has our correspondence made itself & ere it withers into nothing I will kindle up the expiring spark that remains & make a letter by its light if I can but when you sent me the Poems in summer you never sent a letter with them I felt the omission but murmured not it was not wont to be thus in days gone bye so I will shake off this ague warm feeling & this dead living lethargy & ask you how you are & where you are & how our friends are tho most of them I expect are wasted to nothing but a name—I myself am but very middling & I feel that I must take the liberty to write to Dr. Darling agen very soon—I sent my 4 Vols of Poems under cover to you for G. Darley did he get them he has never written to say so—I sent them in September I think & I could not write to him to ask as I cannot make out the direction which he sent me it is some Hill at Staines (I think Chubs or Cherubs but I cannot tell under cover of Honble Mr. Westenra M.P.[1]) so I sent the Parcel to your care & trouble as the best means to reach him—I have wrote to Dewint to thank him for his kindness in drawing the Frontpiece for me & this leads me to reccolect that I asked you for two or three of the engravings when I asked for the books but you never sent them & if you will now have the kindness to do so you might send them to Mrs. Emmerson for me who is going to send me a parcel in a few days & would enclose them in it & as I am going to write to her to-day or to-morrow I can get Mr. E. to call on you if it would be giving you too much trouble to get them there I have been over Castor Field the scene of Mr. Artis's discoverys but have been able to make nothing out further than that every ploughboy & labouring man have a collection of coins to offer you for sale for a trifle for they fancy all are antiquarys that appear there as strangers & I mentioned the substance of your

remarks to Henderson of Milton who told me he thought you
might fancy the pots were Etruscan as some did—Did you think
so I have never seen Artis since last winter & so I had no
oppertunity for further enquiries—Do you see Mr. Hall the
Editor of the Amulet he has sent me the Amulet a good while
back but not the 'needful' yet tho he promised then to write
me in a few days what a pretty thing that is of Conders[2] on the
'late Spring' its the best in the book & that by a great deal
friend Darley has got no 'Green of the Day' in this year &
Conders 'late Spring' is the only thing that can be found
worthy as a successor a favourite of mine yet it is a next
favourite & I wish I could write as luckily myself—you said
you would let me see the Eclectic's Review of my shepherds
Calendar that I might write to Conder[2] but you never did &
why not how does the New Poems sell? Mrs Emmerson told
me that you gave her good tidings of them when they first
came out & I hope they will do better bye & bye but two
gentlemen was with me yesterday who had come from London
of the name of Stuart[3] & they was astonished when I told them
my new poems was out as they had never heard of them tho
they had often enquired about them & this is the case with
many people here I do not know the reason except it is that
they wont know on purpose to dissapoint me with their
ignorance—give my respects to those who may think me worthy
of enquirey & alow me to remain dear Taylor

Yours sincerely

JOHN CLARE

To [Harry Stoe Van Dyk]

Helpstone Novr 1827

My dear Harry

I write to tell you that I have seen the Criticism on my Poems
in the Literary Chronicle[1] & tho I feel highly pleased with it I
cannot dare to take all the praise to myself which you & some
friend of yours has kindly given me I think I understood you a
friend of yours wrote it & if it is so & that no secret I wish you
would tell me his name as I may beg his acceptance of the Vol:

for I feel it is a kindness & moreover I want to make up a parcel
to send you the Poems which I have copied out for you as well
as I can on purpose for you to insert in the first Vol & then it
will be compleat I ruled the lines with a bad pencil so I could
not get them out even with India rubber & that has made a bad
ʲob of it but it cannot be helped now . . .*

To Taylor

[sent]

Helpstone, Dec.ʳ 10. 1827.

MY DEAR TAYLOR,

I thank you very kindly for the Plates and Reviews which are
as usual talking of what I know not and as usual liking that
least which I think best but I like the Eclectic much the best
in fact I always liked it there is a heartiness in the praise and
that coming from a Poet pleases me much better—but what's
the reason here is Darleys Poem[1] without a superscription not
a word is there on the fly leaf nor a letter either and by your
mention in your letter of '*the Poem and Letter*' waiting for
yours I expected both *tell* friend Darley that I am mad at the
omission and feel if there's no mistake there is something in
the difference and if he does not write to tell me I shall give the
matter out as earnest. I don't like this half facing a matter he is
not a Scotchman and therefore I did not expect it from him for
they are very shy of foreigners tell him of the omission if you
do not I shall lay you out as both of a plot—if I could believe
you when you say you intended coming at Christmas and that
you have put it off till Spring if I could raise confidence enough
from old disappointments to believe you in earnest I should
feel happy at the matter for there is no two in existence that
I should like to see better than yourself and Darley and I want
to see you much to talk over a many things but as to Darley if
he does not write me as usual and make a good account of the
omission of not putting his name to the Poem as he was wont
need not look to see me at Helpstone as a brother poet is
welcomed but as a proud high and stiff Professor of English

* Letter unfinished.

Literature[2] and instead of the freedom of a hearty shake by the hand I shall have my fears of fashion in one hand and my hat in the other will he like such reception I think if his present omission has method in it he assumes the fashionable Poet with a vengeance and he shall be humoured if it is so. I like his Poem very much the characters of the peasantry put me in mind of those in 'As you like it' and those unaccountables the Fairys, &c., of the 'Tempest'. What I think of it I will tell himself if he has not grown above me and my opinions. I took this large sheet to insert a Poem for your opinion it has been long written I think I told you I had a Vol for children the Grasshopper was the first and this the second and I have another the Lady cow's dream not finished nor do I like it but if you like this I will try again, a friend of mine has told me that a story of 'The Toad in the Rock' would make a good thing if well done being a history of the terrors and feelings of insects at the Noahs flood told by itself what think you but here's the other.[3]

To his Wife Patty

[*sent*]

p.m. 25. Feb. 1828.

MY DEAR PATTY

According to promise I write to you today to tell you that I got up safe to London & that as you know I am now at my good Friend Mrs Emmersons & I have not been anywhere else as yet

But I ought first to have asked you how you are I hope you are better then I fancy you are[1] & how is my dear children—my Anna—Eliza Frederick & John kiss all & each of them for me & tell them I shall not forget my promises of their little books &c when I return Mrs Emmerson desires her kindest remembrances to you & the children & their grandfather & grandmother Mr Emmersons doctor a Mr Ward[2] told me last night that there was little or nothing the matter with me & yet I got no sleep the whole of last night I have as yet taken no medicine & perhaps I shall not but I shall most likely see Dr Darling before long for satisfaction & I think I shall go to

Taylors tomorrow I shall not trouble you with a long letter but
merely desire my remembrances to Baxter & Royce[3] & to you all
make yourself perfectly easy on my account tho I cannot exactly
feel so on your own for I am in the midst of my best friends & if
kindness & friendship can make me better I shall come home
well where I shall hope to find you well but if that cannot
[be?] Gods will be done & not mine but well or ill I am my
dear Patty yours

Sincerely & affectionatly

JOHN CLARE

20 Stratford Place
  Oxford Street
    London

To [Alaric Watts][1]

[*sent*]

20. Stratford Place,
March 12. 1828.

DEAR SIR

I thank you kindly for the 'Souvenir'† & I assure you that
the one you sent before never reached me & for the absense of
it I cannot help confessing that I felt dissapointed.

I also thank you as kindly for your liberal offer in paying me
for my contributions[1] & tho I would not have requested it if
I could not have done without such means of bettering my
condition yet my Publications have brought me so little real
profit (tho a good deal of words have been wasted to the contrary) that for my increasing needs I am obliged to seek out
other resources.

& I shall feel heartily glad of contributing somthing worthy
of your next years' anual & as I am now in London I should be
happy to call upon you & make arrangements to that effect

I am dear Sir
Your faithful serv^t

JOHN CLARE

To Patty

[*sent*]

20 Stratford Place
March 21st, 1828.

MY DEAR PATTY

I am anxious to see you & the childern & I sincerely hope you are all well I have bought the dear little creatures four Books & Henry Behnes has promised to send Frederic a wagon & horses as a box of music is not to be had—the books I have bought them are "*Puss in Boots*" "*Cinderella*" "*Little Rhymes*" & "*The Old Woman & Pig*" tell them that the pictures are all colored & they must make up their minds to chuse which they like best ere I come home—Mrs Emmerson desires to be kindly rememberd to you and intends sending the childern some Toys —I hope next Wednesday night at furthest will see me in my old corner once again amongst you . . . I have been poorly having caught cold & have been to Dr. Darling I would have sent you some money which I know you want but as I am coming home so soon I thought it much safer to bring it home myself than send it. . . . Kiss the dear Childern for me all round give my remembrances to all and believe me my dear Patty

yours most affectionately

JOHN CLARE

To Taylor[1]

Addressed: John Taylor Esq., 6. Percy St, London.
[*sent*]

Helpstone [April] 3 –28[1]

MY DEAR TAYLOR

I waited till I had made somthing out respecting the 'Roman Coins' ere I wrote & I went yesterday to Milton on purpose & my friend Henderson says he will send you all he has gotten as a sample & if you like them at the price he gives for them he will become your collector & get all he can tho' he says they are not brought to him so plentiful now as they were—he gives a penny each for the common ones & as much as 6^d for such as he thinks good but seldom or ever more he has made several out which he will send you among the rest he would have put them into my charge for you but I told him to send them himself & then he & you could explain matters about them better as to what may suit you best & what he may collect—so much for Antiquity—Tho I have not as yet opened any prospect of success respecting my becoming a bookseller yet I still think there is some hopes of selling an odd set now & then & as you are so kind as to let me have them at that reduced rate when I do sell I shall make somthing worth while for a trifle which I thought so in my days of better dreams becomes somthing considerable now—& even trifles are acceptable for I do assure you I have been in great difficultys & tho I remained silent under them I felt them oppress my spirits to such a degree that I almost sunk under them for those two fellows of Peterbro in the character of doctors have annoyed & dunned me most horribly at times & tho ones claims are unjust I cannot get over him by any other method than paying—but my coming up to town has aleviated me a little & by next latter end of the year I hope to be half set up I have got 4 pieces into Ackermans forget me not for which he has paid me already at the rate of 20 guineas per sheet which is the utmost he gives & with which I am well contented & I am going to write for the 'Spirit of the Age' for which I am to have a pound a page & more when it becomes more established—but promises tho' they produce a plenteous seed time generally turn out a bad harvest—& be as it will I am prepared for the worst I have long felt a dislike to these things but force puts no choice—'Interest makes strange friendships' White the Naturalist says & I feel its truth & its misfortune but thank God I am once more in my old corner & in freedom I am as great as his majesty so a fig for the Babelonians

Will you be so kind as to send me the half dozen sets of my Poems² as soon as you can with an extra half dozen of the Calenders & I shall take it as a great favour by your enclosing those little books as you promised me the Virgil & Homer &c &c as I should like the whole of them with the portion of the Bible & I hope you will compleat the Virgil

I went to A. A. Watts³ but I did not feel at home there for

there was a party of literary men & painters all entire strangers
to me I was unwell & rather in the situation of a fish out of
water struggling for my own element but Watts himself
behaved very well to me & was quite a different man to what I
expected from the first sight of him yet our opinions of poetry
do not agree & I shall never attempt to write for his Souvenir
any more as I sent him one which I fancied my very best but
he did not like it—I shall now advertize my Books in Drakards
Stamford News & if I succeed in selling them all well & good
if not it will not be the first dissapointment I have met with &
now my dear Taylor I will as a man of business say what I have
long neglected as I never liked to refer too but it is a thing
that must be & it will never interfere in our friendship be as it
may—so I should like to know at your leisure how I stand with
you in my accounts & my mind will be set at rest on that score
at once for if there is anything coming to me it will be acceptable at any time & if there is nothing I shall be content the
number printed of the first three vols I have known a long
while by Drurys account but wether I have overrun the
constable or not since then I cannot tell & that is what I should
like to know the first oppertunity I hope you will not feel
offended at my mentioning the matter as I do it for no other
wish than to make us greater & better friends if possible—
than whom no one has a better claim on you than

Yours affectionatly

JOHN CLARE

To Frank Simpson[1]

Helpstone April 9 1828

MY DEAR FRANK

I have been obliged after a good deal of hammering to give
up all trials as dissapointments about the Epitaph for they are
cursed dissapointments to myself more so than they will be
to you for I wished to accompany your monument yet its all no
use I can do nothing for the more I try the worse I am & the
reason why it is is I believe that I never knew Mr. Friar[2] &
therefore I cannot feel the subject at all so here I give it up with

much reluctance for Patty went over to Wilsons on Wednesday
with a letter but more for a Vol which I much wanted & delayed
writing to you by her in hopes that I might be able to do somthing by friday so you see instead of getting better I get worse
& such will be the attempts I doubt at Behnes princess Vittoria[3]
which I am most anxious to attempt as he has flattered me to
desire it but thats all against my success & I have but little
time now to try I expect as Mrs Halls Evergreen[4] the work in
which it was to appear was to go to press on the 6th of April for
so she told me herself & I imagine it will not be far from a first
article so I have as good as gave it up entirely—I have also a
commission to write full stop thats too much a trade word for
friendship The fact is I am to write a Poem for one of the
Annuals To my Kind Friend E.L.E. It is to be called Wreath or
Chaplet I dont know which & wether it will ever get any
further then the trifle I cannot tell—yesterday Mr. Ryde[5] called
on me & told me he was going to London in a few days &
wished for my friend Mrs. Emmersons address which I told
him & he told me about his sons attempts to find out a publisher
for me but really this is a thing that only one word expresses
better than the rest do you reccolect Mr. Burchell in that
immortal Bard of Erin's Vicar of Wakefield when the ladies
were promising the daughters of the Vicar so much & so many
idealitys of successes in life & fortunes thus said Mr. Burchell
[who?] stood rubbing his hands by the fire & uttering rather
audibly to their patronage & pomposity—'fudge'—& tho I
have never uttered it I have often thought of it when Mr.
Rydes sons stories meet my ear for how can it be expected that
a man can further a poor Authors interests in reccomending a
publisher when he has a commodity going the rounds of the
market quite as unsuccessful as the one he would pretend to
help for I have not yet tryed anything of my own for fear of a
refusal any further than small things which have never missed
the success they were seeking its plain that if Mr Colbourn is
his friend why the d–l is it that Mr. Colbourn does not publish
this Classical or Heathen Dictionary I can see thro this farce
of folly & mock patronage this play at chuck ball & catch it
between Mr. R. & Mr. R. the son & egad I'll be a ball no
longer so here the Farce ends for I must tell you my dear

Frank I dont like them at all & I never shall like them that is as friends I do not wish to have indeed I shall give them no cause to be enemies their pomposity & fudge I dislike most damnably & never wish to cross it any more & neither will I so you must manage matters as well as you may for my likes & dislikes are past all cure I feel vext at myself often but I cannot act the flatterer well at all & if one does not lay it on thickish its no use but I like such folks who are too honest to be flattered those John Bull sort of fellows they are the sort for me & shall you take me for a flatterer when I say that the people I prefer are somthing after your own way & that of your family to whom I beg to include my kindest remembrances & to none more sincerely than to yourself while I subscribe myself my dear Frank

Yours most affectionatly

JOHN CLARE

You must have the sincerity to believe my failing in the d–d foh [?] that is not the epithet for an Epitaph they are always sacred as a sincere feeling that is of no other cause than inability to please myself or others for that is the cause & none other

Yours &c &c

J.C.

To Taylor

[sent]

April 12th 1828.

MY DEAR TAYLOR

Having advertized the Books yesterday I write agen to you for the parcel & hope you will send it directly as I have 3 orders for them already 2 for the Calender only & one for the Set & 3 ladies came this morning wanting them & are to call agen tho I did not ask them how many they wanted but I hope to succeed so do let me have them quickly I do not like to give you trouble by this additional letter but I feel anxious about having them & you may as well write to Henderson of Milton in the parcel as he has got some very curious Roman Coins such as will suit you if you really wanted them as you expressed you did & he will think perhaps I made all this talk about nothing if you make no inquiries however be so kind as to forward the Books as soon as you can if you please & I shall write no further this time then being

Yours sincerely

JOHN CLARE

Here is another of those Imitations of the Psalms & this I did this morning look at the original & tell me if such will do as Imitations

[There follows a version of the 137th Psalm:[1]]
By Babels streams we sat & sighed . . .

To Thomas Pringle*

[sent]

Helpstone Aug. 29. 1828

MY DEAR SIR

I return my hearty acknowledgments & thanks for the kind & obliging present of your Poems[1] & the rest of ctceteras with which I am highly delighted & in return I beg your acceptance of my last Vol to which I shall add the whole the first oppertunity & altho I fear they will not meet your expectations as to what I might have done for situations in life however humble afford no apology in this age when we turn to the sun burning exellence of a Burns & a Bloomfield two poets tho of very different powers yet inimitable & perfect in their own exellence for both of whom I feel more than admiration & I dont care who laughs or calls me fool for odd opinions but if I may judge from Pope's Translation (for I have no latin) I would sooner be the author of Tam O Shanter than of the Iliad & Odyssey of Homer

I will tell you which I like best of your Poems as I go on & what parts but why did you leave out your very best song of Teviotdale for I dont find it here—

* See Biographical Memoranda.

In your Excursion[2] I picked out as favourites some beautiful bits of scenery &c P. 5 'Say shall we wander where the swan' to the close of the sentence & something far sweeter beginning on P. 16

> *Yet where the Westward shadows fell* to
> *Still to the wild its music made*

I think this very beautiful & the next

> *Among the banks of tedded hay*

to the end of the sentence & these four lines are so good I must repeat them:

> *& viewed with meek mysterious dread*
> *The moonbeam thro the lattice shed*
> *Deeming twas God's eternal eye*
> *Bent down to bless us from on high*

This is also as good page 27 beginning:

> *The music of the mountain rills* to
> *In living lines of glorious light*

In this passage

> *The starry scriptures of the sky*

appears to me very fine but I'm no critic. The song of the Lady-Well tree I like much & the sonnet to the river Earn. In the second part I like them all equally as I fancy tho perhaps these rather best 'Afar in the desert' 'Wild bushmen' 'Warsong of Makanna' 'Lion Hunt'—capital 'The caffer Commando' & 'Noonday dream' I have read the Vol with eager interest & not with a view to criticize therefore you must not think I have read it all I hope you intend to write more on your sojourn in Africa The notes are uncommonly entertaining & give more ideas to a Traveller at Home of those strange Lands—than one of Mr Murry's or Colburn's table breaking quartos

I shall trouble your kindness with a letter for my friend Allan Cunningham & also return & thanks to your publishers for their kind present of Bailey's West Indies.[3]

And whenever you have leisure I should feel thankful for

your opinion of my Poems & shall recieve any suggestions for
future improvement very thankfully that is a plain pointing out
of my faults in ryhm for I know I have many & as I am now
embarking in a long trial which is if I succeed to be a long
poem advice will do me service—I shall bye & bye be in
London I think when I shall most certainly do myself the
pleasure of calling to see you & anticipate with double zest
the [gap] of joining you & Allan on . . .⁴

To Patty

Addressed: Parker Clare, Helpstone, nr. Market Deeping
[*sent*]

Sept. 29. 1828.

Dear Patty
    I write this note to desire you would send me as quick as you
can the two remaining sets of my Poems as the Mayor of
Boston has ordered them & I want to present them to him—
you must send them so that I can get them this week & for
safety's sake you had better take them to Deeping yourself seal
up the parcel & get Baxter to direct it to 'Henry Brooke Esqʳ
Pump Square Boston' be sure not to neglect to send them as I
have been introduced to the Mayor who has shown me much
kindness & ordered one set for himself & one for a Friend who
is on a visit to him therefore the sooner you send them the
better it will be to my advantage—do not expect me this week
if I do not come I hope the children are all well & believe me
                        dear Patty
                    Yours sincerely
                                JOHN CLARE

To Taylor

Addressed: John Taylor Esq, 30. Upper Gower St, London.
           [*sent*]
                   Helpstone. Oct. 15. 1828.

My dear Taylor

Will you have the kindness to send me 6 more sets of my Poems compleat & 6 of the Calender as I have sold every one & not got a Vol left by me now & I have another set ordered to go to Boston where I have been on a visit & met with a very kind reception the Mayor of the Town sent for me as soon as he heard I had come & treated me in a very hearty manner & wished me to procure him two copys of my whole poems & desired me to insert his name in every Vol he also lent me Leigh Hunts Memoirs of Byron the first time I had ever seen it —The Portrait of Lamb is like him as far as portrait but the life & vivacity of his countenance is lost—the one of Keats I know not what to make of it's bad the books interesting & not so abusive as I was led to believe from the accounts in the Journals &c—have the kindness to send the books as soon as you can as I wish to return my thanks with those I send for the loan of this Book—When I got to Boston I had another invitation to go to Hull but they looked on me in a character that I could not fill up without making myself very ridiculous for several young men in Boston had made it up among themselves to give me a Supper at an Inn where I was to have made a Speech, &c &c but as soon as I heard of it I declined in the best way I could & told them if they expected a speech from me they need prepare no supper for that would serve me for everything & so I got off of the matter—I felt the kindness but I could not tell them I felt it & now Ive got home agen I must write them my feelings & realy this speechifying is a sore humbug & the sooner its out of fashion the better—I heard that Dequincey's Mother had been on a visit to Boston some time back & that he has been expected having relations there— Lamb is a great favourite there as Elia & Dequincey is as the Opium Eater but the worst is that many of the bookeaters laud it as the production of Lamb & you cannot convince them to the contrary—Give my remembrances to Hessey Darley Dewint Hilton &c &c bye the bye Hilton was at Lincoln. I heard when I was at B.

I am Dear Taylor
Yours sincerely

JOHN CLARE

I had forgot to tell you that I cannot procure the Coin without giving more than its worth for the mans been told its worth much more than it really is Artis gave me good advice respecting the purchase of old coins which I mean to abide by & that is never to give silver for anything but silver unless one is sure it is gold (for doubtful gold & silver too is very current among antiquarian fancys) & then one cannot be far wrong the coin I told you of is copper & if I can get it for copper you shall have it but the fellows got it & if he cannot find a customer elsewhere I shall have it brought for a quart of Ale at least I expect so.

Yours &c
J.C.

I have read over those Books you were so kind as to send me the translations* I mean & I like Virgil best & I should like to see Darley undertake the whole version & without the latin for common or universal reading for the interlinings bothers one's eyes terribly

You never sent me Darleys later Mathematical publications I should very much like to see them Lord Milton has sent me 13 Nos. of the 'Useful Knowledge Library' which I expect he intends to continue for there will be no end to it

To Taylor

Addressed: John Taylor Esq, 30. Upper Gower St., London.
[*sent*]

Helpstone. Decr 21. 1828.

MY DEAR TAYLOR

Will you have the kindness to send me my little money as soon as [you?] possibly can for Christmas is nearly here & I

* Taylor's 'Interlinear Series', advertised as 'Locke's System of Classical Instruction'.

want to get straight as near & as soon as I can—I began very abruptly but having got the business over which caused me to write I shall now fill up the sheet with something or other—I should hope you are well as to myself I have had one of the severest fits of sickness I ever remember to have had I was taken soon after I recievd your letter with the books & was ill six weeks it was a very bad Fen fever & I expect I brought it out of the Fens home with me for it went thro the house & my wife & childern were all ill but myself & the youngest child were worse than any of the rest & thank God we are all recovered & well & what is better I never took one dose of phisic tho a kind man a stranger to me heard of my illness & kindly sent me some medicine last week gratis & at a venture but I was well & have been well this 3 weeks or month past I daresay yet the kindness was the same & do you know I am taking the medicine regularly till its gone to prevent a return of the malady which I understand is often the case & then it ends in a consumption & finishes the matter so say the wise folk of the Fens & it shall be a long while ere I visit them agen tho when I wrote to you last I felt as well as ever I did in my life & I had not the least idea of illness tho the friends were I was fell very ill before I left.

I have written to Darley which accompanyes this & I have written to him for advice as I am trying for a long poem & my present intention is a poem on the 'Pleasures of Spring'—I had some desire to try one on 'The Last Judgment' but expecting I shall be on the wrong side in this world as well as the next by so doing I dare not—I shall write to Mr. Cary also for his advice & I should like to have yours as to whether I had better go on with short pieces in the manner of the old poets or attempt something long—I like Darleys Companion* very much indeed & think it far better than if he had enlarged it & I think it would have been more popular if both Treatises could have been compressed in a Vol—The Vol *was charged* against me in the acct with my books but I should suppose without your knowledge for I cannot afford to buy a mathematical library & yet am very anxious to see anything which Darley writes as there is always somthing to interest me—Henderson of Milton

* *The Geometrical Companion*, published by Taylor, 1828.

came over to see me about 5 weeks back & I asked him about the Coins when he said he paid 10 or 12 shillings for them & I am going over to Milton when I will pay for them but my opinion is that he was overcharged & I think if I make inquirey I can get coins cheaper the best way is to offer those who hunt them so much a dozen did he tell you the charge when he sent them if he did not I shall desire him to insert it on a scrap of paper as you may know there is no extra charge of mine— dont doubt but they may cost him that in the lump neither have I a doubt but our friend Artis has had a finger among the best of them & 3 or 4 out of that quantity underrates the value to an antiquarian for I know there was some among them which he thought very good indeed I told him that you wished for more & he said none of those who gather them had brought any to him latterly nor did he say he would enquire for I was ill at the time & could not pay much attention to anything.

I am my dear Taylor

Yours sincerely
J.C.

To Taylor

Addressed: John Taylor, Esq, 30 Upper Gower St, London.
[*sent*]

Helpstone Jan 3 1829

MY DEAR TAYLOR

I recieved the Annuity quite safe & the check from Lord Spencer which I have got changed I know not why his Lordship sent it thus (tho it is quite as well & much better than sending a bill by letter) for I have never wrote to him to do so nor did I ever send the last Vol as he never took any notice of the first 3 Vols which I sent some years ago so I thought I was intruding in so doing & that his Lordship might think it was a fresh apology to his kindness—I believe my illness was caused by the journey & not by any irregularitys[1] while there tho I one night took a little more liquor than I was in the habit of doing & felt ill two days with a sort of fever while there it was

at the Mayors of the Town he was a very jolly companion &
made me so welcome while a lady at the table talked so ladily
of the Poets that I drank off my glass very often almost without
knowing & he as quickly filled it but with no other intention
then that of hospitality & I felt rather queer & got off almost
directly after finding myself so but I was nothing like disordered
yet it was wine & I was not used to the drink & tho it made me
ill for two days or at least helpd to do so for I had a sort of cold
at the same time it was nothing of that kind that caused my
illness after my return which was a bad fever & it is a mercey
I am here now tho I did not feel the danger of my illness till
I had got over it & then I felt it a miracle that I escaped & a
greater that all my family did the same for every one of them
was ill tho myself & least child was worse than the rest—I
dont think I have drank a pint of ale together this two years in
fact I can drink nothing strong now in any quantity & as to
spirits I never touch & yet without them I feel hearty & hale &
have quite recovered from my last ailments & hope to prolong
the lease of life for a good season tho I dont think I am much
qualified for an old man—Your opinion of my intended Poem
is in some instances correct[2] for the same images must certainly
occur of which I have written before yet if I could succeed
others would be added that would do away the impression of
repetition but action is what I want I am told & how action is
to get into the pleasures of Spring I cannot tell

I think many of the productions of the day that introduce
action do it at the expense of nature for they are often like
puppets pulled into motion by strings & there are so many
plots semiplots & demiplots to make up a bookable matter for
modern taste that its often a wonder how they can find readers
to please at all—I still do as you say & go on with little things
—I feel pleased with your opinion because I feel you speak as
you think these Annuals are rather teazing to write for as what
one often thinks good the Editors return back as good for
nothing while another gives them the preference & what one
thinks nothing of they often condescend to praise—Allan
Cunninghams[3] is the best Annual of the whole & a piece by
Procter one by Allan are the best in the book Darleys I do not
like so well as some of his earlier pieces but his Play the more

I look at it the more I like it there is certainly something very happy & clever about it & it will be read of that I am certain for a neglected poem in these days is almost a sure sign of its merit—I have paid Henderson & ordered him that is wished him to collect you more coins & he will seek out for all he can find.

I write to Hessey today who has kindly offered to send me the Nos. of his New Work on Religion[4] which will either be entertaining or else very dull from its intended magnitude but if the prospectus is followed up with the spirit it professes to set out with it will be a very entertaining book & I have no doubt command a good sale—I thank you very kindly for Darleys Book but your kindness only urges me to increase it by reminding you that you never sent me his Trigonometry which at some oppertunity I wish you would as I wish to see everything he writes in english for I feel a great esteem for him & believe he will produce somthing ere long worthy of better esteem than mine & meet it also—I have wrote a long letter & so farewell.

My dear Taylor
Yours sincerely

JOHN CLARE

P.S. What a dreadful Tragedy I have just read in the Trial of that Burke of 'Modern Athens'[5] the terror seizing descriptions of Shakespear are mere farces of horror compared to the simple naration of this dreadful Trial—the party dancing & drinking till midnight as the prologue of the Tragedy—Hunt & Thurtells was nothing in comparison.

To Cary[1]

[sent]

Helpstone Jan.ʸ 1829

MY DEAR SIR

. . . I write to beg your opinion of the enclosed Poem as one of those I intended to pass off as the writings of others—this I sent to the 'Everyday book' as the production of Andrew

Marvel, & the Editor took it for granted that it was so & paid
me a compliment in praising it which he would not have done
had it passed under my own name & as I still have thoughts of
going on with the deception I have sent it to request your
opinion of it. I know nothing of the writing of the old Poets
further then the '*Specimens of Ellis*' & the '*Songs of Ritson*' but
the idea of their manner is all I want to be acquainted with—
I had read that Marvel was a great advocate for liberty & as
death is a great leveller I thought it would add to the disguise
to father upon him that subject. I have written several others for
Sir Walter Raleigh, Sir Henry Wooton &c &c; the old manner
is all that I attempt with sprinkling a few old words [h]ere
& there—but Taylor wished me not to disguise them under the
names of others but publish them under the Title of '*Visits of
the Earlier Muses*' but I thought if I could succeed well I should
like to have published them as old things found in imaginary
Books & M.S.S. There would be no harm in it I think, would
there? You see I want your advice in the matter & I know you
will give it me—Hayley's Poems which you so kindly presented
me with I have read, and I do not like him near so well as
Darwin[2] but perhaps the subjects are the cause—the measure
in which he has translated some passages of Dante is very
curious but it don't strike me as one well suited for the Epic.[2]
Blank verse & blank verse alone appears to be the natural
style of that sort of poetry at least it appears so to me & the
choice of it in your Translation was a very happy one & I
much wonder that its excellence hath not made it more popular
but fashion is no test of merit, thats left to time—I felt very
sorry I did not visit you sooner then I did but the real truth of
the matter was that I was rather shy in doing so feeling that my
visit might be an intrusion on your new employment . . . if
Mr Taylor had not encouraged me by saying you would feel
disappointed if I left london without seeing you I should not
have ventured to have called on you but your usual kindness
soon did away with these unpleasant feelings & I was very
loath to leave london without the further pleasure of a longer
visit but I had booked my passage that morning & could not
alter it but when I come to london again the museum[3] shall be
the first among my reccollections to visit—if I had so many

books to run to I should not know where to begin . . . I beg
my kindest remembrances to Mrs Cary & to your son I saw &
also my dear Sir to remain

Yours very sincerely

JOHN CLARE

[There follows:]

DEATH

Why should man's high aspiring mind . . .[4]

To Allan Cunningham*

Addressed: 27. Lower Belgrave Place, London.
[*sent*]

Helpstone Feb^r 22 1829

MY DEAR ALLAN

Here I am agen with lots of rhyme both for your reading &
Anniversary also—of the three Vols I beg you will accept them
as the completion of my intentions when in London last Spring
as I had not the oppertunity to do so then & I shall be glad to
hear your opinion of them sometime or other—not the humbug
of fashionable flattery for we both of us hear enough of that I
dare say at times but your honest likes & dislikes that are ever
the best & most profitable to correct ones errors for we seldom
'see as others see us'—as to the things for your Anniversary I
have sent the 'Statute'[1] thinking it not amiss & the other was
written & sent by *request* so if you like them both they are at
your service for I do not write as if I expected pay by the foot
or page either but I like to give good measure & throw in an
extra gratis—you gave me too much for my last & I hope you
will keep that in mind next year & not do so for I never feel
the loss of independance worse then when I cannot serve a
friend without knowing I recieve a reccompence in return for
more than the labour is entitled to—tell me if you get the
packet safe & how you like the two trifles—

I am my dear Allan

Yours sincerely

JOHN CLARE

* See Biographical Memoranda.

I forgot to ask you whether you recieved my last letter which I sent under a frank—soon after I recieved the Copy of Anniversary & in which I gave my opinion as you requested I have to add that the Poem to the 'Glowworm' by Mr Fergussen² is very good as I think for it pleases me much—write as *soon* as you can to say you recieve this if you will have the kindness as I shall be doubtful of its arrival tho I have addressed it as particular as possible

Yours &c &c &c

To Eliza L. Emmerson*

Addressed: Mrs. Emmerson, 20 Stratford Place, London.

[April 1829]

MY DEAR ELIZA

Did you think I should ever write agen I hope you did for I have been head over ears at hard work for the last 3 weeks in the field & this last glut of wet has given me a day or twos leisure for [writing?] & the first letter I have written since I recieved yours is to yourself I also waited to give you all the literary news I could respecting the annuals but I have as yet heard little I got a letter from friend Cunningham yesterday¹ who tells me that my trifles suit him one of which are the verses to E.L.E. of which he makes a strange mistake by fancying they are writ to Miss Landon & flatters me much by praising them & also by thinking them worthy of the Poetess so I wish that the first oppertunity you have you would correct the mistake if you feel the matter too delicate to write upon you can tell the Miss Frickers when they next call upon you for he will most like transpose the E.L.E. to L.E.L. which I shall not be able to rectify if he does not send me a proof sheet & I would much rather that they should stand as written & proud as I am of Brother Allans commendation & proud as I should be of Miss Landons commendation also I feel much prouder to know they were deemed worthy the acceptance of yourself to whom they were written I will give you the quotation from Allans letter relating to the verses—'I have placed your contributions in

* See Biographical Memoranda.

the approved box marked with my hearty approbation your verses to Miss Landon are the very best you ever composed & Miss Landon I must say is a very beautiful substitute for these aerial madams I shall show it to her—' How Allan should mistake E.L.E. for L.E.L. I cannot say but in his hurry he has overlooked it, & I hope you will rectify the mistake I did not tell him to whom they were written because I thought it was not nessesary but I wish I had now to prevent the mistake which will get into the proof sheet & remain there if not corrected beforehand so much for this matter I have not heard a word from Mr Pringle to whom I have sent a trifle for his annual & I wonder how he could refuse the sonnet of yours as you say he did for I am sure it was much better than those he inserted of my own last year but there is no accounting for Editors—I am very glad you like the Bust[2] as I thought myself it was a good one but Frank Simpson tells me he thinks Harry's last touches in my absence did not add any improvements to it but rather injured the freshness of the likeness that he so happily caught in the model & as it was when I last saw it*

To Eliza L. Emmerson

August 1st 1829.
Helpstone

MY DEAR ELIZA

To get out of debt in the way of our correspondence is one reason why I write now & having an idle hour to spare another but which of these reasons can make apology for a bad letter I cannot tell so I leave it with you—Yesterday I saw Artis at Milton & he spoke very highly of the reception he met with at your temple in Stratford[1] (for I presume you are now at Brighton) but he did not speak so favourably of the Bust as I had anticipated he says it struck him too forcibly at first sight as being a copy of Hilton's picture & he left it with a stronger impression of its being so now of this I can say nothing I thought it good for Hiltons picture is good & they are two good things together & thats all I care about the matter most

* This draft-letter is unfinished.

of my friends are desirous for me to attempt somthing in prose
as verse will not sell & I am looking round for a subject as
Cunningham anxiously urges me to it & he anticipates my
success so friendly & earnestly that I have determined *to try*
at all events but wether I shall produce a novel or a prayerbook
I am sure I cannot tell Fashion is a fine dog but a very false
one it barks at shadows & lets monsters of every sort pass by
to its ladys library without a growl so if I can manage one of
these successful abortions I must as that success is a much
better payment that² after praise will you excuse this half
sided epistle as I have nothing more to say & do I am in but
little spirits to write my wife being at this moment dangerously
ill & in bed & the children noising round me in all directions
I hope next time I shall be better provided for a longer epistle
hoping yourself & Mr. Emmerson are well I remain my dear
Eliza

Yours sincerely
JOHN CLARE

To [Henry Behnes Burlowe]*

[sent]
Helpstone August 1 1829

MY DEAR HARRY

I shall not make any apology for not writing sooner further
than saying that I have not had the length of a sheet of paper
time to spare for this last four months excepting on sundays &
wet days for I have taken up my old occupation of hard work &
feel quite as happy as I did when 'Hope told a flattering tale'
The fact is we only have to hope the best & to be undecieved by
meeting the worst & then to hope agen as usual & perhaps it is
good that hope should thus be an evergreen—I cannot imagine
how you feel dissapointed in not finding me writing oftener
when you write so seldom yourself for I 'take no note' of these
notes of yours further than mere nothings in correspondence
when paper is plentifull in a time of scarcity they might tell a
little more than cyphers my eyes are not so bad but I can read

* See Biographical Memoranda.

a sheet full from you by candle light if I have no time by day-
light so remember—I have got settled with Wesley[1] &c & I
am now writing to Mr. Hall[2] as to the 'Spirit of the Ages'[1] The
present price is a too near neighbour to nothing to be of much
use writing for—I think I shall be in town before winter now
but only for a few days as I want to get some matters settled
which I feel impossible to do without coming up—Your
Examiners are all safe as you sent them but I am sorry to say
that some of the Times are destroyed for paper is such a useful
article in my house & considering the times papers as waste
time to read after present time had done with them I let patty
use them as she liked untill your last note checked me from
doing so & I shall take the earliest opportunity to return them
all—& give my best thanks to Mr. Hone for poor Humphrey[3]
& believe me my dear Friend

Yours sincerely
JOHN CLARE

To [William] Sharpe[1]

[sent]

Helpstone Oct 1829

DEAR SHARP[1]

On next Tuesday or Wednesday I shall start off the packet
of flowers & having taken so much care of the paper on which
you inserted those you wished for as not to be able to find it
after many searches I am obliged to send you a selection by
guess & to insert as many of those as you liked as possible I
shall send you portions of almost every perrenial I posses—
I send small bits of each to make the parcel as light as possible
for flowers ought never to cost much for if our amusements get
too much hold of our pockets those amusements are far from
being pleasures in the end which is only considered as another
name for pleasure therefore to make the fact consonant with the
maxim I have compressed as many sorts in as small a parcel as I
could make & if you water them when you plant them they will
all most assuredly thrive for they are perfectly hardy for all
weathers & those that were not I declined sending on purpose

that their loss by frost should not dissapoint you—I shall send the names both Botanical & English as well as I can make them out for altho I know wild flowers tollerable well my knowledge of garden flowers is very limited but I have made out the list as well as I could & the number on the plants refers to the corresponding number & name on the paper—I shall wait until I hear from you before I send them because I wanted to trouble you & the packet with the care of a few letters if I *dare* or may do so for as I wish to do nothing against existing laws that may get either of us into trouble I ask your advice first wether I can do so or how I may do so I can send them open if that will be any difference to the matter tell me & I shall act accordingly

I never sent you anything for Mr Hall because I have had no time having been at work in the ground in which you found me untill now but if Mr. Hall will advance the money in *your hands* or his publishers will do so either for twelve months writing for the magazine at the rate of two pages per month I will take care to supply them with somthing either in prose or verse every month but upon no other terms will I do anything for the very trouble in getting the money is as much as the trifling pay is worth—What money will they advance on a volume of poems does Mr. H. state what, when he says he can get me a publisher on those terms the fact is I would rather take a small sum for the volume altogether than a large promise in 'half profits' because I have been disappointed at that game already with Messrs Taylor & Hessey—I shall send you a copy of their accounts very soon which I shall wish you to show to Mr. A. A. Watts for his advice as nobody knows more of booksellers & publishing than he does & he behaved so kind to me when I was last in London that I dont think he will refuse to give his opinion about it*

* Letter unfinished.

To Mrs. Marianne Marsh[1]

[*sent*]

Helpstone Oct 19 1829

DEAR MADAM

I enclose your 'Book of Epitaphs'[2] (which you was so kind as to lend me) with many thanks for the use of it & having read it with attention I cannot help but confess I have been very dissappointed for many of the epitaphs seem to have been inserted more from the merit of the persons they would commemorate than for any merit discernable in the Epitaphs themselves & others are inserted for no merit or reasons at all as I can find out unless it be to fill the book for the Editor must have been a very wise man indeed to discover either wit or wisdom in such vulgar things as the following couplet

> *Beneath this stone lies John Flint*
> *If he gets up the devils in't.*

in my opinion such would have even disgraced the pages of a Jest Book for here is nothing in the shape of humour to laugh at or of wit to praise while there is much in the levity & vulgarity of folly to condemn

I am led to think that a better collection of Epitaphs might easily be collected by such as had taste & leisure to collect them but I am not so sure that a better collection could be written by one individual at least I feel quite sure that I should fail in such an attempt for a good Epitaph should be somthing like a good Epigram so short as to be secure of a reading & so pointed as to attract the attention when read so as to be admired & read again such Epitaphs would make a churchyard a sort of library where even the most careless observer would not fail to meet with somthing to entertain & perhaps instruct him for anything that entertains the mind is often the forerunner of inducements to improve it my idea of a good Epitaph would be better explaind in the following portion of one on Lady Pembroke p. 186 then I can otherwise explain it

Underneath this sable hearse
Lies the subject of all verse
Sidneys sister Pembrokes mother
Death e'er thou kill'st such another
Fair & good & learned as she[3]
Time shall throw a dart at thee

I should like to see good Epitaphs introduced into churches & churchyards in lieu of bad ones but there is a secret charm attached to the bad ryhmes & worse metre of Stonecutters verses which will ever make them favourites of the lower orders & leave them not entirely discarded by the higher ones from whom the example should first come & that charm is that they are so full of flattery to the dead & we may walk into fifty churchyards & be universally told on every stone that its possesor died a good person & scarcely see it hinted in one that the living are not so good but they may improve thus will bad verses with neither moral or merit to entertain or improve the mind be opposed to the use of good ones that might be made to contain both fearing that I have exhausted your patience with my poor opinions I will conclude tho not without repeating my best thanks for the use of the book & desiring to give my respects to his Lordship & also Miss Mortlock[4] & to be alowed the pleasure to subscribe myself Madam
       Your very obliged & most obedient Servant

             JOHN CLARE

P.S. I have ventured to send two or three specimens of Moths for Mr. G. Marsh[5] they are badly set up but thinking there might be one among them which he had not I preserved them as well as I could & waited the first oppertunity to send

To L. T. Ventouillac*

Addressed: 14 *Cumming Str., Pentonville, London.*
[*sent*]

Helpstone Novr 7 1829

DEAR SIR

In answer to your Note sending the money (for which I thank you kindly) I beg to say that the Editors & Publishers of such Annuals that honour me with a request for contributions are kind enough for the safer conveyance of the money to make a small parcel by enclosing the Annual for which I have written & inserting therein the amount for the trifle inserted by this means it comes much safer than it would do by Letter & I have no doubt if that is your intention to do so that it will reach me safely by adressing the parcel thus ' *John Clare Helpstone near Market Deeping*' & if I can I will send you somthing next year more suitable then the one you have gotten if not Mr. Dale may curtail it as he chuses to make it suitable for your Almanack[1]

I am Sir Yours very respectfully

JOHN CLARE

To Drury†

Helpstone November 1829

MY DEAR SIR

Having recieved a statement of Accounts from Mr Taylor I was astonished at finding an item in them of which I had not been apprised & in addition to the debt you claimed & was paid for it is the following statement '*Paid Mr Clare for Copy right per Drury* £20' now YOU KNOW that I never recieved a farthing extra from you beyond the debt which you claimed & was paid for & that the selling of the copy right was all fudge which you

---

* See Biographical Memoranda.
† There are three drafts of this letter (Northampton manuscripts) and none the one sent.

desired me to accord with merely as you want to prevent Mr. Taylor from depriving you of your share as you feared he would do in the end but however well grounded your fears might seem to be at the time is best known to yourself for you have since found them groundless by having your share of the profit granted you on the same ratio as he allowed himself & I should hope my fears respecting the loss of the £20 may be as groundless as yours were for whatever tricks may have been played with my ignorance I cannot think this was a plea of yours to cheat me out of that sum but that it is a mistake which you made in making out the accounts for you well know that I never recieved a farthing beside the debt you claimed which was to be temporally considered as the price of copy right merely for your own interest as you desired to defend you from your supposed enemys who turned out your friends so far as to grant your dues in the end & I hope that by expecting the same treatment from you I shall not be dissapointed for there are a set of people who profess a great deal about character & religion & honour & all that who are often found to want the very profession of common honesty

I understand from Mr Taylor that the publisher of those songs of mine made you a remuneration for them & tho I was to have had a remuneration also you know I have never had anything & tho they may not have made much yet a portion of that little as my right would have done me some good & you no harm as it would tend to show you to the world what we always wish to be considered a fair dealing man you also possess a quantity of my writings & a folio sort of Tax-shaped book in parchment covers which you only borrowed to copy out the trifles it contained & which you never returned & tho they are of little worth either to yourself or me yet you know they are mine & if you would have the kindness to return them at the same time that you show your willingness to correct the above mistake & comply with my just rights in the other matters you will prove by so doing what you often professed to be my friend & I shall feel the proof as warmly as you often made the profession of considering myself your very obliged friend & Servant

JOHN CLARE

P.S. You told me when you & Taylor disagreed that 5000
Copies of the first Vol was printed in my accounts there is only
4000 I suppose this is a mistake also of yours

Yours &c

J.C.

To Taylor[1]

Addressed: John Taylor Esqr, 30 Upper Gower Street, London.
[*sent*]

Helpstone Nov 15 1829

MY DEAR TAYLOR

You have no doubt wondered at my long delay in answering
your two last letters & the long accounts that accompanied
them but the reasons were that when they reached me I was
beginning harvest & have been at work with short intervals of
intermission ever since—& having leisure for the first time I
replye & you must excuse my enquircys if I make them where
none are nessesary for my ignorance in such matters must be
my innoscence of any impertinence that may appear to be so—
as every wish in making the enquirey is to be satisfied of things
that I do not understand & not one utterd with the intention to
offend—so where I am right I feel convinced that you will alow
it & where I am wrong I hope as strongly you will excuse me
of any other intention then that of wishing to be right—The
Account A1 & 2' is I think not far from right tho in comparing
it with my own some of the different sums of money are not
only set down under wrong dates of the month but in several
instances of the year also to that in which I recieved them—&
you have not accounted for my writing for the Magazine you
know I was to have twelve pounds a year while I wrote for it
which was three years but if this be considered too much for the
trifles inserted you may pay me by the article for I am not a
bargain hunter only pay me something—Hessey also had in his
hands in 1824 seven pounds given to him for me by a Duchess
& I never recieved it neither is accounted for as I expected I
want that which is right & nothing more & if you tell him he
will remember it at once—In the Account 'C' Drury led me

235

to believe that there was 5000 Copies of the first Vol printed &
tho it was at the time he & you disagreed yet I imagined it was
true but he has made such a false charge to you on me in these
accounts that one who could claim the one may easily be alowed
to assert the other it is the following 'Paid Mr Clare for Copy
right pr Drury £20' now you will be astonished to hear that
this is a lye—for mind I never recieved a farthing extra beyond
the debt which he claimed of me & which you settled—the
selling the copy right was all fudge & pretence he persuaded
me to agree that it ought to be so merely as he said to prevent
you from hurting him in the end yet whatever tricks he may
have played with my ignorance in my acquaintance with him in
those hours of hilarity with which I frequently indulged at his
house I cannot now remember but this I can say that the selling
of the copy right is all fudge & that I never had nothing but small
sums of a few pounds to the extent of that debt & nothing else &
I have written this day to desire an explanation of the matter & I
shall then if he persists in the falsehood *prove* to you that it is a
false charge—it seems that instead of getting anything by the
first Edition I am the loser by £20 from Drurys mistake or
cunning artifice I cannot say which yet

I think Mr Woodhouse rather hard with me in his charge of
£7 for a deed of trust is he not? & I see also another Item of
which I do not understand the import or the meaning viz for
transfer 2s 6d I have no knowledge of its meaning or nessesity
—There is also the portrait charged for which I did not expect
would be an item in the way of my half profits when it was
painted for you & at your desire[2]—& respecting the copies of my
poems which I had from you these are overcharged for in the
account & a great deal beyond what you voluntarily offered them
to me for on my last visit to London viz 10s the set that is 2/6
each for that was what you told me in Waterloo Place—& now
the matter is got thro so far I am heartily glad tho disappointed
for in losing hope I have cleared the prospect to see a little
further as to how I must proceed for the future & my intentions
are to get a small farm or cottage as soon as possible & I have
written to Lord Milton for that purpose but have recieved no
answer as yet from his Lordship for my family is large & my
means small to support them & all I regret is that matters were

not settled sooner but when I expressed a desire to have a
settlement years back Hessey urged me to patience & told me to
wait & that I should be in the end 'rich & happy' I am not amiss
off for happiness but the other part of his prophecy is badly ful-
filled but I am contented

I long to have a scrap of Dewints sketches for a frame to hang
up in my cottage & if you would alow me to posses the painting
he did for the 'Shepherd's Calender'[3] I should be exceedingly
pleased & when I was at the Bishop of Peterboros this summer
Mr Herbert Marsh his eldest son told me he admired some of
Shellcys Pocms very much & on my asking him if he had read
any of Keats he said not & I much wish to present him with a
copy of the 'Endymion' yet not at the same time be left without
one myself so as you owe me 12s for the Roman Coins perhaps
you will send me a copy down & that at *trade price* & there is
another book I should like which is The 'Guesses at truth'[4] but
if the money will not by [buy?] both at the price send the first
only & never mind the overplus money & if you will spare me
Dcwints Drawing you can place it in the parcel the book makes
excuse my freedom

Poor Hesseys failure[5] astonished me much because I always
thought that his constant attention to business would have
prevented him being caught up in the tempest that destroyed the
more inconsiderable portion of the trade but I hope he will yet
meet some success for his family as like me he has a large one—
I always thought Hessey a cautious monied man give my
remembrances to him—& poor Mrs Wright what a breach
Death makes in our acquaintance every time he pays a visit
among them & what an imperceptible impression such visits
make with the world The newspapers are read by thousands &
the Thousands of deaths in them are passed over as matters of
course but the loss is only felt by the few—I am almost sorry
that I knew her no better yet I knew enough of her warm
attachments to her friends to regret the accident of her loss & to
feel what a loss it must be to others the fact is we never know
half the esteem which we ought to have felt for a friend & little
of the value we possest by such friendship until it is too late to
show our sincerity when everyone hears it but one who would
have been most interested in our esteem yet even these sorrow-

ful reflections are not without their satisfaction for to feel sincerity for friends that are gone is a sure proof that we esteemed them when living or at least feel that we ought to have done so I am sure nobody respected the kind hearted friendship of Mrs Wright more than I did

You threaten me with a visit to Helpstone but had you not said it so often & never proved your doing as you say in that matter but once I can feel it in no other way then that of a compliment if you *mean so* I shall be most happy to see you give my best remembrances to Darley to whom I shall write soon & believe me

dear Taylor
Yours sincerely

JOHN CLARE

To de Wint[1]

Addressed: P. Dewint Esqr, 40 Gower St., London.
[*sent*]

Helpstone Decr 19 1829

MY DEAR SIR

Nay I will not be so fearfully polite as fashionable policy urges people & friends of cold blooded etiquete to be for I hate it so I will say at once My Dear Dewint (a much better commencement to an old friend & I am sure I have known you long enough to be one & you see I have not waited to enquire wether you will alow me to call you so but have taken french liscence for the liberty without asking it—but to proceed your Daughter flattered my vanity in asking me to find time to become one of her (that is one of your family) correspondents now I feel such a respect for the young Lady & her family & am so proud of having an oppertunity of being acquainted with one of the finest Landscape painters of the Age that I will not let slip either time or oppertunity to become correspondent with either yourself or family & tho by the way I have taken an odd oppertunity to commence with I know you will forgive it at least I will hope as the Irishman did that you will grant the favour first & forgive the liberty afterwards

The favour requested & the liberty taken to request it being neither more or less than a wish to possess a bit of your genius to hang up in a frame in my Cottage by the side of Friend Hiltons beautiful drawing[2] which he had the kindness to give me when first in London what I mean is one of those scraps which you consider nothing after having used them & that lye littering about your study for nothing would appear so valuable to me as one of those rough sketches taken in the fields that breathes with the living freshness of open air & sunshine where the blending & harmony of earth air & sky are in such a happy unison of greens & greys that a flat bit of scenery on a few inches of paper appear so many miles for so some of those beautiful little things appeared to me which you so kindly indulged me with a sight of in your study 8 or 9 years back—alas that it is so many for time has made a sad gap in my little catalogue of friends since then I dont know how it is but nothing in the Royal Academy & other Exebitions struck me so forcibly as representations or rather fac similies of *English* scenery as those studies of yours— now I think many Painters look upon nature as a Bcau on his person and fancies her nothing unless in full dress—now nature to me is very different & appears best in her every day dessabille in fact she is a Lady that never needed Sunday or holiday cloaths tho most painters & poets also have & still do consider that she does need little touches of their fancies & vagaries to make her beautiful which I consider deformities tho I should have given up the point in fancying that they might be right & I wrong if I did not feel that your sketches I speak of illustrated my opinion—The reason why I dared to take this liberty of a request is that on hearing you had the kindness to make a drawing for the frontispiece for nothing I felt heartily anxious to thank you for the kindness & having done so (excuse my vanity) I felt as heartily hopeful that I should one day possess the drawing but never having those hopes gratified my dissapointment has at last grown up into a determination above timidity to request something of the kind which would give me a pleasure to posses[3] & having done so if I thought it needfull I should ask your pardon but feeling it otherwise I shall ask nothing about it but go on begging you will kindly remember me to Mrs. Dewint & to your Daughter to whom I shall take the liberty to

write first oppertunity also to friend Hilton & Mrs H to whom
my respects are not less sincere from being strange & unfamiliar.
—Miss Dewint asked me when I came out again in the shape of
a vol: of Ryhmes in fact I cannot answer the question but being
strongly urged by my Friend Allan Cunningham to try something in prose I am doing so but wether I shall succeed or not I
cannot tell I hope on as usual and with the assistance of these
hopes I scribble my leisures into the bulk of a sizable volume &
if it be deemed worthy of reading so much the better I shall most
assuredly solicit Miss Dewints earliest opinion of it as soon as
published if it ever arives at that honour—if you see Mr
Herbert—Reynolds—now give him my remembrances for I shall
never see him perhaps to give them myself—I am

Dear Dewint yours very sincerely

JOHN CLARE

To Drury

[Dec. 1829.]

SIR

I am sorry that you have gave my enquiries so little satisfaction respecting the mistake of the money but I am not
dissapointed in your explaining the matter against me because
when I saw it inserted in my accounts from Mr Taylor I knew
that the impudence that claimed it would not be without an
excuse to justify it

As to what you say respecting settling the accounts (at the
time you executed the instrument not I) this is a lye for you
never gave me any account at all the reccolection I have of the
matter is this that you wished me to say you had bought the
copyright for £20 & you wished me to write that down in your
account book one evening which I did remarking at the same
time that you should cross out £20 of the accounts & not trick
me into an additional debt by my agreeing to your desire

I now find I acted foolish in the matter but thats no use all I
know is that your explanation of the matter is as utterly void of
foundation as the instrument you talk of was of honesty for Mr

Taylor declared he never saw a more impudent attempt at imposition on my ignorance in his life

I should not have written again to you in reply had not you chose to be very pathetic towards the conclusion of your letter respecting me & my affairs all I wanted from you was what I considered my just rights & as you have denied them all I have nothing further to [say] on the matter only that I am happy my affairs are out of your trust & heartily [wish] I had been out of it sooner as feeling such an occurance would have been a benefit & I earnestly hope I may never encounter such zeal as yours again I never entertained the least idea of your
[1 line scored out]
with my comfort & happiness I do not think you have much to do

Mr Taylor said right I think in respecting you he did not consider you were entitled to participate in the latter publication & its my intention you should not have any further concern in the earlier ones*

To Cary[1]

[sent]

Helpstone Jan.y 25 1830

MY DEAR SIR

. . . I value your correspondence & friendship so much that I will not loose either the one or the other by any neglect on my part . . . remembrances to Mrs Cary . . . & friends also that you may fall in with & whom I may never chance to see again. I am often sorry upon that account that the Magazine dropped into oblivion, it took so many pleasant meetings along with it.

Do you ever see or hear anything of Wainwright that facetious good-hearted fellow I long to hear something of him agen & where is Charles Lamb I have never seen him since the year 1824 what a season—do you ever see or hear anything of him now or do you know where he is to be found if I could procure his address I wanted to write to him but nobody can tell me where he lives now, farther then that it is 'some distance

* Letter unfinished.

from london' which is a bad direction to find him with . . . [his settlement of accounts with Taylor: prevalence of bankruptcy]

I am dear sir

Yours sincerely

JOHN CLARE

[a postscript about Sir T. Lawrence's death, much regretted by Clare]

To Taylor[1]

Addressed: John Taylor Esq, 30 Upper Gower St, London.
[*sent*]

[Jan–Feb 1830]

MY DEAR TAYLOR

I ought to have told you long ago that I got the annuity safe & thank you for sending it—& the reason why I did not do so is that I have fell in with a very violent cold which is now getting better otherwise I have been well & hearty for a long while— the times as you say are bad & the worst is that I fear all this bother about country meetings & other rigmarole pretentions will not better them—tho there are many voices mixed up in the cry—common sense is seldom among them for self interests & individual prosperitys are the universal spirits that stir up these assemblages of reformers the Farmer is on the look out for 'high prices & 'better markets' as he stiles them tho these markets are always curses to the cottager & the poor man—the Parson is now rather stirring into radicalism for a partial reduction of individual taxes merely because he sees somthing must be done & as he wishes to keep his tythes & his livings untouched he throws the burden on government The Specula- tor—he is looking up to a paper currency which placed a false value on his bargains & thereby enabled the cunning to cheat the honest & the unprincipled to ruin those who had a principle for so long as county banks are alowd to accumulate their three farthing bits of paper on the public as money without any other check then a trust on their honesty so long will a few build their prosperity on the ruin of thousands—I think a paper currency upon just principles a very commodious way of trafic much

better than gold—but I would have every bank issuing one
pound notes dependant as branch banks on the bank of England
nay every bank issuing paper at all ought to have that check
upon them to prosper but you are a far better politician than I
am—yet I feel as common sense dictates & I think that a
universal reduction of tythes, clerical livings, placemens pen-
sions & taxes & all renovated & placed upon a reasonable
income suitable to the present decreased value of money &
property is the only way to bring salvation to the country I
know such thoughts some time back would have been considered
as proceeding from a leveller & a radical—the meaning of the
last word is like wigs & torys indefinite but I am no leveller for
I want not a farthing of any one's property all I want is to keep
the little that fortune alowed me to call mine but if government
goes on patiently [?] taking a little from those who have only
a little & leaving the wealthy untouched—I shall quickly be
what I have been but no matter times must change & if for the
better I am willing to suffer my little with the rest—heavy
burdens with proper assistance become light ones & when there
is not so many idly looking on who have no burthens to suffer &
immense strength to bear them they ought to bear a part
wether they belong to church or state—I am delighted with
Dewints kindness & shall look for it with delighted anticipa-
tions—Sir T Laurence is gone I hear—he was a kind hearted
man & the reccolections of his kindness to me when at his house
affected me greatly to hear of his death—if merit has anything
as usual to do with the choise of another president Hilton or
Etty wd be prominent in the group if the first happens to win it
I shall be heartily delighted for he would confer more honour on
the appointment then the appointment conferred on him & if
Etty wins it I shall think he highly deserved it—both are
amiable kind hearted fellows who seem to have nothing in their
composition but good will to others & a carless indifference to
themselves—I shall write to Darley this week—I had many
things to say but have no room Give my remembrance to Hessey
& all other friends & believe

Dear Taylor
Yours sincerely
JOHN CLARE

To Darley

[1830]

MY DEAR DARLEY

How are you & where are you in the land of the living or among the monuments of the worthies in 'Westminster Abbey' for it is so long since I heard from you in the shape of a letter or otherwise that I cannot tell where you are or what you are neither can I say wether you are a sheet of paper in my debt or wether I am one in yours & the very reason why I write is to clear up the mystery & come to a correct conclusion as soon as possible for I hate that any obstacles should lie in the direct road to friendship most d–d–ly they are as troublesome to me as those toll bar creeds are in the road to heaven or the hereafter which you please

How the times have altered the opinions & views of the people even here we have our villages mustering into parliaments & our farmers puffing themselves up into orators & there is scarcely a clown in the village but what has the assumption to act the politician & I hope this general stir may produce general good but the farce of the thing is that our tory folks should be grown into radicals & be brawling after the reform which they alone have so long & so obstinately prevented—what is the reason—it is a known fact in natural history that foxes will do all they can to drive badgers out of their holes—that they may get in themselves—& I think there is a parralel in this matter true enough to alow the comparison—such ridiculous inconsistences in public characters make us ready to exclaim with Mrs Winnifred Jenkins[1] 'O Molly these sarvants at Bath are devils in garnet—they lite the candle at both ends'

I heard from Taylor a little while back & he says he seldom or ever sees you now—I have had a very unpleasant business to settle with him which thank god I have nearly got over & that was to settle my long pending accounts of 'half profits' which taking everything into account is I think a bargain that goes under a wrong name—in the first instance I was so far taken in by a Drury of Lincoln (a trafficing hugster after self interest rather than a book seller) as to loose entirely the profits of the first edition of my trifles which is past John Taylors power to prevent or remedy & I cannot expect him to loose it so I must— & all I am sorry for is that such a fellow as Drury should be found professing every virtue under heaven & wanting even that of common honesty & I am happy so far to find that altho in the first instance I mistook Collins Ready Reckoner for a Treatise on Friendship John Taylor is not among the number of those professions for I should have been very down at heel to find at last that he had not been a Friend & I am happy to find that I am not dissapointed for dont you think that the situation of book-sellers is something like that of lawyers & that the mystery of a many of their items appear rather more consistent to custom than to fair play

Where & how is our friend Allan give him my kindest remembrances as soon as you see him & also to Mrs Cunningham & all I hope is that you & they are all well—Sir T Laurence is gone[2] I understand & the loss is attempted to be filled up by Mr Shee[3] did they forget in the hurry that there was such names as Wilkie[4] Hilton & Etty[5] or was it deliberately considered— Mr Shee may be a great artist as far as I know but of the others I did now [know?] as the opinions of many confirmed that of my own—I am at the end of the sheet & beg to remain dear Darley

Yours sincerely

JOHN CLARE

To Cunningham

Addressed: Allan Cunningham Esq, London.
Favoured by my Friend Mr Nell
[sent]

[1830]

MY DEAR ALLAN

Here is a Friend of mine a Mr Nell[1] a very hearty fellow & one who is very desirous of seeing yourself as a Poet & as I have convinced him as hearty a fellow as himself & therefore I have taken this liberty of introducing a stranger without any apology feeling that such an introduction needed none & he will be par-

ticularly gratified in seeing what you can show him of the
immortal specimens of Chantrys[2] Genius & any other matters
that can interest a literary man for his profession as that of a
Bookseller is not his only recommendation being a man of no
common taste & also a great admirer of Painting & Sculpture &
a lover of the Muses here ends my introduction of my friend
Mr Nell & now my dear Allan how are you how is Mrs Cunningham & your Family & our old Friend George Darley as for
myself I am as dull as a fog in november & as far removed from
all news of literary matters as the man in the moon Therefore
I hope you will excuse this dull scrawl & the blunders attending
it & believe me as I really am
Yours heartily & affectionatly

JOHN CLARE

Has Hogg[3] visited London yet when he does tell me & I'm
d–d if I dont muster up every atom of my possibility to have a
sight of him
Angel Inn
 Peterbro

Having left your address at Helpstone I am obliged to trust
this letter & my friend to providence to find you which I trust
he will readily—yours

J.C.

To Miss Jane Mossop[1]

[sent]

Sept 9 1830

DEAR MADAM
 I beg you to do me the favour of accepting the enclosed
Volumes as a small Token of regard for the kindness I recieved
in my illness from Mr Mossop & yourself & for which I beg
to remain not only now but always
Yours sincerely & respectfully

JOHN CLARE

246

To Taylor[1]

Addressed: John Taylor Esq[r], 30 Upper Gower Street, London.
                    [sent]

[late September 1830][2]

My Dear Taylor

I have not been able untill now to write to you—for I have
been dreadfully ill—& I can scarcely manage even now to
muster courage sufficient to feel myself able to write a letter but
you will excuse all—I have been bled blistered & cupped & have
now a seaton in my neck[3] & tho much better I have many fears
as to recovery but I keep my mind as quiet as I can—& am able
to read a Newspaper—all I regret is that I cannot describe my
feelings sufficiently to benefit from our friend Dr Darlings kind
advice in whom I always had the greatest confidence—my
fancys & feelings vary very often but I now feel a great numbness in my right shoulder—& the seaton tho I cannot bear it to
be dressed for 3 or 4 mornings together discharges so much
that I fear I shall fall into a Decline at last—but thank god my
head is more relieved tho it stings now & then as if nettled I
cannot describe what I have suffered but all I now dwell on is
that I am getting better—I thought once that I should never
have met health thus far so as to be able to write or read any
more I can do both & I am thankful to that power who gave me
the means to think & be happy & who can take both away when
he chuses—how is Hessey I often thought of his kind attentions
to me in my first illness when I could think—& tell him I desire
to be remembered to him—I have got another addition to my
family a Girl a few weeks old[2] There is now six of them—& all
I want is a cottage & a few acres of land but do you know I cannot get any thing of the kind either for love or money—I have
sold all the copys of my poems & I wish you would send me
down another packet of them as soon as ever you can for I have
several copies spoken for—so send me 6 copies of the first
Vol 6 of The Village Minstrel & 12 of The Shepherds Calender
& dont forget me There is nothing that would give me more
pleasure then the revival of our correspondence but as the fault
is not mine I cannot mend it—still my old feelings have never

forsaken me & I look upon the early acquaintance which my ryhming trifles provided me as constituting the happiest period of my life I wish nothing had broken in upon those asociations for they had grown as dear to me as my own fireside—but some are in the grave yet Death shall not have the warmth of their memorys that lives with me untill this hand is as cold & insensible as the moulds which cover them—where is Darley he never writes & Dewint tho I have written two letters to him [he] never noticed them—did I offend him if I have done so I cannot make out how I did it because you told me he intended to send me the drawing which emboldened me to repeat it—thats all I can say about the matter I have felt the dissapointment long & have not forgotten it yet

I am Dear Taylor
yours sincerely
JOHN CLARE

To Taylor

Addressed: Mr. George Stothert, c/o Mrs Taylor, Bolham Hall, East Retford.
[sent]
Helpston Oct 2 1830

MY DEAR TAYLOR

I am very disappointed in not receiving an answer to my last letter because I wrote it under such difficulty when I was scarcely able to manage the pen as I wanted some copies of the Poems down as quick as possible & I expected to see them long ago but I fancy you was not at home when it arived & therefore I have written again & hope you will reply as soon as you can—I have been dreadfully unwell & I am sorry to say that I often feel apprehensions of a return of the illness that distresses me very much by times tho I do all I can to keep up my spirits—I again repeat the desire that I expressed in my letter to send the books as soon as you can—I have no other news to write about & as to my road at this present in the wilderness it is all barren still I am

Yours sincerely
JOHN CLARE

Have you seen Dewint if not have the kindness to remind him
ere you send off the books & let me hear from you by letter that
you recieve this—& when I may expect the parcel as I will send
over to Deeping for it

yours

J.C.

To Hessey

Addressed: J. A. Hessey, Esq, 263 Regent Street, London.
[*sent*]

Taylor's date: 1830 ? Oct.

MY DEAR HESSEY

I recieved your kind letter with great pleasure that accompanied the parcel & was very glad to hear from you & also to
hear that you was so well & the account of your healthy
catalogue as a first attempt pleased me as much but I had long
heard of your success by my excellent Friends Mr & Mrs
Emmerson (them whom two of kinder intentions & warmer
feelings never existed for time hath made no change in them)
& the success of so old an acquaintance could not fail of giving
me pleasure which next to my own interested me as much as
any thing could do & I was as sorry to hear of your late
struggle[1] but honesty is proof against every thing but misfortune—& poverty never disgraces it—it only leaves it to its
own lustre & shows its value—As to religion my mind is
compleatly at rest in that matter my late deplorable situation
proved to me that I had read the Bible successfully for it was an
antidote to my deepest distresses & I had not the least doubt on
my conviction of its truth—but I recieved a relish for reading it
from some Numbers of Scotts Octavo Bible which is a most
excellent work & it also gave me a relish for thinking—I studied
the Bible often & found it long before my illness The one book
that makes the carnallitys of life pallatable & the way to eternity
pleasant—the one & only book that supplys soul & body with
happiness—I also find in it the beautiful in poetry in perfection
—I had read Homer but a greater than Homer is there—I found
in it gems of the oldest excellence in sublimity which the greatest & oldest poets had borrowed to enrich their own lustre &

249

what astonished me most was that I found beautys that I had
never met with before tho I had read it over time after time
when I was the happiest fellow in existance when I had no particular friends & no enemies at all neither wanting the one or
fearing the other—it was then the cottage book The only piece
& part of the cottage furniture in the shape of a book which I
could lay my hands on & tho I read it with the customary
reverence instilled into my mind by my parents I read it with a
lack of reflection & rather more for amusement than profit—I
am glad to hear that your family are well & to Mrs Hessey & all
you will remember me—& I am as happy to tell you that mine
are all well & hearty & as to Patty she is never or so seldom ill
that she forgets from time to time what illness is & I have heard
her declare that she never knew what the head ache was in her
life untill within these last few years—she has been of much
comfort to me both in illness & health & I always feel happy that
I met with such a fortunate accident that brought us together for
'an honest woman is the honour of her husband' & Solomon who
said it might no doubt have given his whole inheritance of riches
for such unpurchased sincerity (as the poor man posseses) &
been never able to meet it—my children are comforts in their
kind but the thoughts of their future welfare often makes me
uncomfortable about them I wish to make them all good common
scholars & wish also to instill into all their minds the innestim-
able value & the upright integrity of common honesty Mr
Mossop our Vicar has been uncommonly kind to me in my
illness & he wrote as kindly while I was ill to Mrs Emmerson to
ask her to get my eldest boy Frederick into a school & he has
told me to mention it again to Mrs E. but the shock that his
success will give me in being obliged to part with him (if the
attempts of his friends are successful) will be so great that I
never have had the courage to alude to it—tho the Boy says that
he will go if he can get in & often aludes to it with childish
satisfaction—the names of our old friends which you mention I
am extreemly happy to hear of & Charles Lamb I want to write
to will you tell him so when you see him that he may leave his
address with you poor Miss Lamb I hope she will recover—
there is hopes & there is mercey to hope it—Hazlitts death I
saw in the papers I read it twice over before I dare believe

it was Hazlitt that I had met & whose writings I had read with
much gratification & it shocked me much to think another
acquaintance had made a blank on our memorys & in our esteem
for the tallents of Hazlitt was of no every day matter—what I
have read are the works of a man of original Genius & it seems
that he died in the character of Genius—neglected & forgotten
—when will the cant & hypocrisy of trifling be put aside & the
sterling merit of inferior [superior?] minds be so valued as to
be considered worthy of universal reward & the humbugs of
party cavils & party interest be done away with—I doubt never.
Give my respects to all friends & believe me dear Hessey

yours sincerely

JOHN CLARE

To Taylor

Addressed: John Taylor Esq, 30 Upper Gower St, London.
[*sent*]

Helpstone Jany 15 1831

My DEAR TAYLOR

I recieved your letter & I was rather dissapointed at the task[1]
you wish me to undertake for I am such an unsuccessful
manager of such matters that I cannot get my own & I am sure
not to succeed in yours—time only could prove the success but
I have *no time* to try it—I have at this moment twenty three
pounds due to me from different parties & not a farthing have I
gotten of it I have been waiting & waiting—for the seedtime
was rich in promises but the harvest is worthless & barren of
benefit—& therefore I have given it up—nessesity is trampling
my shoe heels off & therefore if you will send me the money in
the old way I shall be greatly obliged to you & esteem it as a
favour—I will try sometime or other—at least I will send your
bill & say it is on your account &c—but as to try to get anything of the kind for my present nessesitys tho a mere trifle—I
might as well have a checque on the man in the moon

—For the use of Chaucers Works I shall thank you & return
them when I have read them as to our friend Dewints Drawing
it had grown into a hopeless anticipation untill you revived it—

251

I care not what it may be if so it be one of those off hand
Sketches in which his truth to nature stands as visible as day-
light—thats all I care for—there was a stranger with me sometime back a very intelligent man who admired Spenser &
Burtons Anatomy & Keats[2] & who knew Keats (as he told me)
from a boy—I have forgotten his name but I think he was an
Artist by the manner in which he was struck by Hiltons Wise
bird the Owl which he seemed very pleased with

I have met with much trouble in 'myself matters' for my
youngest boy William Parker a fine little fellow has been
dangerously ill of an illness very prevalent here & my Sister
Sophys eldest daughter a very fine child of nearly the same age
is gone into the hopes of eternity which calamity entirely
incapacitates me from any exertion of even only a letter & added
to that my last summers illness expences have just been brought
in to the length of nine pounds seven shillings & fourpence—
trouble has got the start & he seems determined to keep it—so
that I often wish I had never been known beyond 1818 when I
had no enemies that I cared for or no friends that I knew of &
yet was so happy that I fancied I had more then I wanted—I
have been very unwell this last fortnight & for the last three
days I have been so distressed in mind & body that I was
obliged to take medicine again—but to night I fancy I am
somthing better—& no further can I get—& hoping I shall
hear from you soon

I remain
Yours sincerely
J. CLARE

To Taylor

Addressed: John Taylor Esq, 30 Upper Gower St, London.

[sent]

Taylor's date: Mar 7 1831

MY DEAR TAYLOR

I must trouble you with this request and I hope you will
speedily answer it—for you are of late some letters in my debt
—but as to that I never minded when entertainment was all—

it is now nessesity for I am ill & very ill & as I cannot get a frank soon enough (for Lord Milton is not in parliment) to write to Dr Darling I trouble you to tell him & I hope you will write to tell me you have done so—I was taken 3 weeks back or more—with a pain at the stomach which would not go off & as it affected my head very much I felt alarmed & took a part of Dr Ds last prescription which checked it & subdued the humour in some measure but whenever I attempted to walk friction brought it on as bad as ever & the pain at my stomach started again as bad as ever & I then finished the packet of powders & on last Saturday night by the recommendation of Mr. Mossop (having nothing left of my last prescription) I took a blue pill & on monday morning I waked with a dreadful burning humour in my lisks & a contraction so as almost prevented me from making water on monday I commenced a second course of Dr Darlings medicine & the humour tho abated is not subdued —for I awoke this morning with a burning heat in my funda-ment where the humour again made its appearance with prickly pains in my head arms & shoulders & they are as bad just now —I fear I shall be in the same state I was in last summer—for unlike last night I got tollerable rest but the pain at my stomach was more frequent in its attacks & I awoke in dreadful irritation thinking that the Italian liberators were kicking my head about for a foot ball—my future prospects seem to be no sleep—a general debility—a stupid & stunning apathy or lingering madness & death—my dreads are very apprehensive & uneasy I dislike this prickly feel about the face & temples worse than anything & a sobbing[1] or beating when I lay my head down on the pillow was first felt last night for a long time—my appetite was gone & from monday to this morning 4 Eggs & a bit of bread have been the whole of my food—it never attacked my appetite before as I know of & I am so alarmed & so anxious to get better that if I cannot in no other way I will draw upon or sell out my fund money (if it can be done without entravagant loss) & take lodgings in an humble way as near Dr Darlings as I can & the steam bath in great Marlboro Street which did me uncommon benefit in 1827 [1828 ?] & would do me as much benefit again I write this not as a resolution but for your *advice as a friend* for I want to get better & Dr Darling in his last

253

letter to me ordered a steam bath but there is no such things
here—at all events write by return of post with Dr Darlings
advice I shall wait with impatience for it—I have been favoured
by a friend with a sight of the Quarterly Review for January in
which is an article on some poems of one Jones[2] which Mr
Southey has published & the poem which induced him to do so
is so much like a facsimile of a trifle of mine put in Pringles
Friendships Offering for 1830 To the Autumn Robin & as
most of Mr Jones Images are the very same—I should like
you to see mine & if you have not got a copy of Friendships
Offering—I will write out the verses for your opinion—the
coincidenses as such things are called might be construed into
imitations by many & as mine was first published I like to be
correct on that point tho in trifles—for Mr Southey seems to
hold uneducated poets in very little estimation & talks about
the march of mind in a sneering way—as to education it aids
very little in bringing forth that which is poetry—& if it means
[a] humble situation in life is to be the toleration for people
to praise him I should say much admiration is worth but little
the whole review for a leading journal exceeds all the twaddle I
ever met with—there is a line or two in Notice about a bell not
being rung a silence pervading at dinner time—are these—
beauties I feel anxious that a selection of my fugitives should
appear the earliest oppertunity—as the best things I have
written are among them & I wanted to get them written out
for your opinion but I cannot—I am dear Taylor

Yours sincerely

JOHN CLARE

I had intended a good while back to send you some sonnets
viz Poesy a Maying but you are a matter of fact man now in
literature & may deem such fancys intrusions

To Taylor

Addressed: John Taylor Esq, 30 Upper Gower St, London.
[*sent*]

Helpstone 24 July 1831

MY DEAR TAYLOR

I recieved the parcel & thank you for sending it for I assure you that I was troubled in consequence of not being able to meet my expences & even now I cannot get clear of them by a long way but I must make the best shift I can—I will mark out the passages which I fancy sublime or beautiful in the vols you sent me[1] with remarks &c at my future leisure & then I will send them to you to do as you please with—as to what you say respecting the Poems I cannot say anything in the matter further than that you may act with them just as you would do if they were your own property for I know you are my friend & I see no fear in what you may get for them or do with them—for it appears that they are of slow sale—but why do you think they will fetch no more than one shilling per copy—if that is your opinion as you know such things better than I do I expect use liberty & do as you like in the matter but at the same time I should like to get out a new Vol with someone if I could & I have long intended & am now resolved in putting together what I have at the different intervals written for that purpose Viz Letters of Advice to my Childern & Essays on commonplace matters in life & when I get them in a form I will send them to you for your perusal[2]—In the Vol of old Poets I very much admire those of William Brown[3] There is a freshness & beauty about them that supprised me & with which I was not acquainted —there is much english landscape about them & the second song of Brittania's Pastorals commences with one of these

> *The Muses friend grey eyed Aurora yet*
> *Held all the meadows in a cooling sweat*

Although not of the beautiful but Surrey is beautiful

> *The sunne hath twise brought forth his tender green*
> *Twice clad the earth in lively lustiness*
> *Once hath the winds the trees despoiled clean*
> *& once again begun their cruelness*

255

Surrey's Sonnets are tender & very poetical there is a breathing
of Shakespearean healthfulness about them that is evergreen—
& there is much more to say about this volume which at my
earliest leisure I will look over & make notes as I go on—but
I think it very slovenly edited thats all & many names left out
that ought to be in & some that occupy much room [3 words
unreadable] less by abridgment but after all what dissapointment to see Wither in little only filling a few pages—I am my
Dear Taylor

Yours very sincerely
JOHN CLARE

To Taylor

Addressed: John Taylor Esq, 30 Upper Gower Street, London,
[*sent*]

Helpstone Oct 1831

MY DEAR TAYLOR

I have again been very unwell & unable to write or read or in
fact to do anything—but thank God I am now well & mean to
keep so if I can—[one line crossed out] I have not been able to
read the old poets with any intention to select & there is no
room on the margin to make any remarks so that I shall be
forced when I do start to pass them without any—how is it I
cannot find the sublime or beautiful which I expected & I wish
I had you by me to read to me for the defect must lie in my
imperfect way of reading them but if Mr Southey's Judgment
as a collector of the beauties of old Poets be correct I am sure
mine must be very imperfect for it appears to me a most
imperfect collection & would rather seem as a sample got
together by a painter as chance directed rather than by the
Judgment of a poet & that Mr Southey—Where is Suckling &
where is Herrick & twenty more that ought to have been there
for the Lyrics of Suckling have never been surpassed & only
equaled by Shakespeare

All I want to go on is a stimulous an encouraging aspiration
that refreshes the heart like a shower in summer—instead of
that I have nothing but drawbacks & disappointments I live in

256

a land overflowing with obscurity & vulgarity far away from
taste & books & friends poor Gilchrist was the only man of
letters in this neighbourhood & now he has left it a desert—
I see things praised that appear to me utterly worthless & read
criticism in the periodicals when I do see them that the very
puffers of Blacking & Bearsgrease would be really ashamed of
—& I lay my intentions aside having no heart to proceed
but I am resolved to show them I can judge for myself & whatever remarks I may make on the ryhmes of others they shall be
done honestly & with as little vanity as possible

& now respecting 'self' have [you?] made out anything
respecting the publishing my Poems because I now want to try
to get them out as I am going to leave here & commence cottage
farming & therefore I shall want somthing to begin with & as I
am rather unwilling to interfere with the fund money if I can
help it I should like for you to use your interest for me & to do
all you can for that I am going is positive & that I want somthing to start me is positive & these two cases make it necessary
that I must do somthing therefore I trust to you for advice & I
hope you will write to me immediately—of one thing I am
certain that if health keeps on my side I shall become an
independant man & care a fig for nobody but friends—I shall
have a good landlord & I am told the place is a good one &
therefore it is all on my side further I shall have fewer regrets
to leave this old corner where I now write this letter the place
of all my hopes & ambitions for they have insulted my feelings
latterly very much & cut down the last Elm next the Street &
the old Plumb tree at the corner is blown down & all the old
associations are going before me—I can send for your inspection all the Poems for the pres Vol I have written—I thought of
you very often in my illness & wished then to say what I now
can say which is that if you outwear* me that everything I have
written may pass under your observation & nothing be published without your opinion I find that true friends are scarce—
illness has not shaken my confidence in yourself but confirmed it

How is Hessey & Hilton & where is Dewint have I offended
him that long promise has never reached me—How is Cary you
have another Ed of his Dante I see in the popular size & it will

* Taylor 'outwore' Clare by about six weeks, dying in July 1863.

be popular—where is Charles Lamb are 'Album Verses his own publishing or the collection of a bookseller—I have not seen anything but the title which I thought in bad taste

Yours sincerely

JOHN CLARE

To Taylor

[January 1832]

MY DEAR TAYLOR

I have again been very ill & all unable to write or think or do anything but thank God I am now better & I mean to keep so if I can—I should have written to you three weeks back[1] but a matter fell in my way that occupied my attentions which were not then fixed but they are now & I hope I have luck in the wind—for I'm going to leave Helpstone at Spring to occupy a cottage with about 5 acres of land—& the best is that when I get fixed in it it will be as certain a home as if it was my own—for I shall have a good landlord as Lord Milton owns it & altho I have had some difficulties to leave the woods & heaths & favourite spots that have known me so long for the very mole-hills on the heath & the old trees in the hedges seem bidding me farewell—other associations of friendships I have few or none to regret—for my father & mother will be often with me—& altho my flitting is not above three miles off—there is neither wood nor heath furze bush molehill or oak tree about it & a Nightingale never reaches as far in her summer excursions—would you believe it but the fact is it is so—but we must put aside such fancies for a season to live in the world by taking it as we find it—& my wishes have grown into resolves to better myself & I feel that I am commencing with a good oppertunity that keeps up my spirits & do you know I feel as happy at this moment as ever I did in my life—for I am looking at a sunny prospect—(there may be clouds but where is the sky without them) & I think that I shall yet live to see myself independant of all but old friends & good health & as the best way to end well is to begin well my desire is to start upon a new leaf—to get out of debt before I leave here & to keep out when

I commence a cottage farmer—the place I hear keeps two cows
& therefore I shall want a great deal to set me up & start me—
I dont much like to meddle with my fund money that is to
break it but I cannot get on without it so I must do it yet if I
could draw a sum upon it I would do so because I fancy I shall
be able to replace it as I think of saving somthing yearly by my
labour as its poor doing in working for nothing—therefore I
want your advice & that directly for my mind is made up & all
that remains is to make a beginning

I have never heard from you since you sent me the old Poets
neither have I written[2] but that vacancy is under such a heavy
cloud that I cannot even turn back to view the prospect I hope
the future will find me a good stock of health for without it all
else is nothing[*]

To Taylor

[January 1832]

My dear Taylor

In the paralyzing suspence your silence completely stultifyes
my intentions—I was in hopes that I was at the end of my
pilgrimage & that the shadow of independance if not the substance was won as all I wanted was to use my own means to sink
or swim as good luck or bad luck might hereafter alow me—&
to free myself from talking & writing kindnesses that hang like
a milstone about my feelings—I thought that one word to you
would procure this & that I should launch into the broad ocean
of liberty in my own boat—but no such thing the conclusion of
your letter to my neighbour[1] came like a broad big wave over-
powering every struggle & throwing me back upon the shore
among all the cold apathy of killing kindness that has numbed
me into a cypher for years—I am ready to stand if not able for I
wish to start out of debt & if twopence would do it I could get
no such bond here[†]

---

* Letter unfinished.   † Letter unfinished.

To the Rev. Charles Mossop[1]
[*sent*]

[Jan 1832]

DEAR SIR

Will you do me the favour to read this note of Earl Spencers
—it would appear that my money was sent on the 22nd of Dec[r]
& if so I never got it—therefore somebody else must & if there
is any deception used by anyone in the matter it should be found
out—I sent several times to the post after it but it was always
'not come' & yet if it is lost or made way with it is not too late
as I should hope to find out the mistake for that satisfaction
would be better to me than money itself—for though I am poor
I wish to be honest—& Lord Spencer may imagine that I got it
& then decieved him by not noteing it & I do assure you that
to my feelings suspicion is as bad as robbery—& I feel it
nessesary to make strict inquiry at Stamford & Deeping Post
offices & as I write for your advice if you think the same I will
do so for I cannot rest easy on doubts in such matters—& then
there is Taylors letters not as yet come & it would seem that
trouble had made use of every difficulty to urge my flitting—&
I shall be glad when time prepares me for starting

I almost feel that a poor mans honesty is mistrusted—while
the rich mans 'faults make graces' & I am ready to believe
Solomons advice to his son that 'it is better to die than to be
poor' in fact I am terribly troubled & I cannot help feeling that
the writing for & the hunting about & other appendages due in
apologys & thanks repeated & expected as eternally as the
ticking of a clock are of more trouble than the profits worth in
fact my spirit works up with independant feelings but she is such
a cripple that she cannot overtake them just yet—

Will you have the kindness to send me the book of the Plague
it should have gone home on Saturday last but I could not write
& so I neglected to do so—& if you have done with them—Mrs
Marshs Tracts—Lord Radstocks Sermons—& Hills Herbal—
as I want to look into them the rest you may keep as long as
you please—I do assure you my mind is in such trouble tho I
divert it as well as I can

Yours sincerely

JOHN CLARE

To Taylor

[1832]

I had been very troubled in mind when your letter reached me for I really thought that the difficultys the 'red sea' that now lies between me & the 'land of promise' would become impassable for do you know enemies have sprung up where I did not expect them—& the neighbour of mine had told me this morning that mine landlord had been talking it about the town that of my back rent—the fact is I owe him now for two years but I thought that my honest intentions would have given him feelings of more delicacy towards me then throwing tokens of my poverty into the mouths of my neighbours for no other purpose than that of insulting me because he is offended at my going to leave his house to better myself—these hurt me in such a manner that I felt the truth of Solomons advice as just 'My son it is better to die than to be poor'—now to get out of these difficulties about twenty pounds would release me for the present can you send me that sum to be settled hereafter & it would be now as a godsend—& then there is the great desert to be crossed & I shall want to start in April & if the money cannot be sold out surely we may get a less sum on its security—I have hopes & they are strong ones that I shall see the expected haven but I am so cast down by times that I dont know that I shall wether the storm*

To Jane Mossop

[sent]

[Spring 1832]

DEAR MADAM

You did me a kind favour in kindly offering to copy out Mrs Emmersons Song for the Bee† & I should have sent it in the letter long before this but I thought that as you had company

---

* Letter unfinished.

† *The Bee*, or *Stamford Herald and County Chronicle*, was founded in 1830 as a result of the political terrors and agitation of the times. Clare and Mrs. Emmerson contributed poems, but the old story was repeated—payment precarious or non-existent.

you would not have the time to spare & that was the only reason why I delayd it—your kind offer of taking it to Stamford for the Bee leaves me doubly indebted to you & for both kindnesses I doubly thank you as I should have had no means of sending it sooner than Friday

This weeks 'Bee' has not come to hand as yet & I cannot imagine what causes the delay but you know I am not a subscriber & therefore I must be content to catch it when I can—my head is better today—my best respects to your fireside—& to yourself dear Madam alow me to subscribe myself

Your very humble & obedient servant

J. CLARE

To Marianne Marsh

[sent]

[Spring 1832]

MY DEAR M.M.

Have the kindness to thank the Lady[1] for her opinions in my favour of wishing to have the names of my subscribers in the book—to please them was the first ambition that made me ambitious of the name of a Poet—& as to profit I never thought of it & have only just reccolected that I wanted it—yet my ambitions burn as proud as ever & womans praise is still the manna in the wilderness the Ladys opinion delights me & their names shall be printed & if they only left me one page to return my best thanks in their service that book would be to me the proudest I have published—but these reviewers who begin like bill stickers to vex me very much they would force it down the throat of the world that I am evoking charity when I am only seeking independance—yet while the ladys commend I will say to them

Go on ye shadows & let the sun shine

[There follows:]

I loved thee tho I told thee not . . .[2]

[and]

Critics tis vain to urge your spite . . .[3]

262

To Frank Simpson

[*sent*]

[Spring 1832]

MY DEAR FRANK

I never got the Paper last week & if it was omitted by mistake I wish you would correct it & send it by Patty but if it was not intended to send one—be sure you dont ask for it—I have been ruminating over 'A scene in the Election' & the Song on the other side* is a part of it—I thought of introducing 3 old women singing a song under the tricolour which they had made jointly by tearing up their petticoats & I thought of heading them or the mob by a sergeant in a blue sash who figured in the Election & who after being defeated by the constables commences with an harangue—& joins with the Mob in tempting the sailors who are passing by accident to join them—if you think anything of it I will go on with it for the pomposity of such scenes is cursed ridiculous—be as it will burn this scrawl after you have read it

I am dear Frank
Yours sincerely
JOHN CLARE

Send Mrs Emmersons letter back when you have done with it & a few words from yourself

To Jane Mossop

[*sent*]

[Spring 1832]

DEAR MADAM

I thank you very kindly for the favour of sending to the Bee on Monday altho I have nothing to send myself yet I felt desirous of sending Mrs Emmersons & as she sent me a fresh packet last night I send them also wishing you will have the kindness to send them altogether with the one you copied—your opinion of it is right & these too are no better—she writes

* *The Blues and the Sailors*, by 'Peter Pindar, Junr.,' —unpublished.

263

too much & that much too hasty but my task is not that of the critics & therefore I pass them as I recieved them—she often writes well—I have not wrote any reply about the song there is too much humbug in the stirring up [?]* to be of any use to me—but if I so far settle the bargain as to get hold of the money the dedication will rest with the publisher & not with myself & you may depend he'll have sufficient tact to select a fashionable name or somthing that suits his own interests & views

I shall feel very happy to enjoy Mr Mossops & your kind invitation on Monday evening if I am well for I am very unwell now & have been all day

I am yours sincerely

JOHN CLARE

To Charles Mossop

April 28 1832

J. Clare returns his best thanks to Mr Mossop for the use of The Comparative View'[1] &c & begs also to state that he will in a few days settle the little debt which he owes him & also thanks him for the kindness in lending him it—in the mean time as a preparation for starting to Northborough early on Monday morning he is obliged to say farewell to Mr & Miss Mossop for a little while & heartily wishes them both—health happiness & prosperity†

To Artis

[sent]

May 1832

DEAR ARTIS

I was very glad to hear of you & very sorry that the weather did not permit me to come or I would have been there on

* Word unreadable. We have not traced what the song was, but the implication is that it was political and Clare wished to have nothing to do with the politics of *The Bee* or any other paper.
† Letter unfinished.

Sunday perhaps you can ride over with Henderson before you go your journey & see me I should be glad to see you what are you doing in the book way anything I want to get out a new Vol but the way on which I have started is not very practicable for I want to make it a source of benefit[1]—give my respects to Mrs & Miss Artis & believe me yours very sincerely

JOHN CLARE

To Charles Mossop

[sent]

Northborough Aug 1 1832

MY DEAR SIR

I wish to ask your advice respecting a paragraph copied from the Athenaeum into most of the local papers pretending to know of a matter of which I know nothing viz. that Lord Milton has given me the cottage to live in &c &c.

Not that I should take any notice of the folly of such gossip further than it troubles me & injures my feelings of a propinquity of independence for I came into the cottage with no such feelings or expectations & it is too bad for anyone to surmise & publish their surmises for truth—I should hope his Lordship will not be offended at such stories for I cannot help it—nor did I know anything of it untill two or three days ago when the Editor of the Bee[1] with a friend from London came to see me & they were supprised at my ignorance of the matter saying it was first printed in the Athenaeum & copied into most of the others—but I positively told them my expectations were never so high & that I expected to pay rent the same as my neighbours—& that was all I knew of it—what is to be done should it be contradicted or should it be taken no notice of—I am very unwell & it troubles me in fact a trifle upsets me & my spirits are either elevated to extacy or depressed to nothings— but my intentions as to publishing are earnest—& I expect the prospectus will be finished to night—give my best respects to Miss Mossop.

Yours respect^{fy} & humb^{ly}

J. CLARE

To Jane Mossop

[sent]

Northborough Aug 1832

MY DEAR MISS MOSSOP

You see I have started in earnest—Clifton* offers to print the Verses at a reasonable price but I fear anything printed out of London will go a good way towards crushing the matter so I must wait before I promise it & hear from London

I shall be harping over success untill it goes to press & when published come what may if the trifles deserve favour they are sure to meet it so all I want is a sufficient number of names to start it & then 'God speed the Plough'

I have been very earnest in making up the Tales Ballads & Songs that I want for the Vol & very unwell but the thought of untying these tethers of difficulty that hopple both legs hands & all & numb my best resolution into nothingness—this thought makes me go on & the labour is as entertaining as play

I could not send any more this morning not knowing what I shall want but bye & bye I will send some for your friends—in the meantime I need not urge your endeavour for success because you was in earnest whèn I was doubtful & as my little boat only wants a push from the shore I've too good a faith in the Ladies to think they would hesitate to lend a hand for to their praise I owe much success—

I am

Yours sincerely & respectfully

J. CLARE

[To Cary]

[sent]

August 1832

MY DEAR SIR

Your kind letter was to me an happiness your philosophy of quietness was better than medicine to my mind for I was enduring ill health & impatience when I recieved it as it was

---

* A Peterborough printer.

accompanied by a very disaggreable fiction inserted by someone
in the Athenaeum & for what purpose I cannot tell for if he had
any knowledge of my affairs he must know he was uttering a
falsehood & if he had not he ought to have had some charity for
the feelings of another when he seems to have such high minded
qualities of his own diction & self pretentions as to become a
self authorized counsellor in my affairs & a dictator in the affairs
of others—it hurt my ambitions for I was seeking independance & not asking charity & had published a prospectus of my
intentions to publish a small vol for my own benefit—as I could
not get any money from Mr. Taylor of my own which he placed
in the funds & as he said he had nothing more in profits to
recieve then from my publication having recieved not a farthing
by the first Vol—it was my only remedy to try my own means
to accomplish what I wanted to cover my necessity & to set up
as a cottage farmer—I felt some vanity that I had a claim to the
title of a poet & it was the praise & commendation of men of
genius that fostered that ambition & your commendation given
early & continued long gave me a pride that the ephemeral
opinions of unknown interferences cannot take away—I thought
the offering a volume by subscription could neither hurt my
independence or lessen the claim I had to public notice—I
wished to be judged of by the book itself without any appeals to
want of education lowness of origin or any other foil that
officion [officiousness ?] chuses to encumber my path with but
it seems I must be encumbered never mind I must also write on
for ambition to be happy in sadness as verses make me urges
me onward & if I have merit summer insects may envy but
cannot destroy me & if I have not their buzzing authoritys are
nothings—they neither mar me nor make me—& yet I am
sadly teased & annoyed by their misrepresentations as they
must come from enemies in disguise I here send you a prospectus of my little cockleshell—your kindness in my affairs
makes me add this trouble to your judgment which my diffidence
would not have done had I not recieved your letter yet I wished
to ask your advice in the matter & now I shall ask your advice as
to a publisher for I think I have as many subscribers as will carry
me into the ocean of public opinion where merit will have its due
& that is all I ask for & when I hope success if you laugh at my

ambitions I am ready to laugh with you at my own vanity for I
sit sometimes & wonder over the little noise I have made in the
world untill I think I have written nothing as yet to deserve any
praise at all so the spirit of fame of living a little after life like
a name on a conspicuous place urges my blood upward into
unconscious melodys & striding down my orchard & homestead
I hum & sing inwardly those little madrigals & then go in &
pen them down thinking them much better things than they are
until I look over them again & then the charm vanishes into
the vanity that I shall do somthing better ere I die & so in spite
of myself I ryhme on & write nothing but little things at last—
& these trifles I would willingly trouble your judgment with if
you would do me the favour to waste a few hours over them—
I thought my old friends had all gone away with the world but
I find I have one almost 'the last of the flock' living still in my
ways so never mind our affections increase as our fellowships
diminish & I may be happily disappointed by the enemy[1] & once
more see the old familiar faces, as earnest in their affections &
then I shall shake hands with old time & be more happy than
when old time was new to me

God bless you my dear Sir
I am yours affectionately
JOHN CLARE

& thank God I am nothing in the sad situation they describe
& though some people thinking my promises were put up never
to pay applied at first the rash epithet of law threats to frighten
me out of their debt it was but for trifles—& having been
frightened for a season & having written to Taylor in this tenor
several letters & finding his impossibility could give me no
remedy I took heart faced my pursuers & told them candidly
that they had a good oppertunity for I could not prevent it &
this avowal which I expected would be the commencement of
hostilities against me brought me peace & turned threats into
kindness[2]—so in this truce I wrote this prospectus, got it
printed & sent it among well known friends about the neighbourhood & candidly asked for their assistance in making my
intentions known to their friends & the hearty readiness in
which they all enlisted in my cause set me in good earnest to

complete the scheme as the very best independance I had to get
out of the difficulty & I sent a printed sheet to Mr Taylor wishing him to aid me with a few subscribers & telling him he should
publish the book if he chose but I have not heard a syllable of
him either disapproval or commendment

To Taylor

*Addressed: Mr. George Stothert, c/o Mrs Taylor, Bolham Hall,
East Retford.*

Northborough Sept. 6th 1832

MY DEAR TAYLOR[1]

I had hopes that I should have heard from you about the
arrival of Mr Woodhouse & that I would have had the happiness
of making use of my own money but 'while the grass grows the
steed starves' & I am so tethered in difficultys that I can wear
against them no longer nor can I put up with the coldness &
insults of those to whom I am indebted any longer—for those to
whom I owe a few shillings even take advantage of my inn-
abillity to pay & look on me as if I owed them pounds & others
to whom I am indebted a few pounds seem to row over it as if
I owed them thousands & all because they know I am poor—
therefore with the advice of a few friends (& that of a young
lady[2] here whose [particular?] success is so great that she talks
of it as accomplished I have started to collect subscribers sufficient
to enable me to offer the Vol. to advantage to any publisher who
chooses & if you like to publish it for me it is at your service if
not you will procure me some subscribers which will do me a
favour & perhaps reccomend me to a publisher I feel the situation in which difficulty places me dreadfully but as my staff of
independance is broken by that accident that nobody foresees
viz. a large family an accident that is as dear to me as happiness
now—I must do as I can & I should think it is no shame to state
the truth of my difficultys as the cause of wishing to make an
attempt to get out of them & when I was ill last year my father
& mother often said 'John I should like to see another volume
printed before we die' I feel at times that I could not rest if they

were absent had I not attempted to gratify their wishes as well as my own nessesitys—

If Mr Woodhouse is returned do your earliest opportunity to serve me for I am as helpless as a child & every thing is going wrong with me.

Yours sincerely

JOHN CLARE

I have nothing as yet on the ground neither cow nor pigs nor anything else & am in fact worse off than before I entered on the place[3] & to add to the Depressions that distress me there is a paragraph going the round of the papers which is not true not even in shadow & therefore no body could know that which I know not myself & it obliged me to write to the Steward to show that I was no party in giving such a statement publicity for I thought such a feeling might be entertained by some who did not know me—I heard of it by a person from London of the name of Clarke[4] who called to see me but I thought it a mistake of his own untill I read it myself in the 'Observer' & it hurt me dreadfully—O for the [friendly friends?] & the unobtrusive quiet that I enjoyed twenty years ago when I was happy without knowing it & independant without a friend.*

To Charles Mossop

[sent]

Northborough

Sept 1832

DEAR SIR

Would you be kind enough to send me a few slips of the 'Irish Ivy'—rooted slips would be best if you could get them— I could not find time to call when last at Helpstone—but I shall be there again in a few days I have got subscribers for 49 copies of my intended publication but 18 are rather doubtful the rest are sure & I have not yet mustered the forces which friends & neighbours are enlisting for my benefit but I rather fancy I shall succeed & that beyond my expectation But I have not yet

* Letter unfinished.

270

finished the book & when I have I shall write to the London Publishers directly & the best bidder shall have it—Give my very best respects to Miss Mossop & I am Sir

Yours sincerely

J. CLARE

To the Editor of *The Athenaeum*[1]

[Autumn 1832]

DEAR SIR

Would you do me the favour to give my disapproval of these misstatements that are going the rounds of the papers in the shape of inflated pictures of my affairs—surely I have the same common right to come before the public as any other man & all I wish of the public is to judge of my productions as they please but I think no man can have the right to meddle with my affairs & make my poverty a peg to hang up his own prejudices & dictations as though he were a counsillor pleading a cause having authority only in making me a public beggar—I was not aware that my attempt to benefit myself would be the excuse for anyone putting forth these officious commentaries on my best intentions I need no such sympathy as these dictations put forth I am poor but my independence is not at so low an ebb as these antipathies testify & I feel them as little better than insults which harass me very much—I wish not to have my difficulties trumpeted by everyone who chuses to pen his spleen in my favour—I cannot imagine why these things should be thus represented & why one falsehood should be started before the other is cold by way of explaining it away I wish for peace and quietness & whoever abuses that is not my friend—officious interferences as to my adversity add nothing to my prosperity— let every tub stand on its own bottom—I gave no authority for such matters being published & when I put forth these prospectuses I did it with the intention of getting out of difficulty in a quiet way—never expecting to have my affairs bandied from pillar to post by everyone who has a place in a paper to put forth his opinions in the shape of likes & dislikes as though that writer was all the world & the world itself nothing—I never solicited praise or profit from any individual in my life & I am sure I should not be willing to have my little cockleshell set afloat in your paper the way it has been—I am not seeking charity but independence & if the writer of that commentary has any charity for my feelings he will excuse this attempt of mine to correct his information so far as to assure him that I am as independent of individual favours as himself.

With the manner which my first production came before the public I had little to do friends & real friends exerted their interests.[2]

My proposals for publishing my little Vol has by some means or other got into the columns of the Athenaeum newspaper & for the publishing my intentions more extensively I am certainly thankful but for the manner in which it is published I should have thought it a kindness had it been omitted altogether*

To Cunningham[1]

[*sent*]

Northborough Nov 11 1832

My dear Allan,

I was heartily pleased & pleasingly disappointed to meet with yourself in the shape of a letter, for I hardly ever expected to have seen you more, so it was a double pleasure which is much better than a single disappointment & as to my scrawl excuse it for whether to lay it to the pen or to myself I cannot tell—but the fact is I can write no better, for if I pause my hand trembles there out of all shape & I must go on at a gallop to be understood if so that you can read it at all.

I thank you heartily for your encouragement in the offer of assisting me in my endeavours to get up to the hill-top, for one volunteer, as the old saying has it, is worth fifty pressed men & as the greater part of my ambition is profit & not fame I have little diffidence in telling you my wishes which is to get as many subscribers as I can. For the money that was gathered for me by Lord Radstock on which I depended by drawing a portion to

* Letter unfinished.

start me is so placed in the funds that I am told I cannot get a portion from it & tho I do not doubt it was done with the best intentions yet it put my best intentions in jeopardy—for the first volume brought me nothing & the others when I got some accounts which I cannot understand seem to leave me in debt so I thought there was neither sin nor shame in trying to escape my difficulty in the best way I could & nothing but the publishing a volume by subscription seemed to make me certain of profit—So I wrote out a prospectus, & sent it to the printer before I had any inclination to waver, & sent one to Taylor telling him my intentions, & giving him the offer to print it if he chose, but he has not replied. I wish to hurt nobody but I have those around me that make me turn to the practical matters of pounds shillings and pence & although Mr. Taylor may have got nothing by the others to induce him to buy, I must turn so far a man of business myself as to make the best bargain I can. For of the first Volume I never got anything by a mere trick of the person who introduced it to Mr. Taylor stating he had bought it of me & giving me nothing but charging my little accounts with him to Taylor so that in fact I have lost, & that if I interpret rightly at not less than £40, but as I cannot make out the accounts I must wait the settlement & then I shall see.

I have a strong opinion of Taylor, & shall always respect him & I think if the matter had been entirely left to business & I had sold them out & out even for a trifle I should have been much better off & much better satisfied. The charges are so much in these accounts & the items so many that I could but fear & tremble for profit ere I tried my eye to the bottom to look for it, & I cannot but say God protect all hopes in difficulty from the patronage of Trade. When the Cow grows too old in profits in milk she is fatted & sold to the butchers & when the Horse is grown too old to work he is turned to the dogs, but an author is neither composed of the materials necessary for the profit of butchers meat or dogs meat—he is turned off & forgotten. But I anticipate success for I think I shall succeed very shortly to definite conceptions of being ready for print & I wait anxiously to hear from Mr. Burlowe[2] which I have not yet done. I send him to-day a letter with a few verses on the death of the Sun I mean Scotlands for I saw his end in the papers & felt it. He was kind to me in a notice in my early days of giving me 'The Lady of the Lake' & a gift to the care of a friend Captain Sherwill which I wished to be converted into books: viz Burns Works, Chattertons Poems & Southeys Nelson & I still possess them among the best valuables in my bookcase.

I have said so much of self that I have but little room left for what I most wished to say—I saw some account of your new Poem[3] in the papers & several extracts from your Lives of the Painters which I thought excellent & just what they should be full of anecdote & common sense & that makes me wish you to go on with your intentions of writing a biography of the Poets. The old ones are the most wanting of notice & when I saw Mr. Southey had engaged in the matter I was anticipating a treat, but all my old favourites which had been made so by Ellis Specimens were here either cut up into living skeletons or omitted as nonentities unworthy of a shadow of a name. A biographer may give his opinion on what he likes or dislikes but I like to see Editors give up their gardens to the reader's leisure to choose what flowers he pleases & not leave us to morsels & lock us out from the whole

Give my best respects to Mrs. C.

JOHN CLARE

To Eliza L. Emmerson

Northborough Nov 13 1832

MY DEAR ELIZA

I was delighted to see your handwriting for I have been in such an excess of melancholly that I was obliged to-day to send over to Deeping for some medicine which I have commenced taking for last night my very brains seemed to boil up almost into madness & my arms & legs burnt as it were with a listless feebleness that almost rendered them useless & I got so fearful of myself that I determined to-day to seek a remedy which I am now taking & which I doubt not will relieve me for the doctor is well aware what medicine my constitution needs but it is a sad thing to feel such a debility that will neither bear rest or fatigue long together & I am truly sorry for yourself but you must cheer up & keep on & live to write my epitaph for the great stone which I once mentioned—I am truly sorry that those things should have got into the papers about Mr Taylor & it hurt me much more than if my name only had been mentioned because such things can neither mar me nor make me & all I wish now is to stand on my own bottom as a poet without any apology as to want of education or anything else & I say it not in the feeling of either ambition or vanity but in the spirit of common sense—last Saturday I recieved a parcel of books from Mr How as a present whose residence I gave wrong in my last to you it is No 13 & in them the numbers of the 'Alfred' & the 'Athenaeum in which those paragraphs were inserted Mr How writes as though he caused the one to be inserted in the 'Alfred' & Allan Cunningham has written to say he inserted the other in the 'Athenaeum' & if I did not believe that the best intentions of serving me placed them there I should have certainly fancied them as no compliments & I wrote to Mr How to tell him that I did not wish to have my poverty printed twice over & also that I felt a stubborn belief that Taylor was a sincere friend & I also corrected the misrepresentation by telling him it was the persons misrepresentations who introduced my poems to Taylor that deprived me of all profits in the first Vol.* in fact I have brunted the loss of £40 by it if so that the matter is to pass uncorrected—for he never gave me sixpence further than what he charged for to Mr. Taylor & when Mr Taylors accounts came down I was astonished to see an item of £20 for copy right & another item of £20 for which I had had nothing—I wrote to him wishing him to correct the mistakes but as reguard the Copyright he was silent & as to the other it was he said 'for moneys & goods' & there was the burden still on my back & no remedy to remove it—when I thought him a friend he was always whishing me to appear as if he had purchased the Vol as he said Taylor & Hessey would deprive him of the profit so I was easy & consented it should be so but I never expected he intended to cheat me into a charge for what I never had—it was to have been *deducted* from the accounts & he *added* it to them— though I never sold the Vol I am made the loser & have been

---

* In spite of Clare's efforts, Taylor also saw the articles in *The Alfred* and *The Athenaeum*, and by January was threatening litigation.

duped as it were to purchase my own which is a most damnable heresy—& seeing these things before my eyes I felt determined to do as other folk did sell for the sake of a bargain—when Drury got to Lincoln he wrote two letters to me that if I did not pay him my accounts he should proceed in another way I then wrote to Taylor in fear wishing to turn over all my little property into his & Hesseys hands as I expected the Shark called Law would swallow the whole they then sent down for Drurys bill which he had entered to make out into nearly as much more as it ought to have been & on my objecting to it he took a great portion off & then I knew it was too much but I had no means of correcting it for I kept no accounts against him so it passed on till I after repeated wishes got Mr Taylors accounts down & to my astonishment I found that Drury had sent in in a secret way the above £20 accounts to Taylor a fabrication to a faction which I expect he paid & so you see who is the cheater I am always mad at the meanness when I think of it but I am very sorry that Taylor should be brought into the matter for I am sure he is utterly above such things & like myself a man of business only by necessity—all I wish is that he would clear up a settlement so far that I might be enabled to know how matters stand in his hands it is an happy thing to be free & if the ballance should turn out against me he shall not lose by me if I can get profit enough by this for I will pay everyone to the last farthing & then I shall be happy my creditors if I may so call them to whom I owe trifling sums of money have till lately acted as friends that is depended on my promises & let me alone but a few of them have got rather impatient with dissapointment & threatened me with law but I turned round like the dog at bay & took the resolution to state how matters stood with me & that if they chose to put their threats into execution I could not prevent it & although I expected this confession would commence hostilities it produced a feeling in my favour & one wrote to me in the warmest terms of friendship & gave a proof that he would never hurt me which pleased me much & I shall never forget the kindness

　　Two or three days ago I wrote a few stanzas on the memory of Sir Walter Scott & thinking them at first much better then I think them now I wished to have sent them to you but as I had heard nothing I thought 3 letters would bother you so Harry who had been wishing me to send him somthing for a paper or Magazine got into the trouble of them & I have heard nothing as yet from him

I will send you next a copy of the accounts of my bill so that you may see what it is for I cannot understand it at all though I have puzzled over it with the very excess of my wisdom in pounds shillings & pence

Yours &c &c &c

untill I get into sufficient room to subscribe myself yours very sincerely

JOHN CLARE

Remember me to Mr. E.

I must tell you this letter is only half finished & for the want of room I will write you another before the weeks out & fill it up with other trifles

To T. Henderson

[sent]

Northborough
April 22 1833

DEAR HENDERSON

I should be much obliged to you for a little spinnage seed Lettuce seed Carrot seed & Turnip seed—I have been unwell or I should have sent for them sooner or made a journey for them myself—excuse a short note for I have little inclination to scribble at present

Yours &c &c

JOHN CLARE

To John Taylor[1]

Northborough Sept 1833

DEAR SIR

I recieved your kind letter & should have answered it sooner but from severe indisposition I have not been able which I feel you will kindly excuse

277

The Poems are now in preparation for the press & will be published I dare say very shortly at least I hope so I thank you very kindly for the liberal manner in which you have become a subscriber*

To Thomas Emmerson†

Northborough 1834

MY DEAR EMMERSON

I thank you very kindly for the trouble you have taken in the book[1] & am pleased that you have succeeded so well—but my indisposition still makes me unable to say much I return the check as you desired & you can send it in any way you think best—& I shall try to get out of debt as soon & I feel thankful for your kindness in wishing to look over my accounts which I will send up as soon as I can get them in & I think they do not exceed the sum I have stated—The bills sent in by one man exceed are almost‡

To Taylor

Northborough April 12 1834

MY DEAR TAYLOR

I feel anxious to write to you & have but little to say I am sorry that I am but little better though to all appearances as well as ever I was in my life & though I have had a good nights rest I feel little better I am still troubled & fancy§

To Eliza L. Emmerson

Northborough May 1834

MY DEAR ELIZA

I feel so little better in fact I feel so ill that I feel an inclination to come to London to see Dr Darling he has prescribed for me & the things he sent has done me no good but I think if I could get up he would do me good & that directly‖

* Letter unfinished.   † See Biographical Memoranda on Mrs. Emmerson.
‡ Letter unfinished.   § Letter unfinished.   ‖ Letter unfinished.

To How of Whittaker's

[*sent*]

Northborough 1834
p.m. ' 13 ' or ' 25 Ju '

My ' Dear Sir

You will have considered me very neglecting in not having acknowledged your many kindnesses from time to time in sending me the Journal[1] but the fact is & it hurts me to own it that I have not been able & I have recieved many kind letters from strangers which I have never answered from inability to do so & I have suffered much in not being able to tell them I could not—I feel an anxiety sometimes that the book should be out & if I am any hinderance in its way I am sorry but I feel more & more that I am not able to assist in its publication but my old friend J. Taylor has offered to do anything I wish & I should like the proofs to go through his hands[2] as I shall be quite satisfied in any thing he wishes & thinks should be altered or ommitted I have written the preface[3] but am little satisfied with it & the dedication may be worded as custom generally does but I think the shorter the better—you have published a book on birds[4] & though I read but little it is a book I have long wished to see & if you will send it me at the trade price I shall thank you for the kindness

Yours etc
JOHN CLARE

To Taylor

Northborough July 10 1834

My dear Taylor

I am scarcely able to write to tell you that I am anxious to hear from you & to have your advice I want to get up to London if I can for I feel if I could see Dr Darling I should get better*

* Letter unfinished.

279

To Behnes Burlowe

Northborough Nov 12 1834

MY DEAR HARRY

I wish to hear how you are & I hope you will write directly
to tell me I am ill able to write & little able to bear dissapointment so write to me directly & it will give me great
pleasure to hear from you how are your brothers* & all your
friends & what are you doing I thank God my wife & family
are all well but as for myself I am scarcely able to do anything
yet I feel if I could get to London I should soon be right & I hope
I shall be able to get there before long my eldest boy wishes to
be remembered to you & is very anxious to get some instruction in drawing he has often wished me to write to you to get
him a drawing book but I have not been able to do so before
now—he has got a box of paints & only waits for some instructions which I hope you will put in your letter & write as soon as
you can will you call on Mrs Emmerson as I wish to write to
her but cannot tell whether she is at home send me all the news
you can & write as soon as you can excuse a short letter &
believe me yours very sincerely

JOHN CLARE

To Henderson

Northborough Novr 1834

MY DEAR HENDERSON

Will you give me a few flowers I have been very ill & am
scarcely able to do anything I have just got a proof of the new
poems to correct but I can do nothing with it†

---

* Behnes Burlowe had but one brother, the unregenerate one who had caused
him to change his name.
† Letter unfinished.

To Taylor

[*sent*]
Northborough Dec. 1. 1834.

MY DEAR TAYLOR

I am anxious to hear from you will you write to me directly I
am not very well a nobleman* has been to see me but I could not
talk to him neither did I know who he was untill he was going
away but I am scarcely able to see anybody I feel a great desire
to get to London if I could & think I should soon be better I
have little to say just now & hope you will excuse a short letter
I have seen the engravings for the poems & I expect they will
soon be out God bless you my dear Taylor write to me directly
thank God the childern are all well again God bless you

I am yours sincerely

JOHN CLARE

To Taylor

Addressed: John Taylor Esq, 30 Upper Gower St, London.
[*sent*]
Northborough Jan. 6th 1835.

MY DEAR TAYLOR

I am very anxious to write to you & though scarcely able I do
so to know how you are & I hope you will write directly for it
always gives me pleasure to hear from you so write as soon as
you can I am rather anxious to hear about the Vol & all other
news you have to tell me I am sorry to say I have not yet got
Earl Spencers Sallary & I do not know when I shall what would
you have me do have the kindness to tell me for it is past the
time I used to have it formerly have the kindness to write to me
as soon as you possibly can & excuse me a short letter for I am
not able to write a longer yet I am as usual yours very faithfully & sincerely

JOHN CLARE

* Perhaps the new Earl Spencer: it could hardly be 'Lord Carborough'
mentioned in the letter to Taylor 16 February 1837.

I am so very afflicted that I am scarcely able to get across the house & have not [been] to Helpstone this two years God bless you & I am happy to say that the childern are all well but we have had the loss to bury the youngest[1] my father also has been very ill all the winter & under medical advice but he is now better

Yours sincerely

JOHN CLARE

To Earl Spencer

Northborough nr Market Deeping

Jan 12 1835

My Lord

Your noble Father has been for many years one of my greatest benefactors sending me £10 a year which with 15£ a year from the Marquis of Exeter & £13 15 6 a year from money subscribed for me & placed in the Funds mounting altogether to £38 15 6 makes up the whole of my income I recieved* to recieve it in a check every midsummer†

To Taylor

Northborough Jan 15 1835

My dear Taylor

I recieved the money very safely & thank you very kindly for the parcel of books though I am little able to read yet the Magazine always entertains me I thank you also for telling the best way to write to Lord Spenser[1] for though I could scarcely do without the money I had not the resolution to write for it & I think never should have done so I am sorry to hear your account of poor Charles Lamb[2] & the loss of our friend Reynolds[2] & I am sorry to hear that your own health is so much like my own

---

* Used ?   † Letter unfinished.

To Taylor

Addressed: John Taylor, Esq., 30 *Upper Gower St, London.*
[*sent*]

Northborough August 27/1835

MY DEAR TAYLOR

I ought to have written long ago but I have not been able I
thank you kindly for the parcel & am very pleased with the
review[1] but I am scarcely able to do any thing I feel anxious to
get up to London & think I should get better how would you
advise me to come I dare not come up by myself do you think
one of my children would do to come with me write to me as
soon as you can God bless you excuse a short letter for I am not
able to say more Thank God my wife & family are all well
believe me ever yours

JOHN CLARE

To Dr. Darling

[Autumn 1835]

MY DEAR DR DARLING

I write to tell you I am very unwell & though I cannot
describe my feelings well I will tell you as well as I can—sounds
affect me very much & things evil as well [as] good thoughts
are continually rising in my mind I cannot sleep for I am asleep
as it were with my eyes open & I feel chills come over me & a
sort of nightmare awake I got no rest last night I feel a great
desire to come up but perhaps I shall not be able & I hope you
write down directly for I feel you can do me good & if I was in
town I should soon be well so I fancy for I do assure you I am
very unwell & I cannot keep my mind right as it were for I wish
to read & cannot—there is a sort of numbing through my
private parts which I cannot describe & when I was so indis-
posed last winter I felt as if I had inflamation [?] in the blood
& at times as if it went round me & at other times such a
sinking as if I was going to sink through the bed—& though not
so bad now I am really very uneasy in fact I have never been

right as it were since then here is all I can say just now but I hope you can send something to benefit me give my respects to Taylor & I remain

Yours sincerely
JOHN CLARE

I fear I shall be worse & worse ere you write to me for I have been out for a walk & can scarcely bear up against my fancys or feelings

To Henderson

[sent]
Northborough Jany 13 1836

MY DEAR HENDERSON

Will you have the kindness to give me a few shrubs & flowers a few woodbines & somthing my wife calls everlasting have you got a drooping willow & double blossomed furze my wife also wants a red japonica I am hardly able to say more God bless you

Yours ever JOHN CLARE

To Taylor

Addressed: John Taylor Esq, 30 Upper Gower St, London.
[sent]
Northborough Feb 16 1837

MY DEAR TAYLOR

I am scarcely able to write but I have met so many kind-nessess from Scotland that I wish to send a friend of the Aloa Bank[1] my poems would you have the kindness to send the four Vols he wished for a picture & I wrote to Mrs Emmerson for one but she never writes he will give from thirty shillings to two pound could you get one write directly I think Rippingille would do one a sketch will do I wish to return his kindness can I get a Bust will you enquire I have many poems here I want you to have the best I have done my wife & family are all well God bless you

Yours ever
JOHN CLARE

To Taylor

Addressed: John Taylor, Esq, 30 Gower St, London.
[*sent*]

Northborough May 5 1837.

MY DEAR TAYLOR

I thank you kindly for sending the parcel you sent too many
I only wanted the four Vols & the two others they dont know
I am scarcely able to write I have got the drawing done here you
& Mrs Emmerson are the best friends I have & just as you was
the Lord was Lord Carborough I did not send to Earl Spencer
because I could not write & I sent to the others without any but
Lord Fitzwilliam & Lord Exeter know me & take no notice
many have left me because I cannot write but the best are just
as they was Sherwill wrote & told me he would send me some
books he had written but he never did have you seen his travels
I should like you & Mrs Emmerson to see all I have & more
but yourself can make out what I have done if I get better I shall
send them I should like to see Hilton & Cary The Curate* here
draws well & has made many sketches from the poems God
bless you

Yours ever

JOHN CLARE

To Frank Simpson[1]

Northborough
[1835–7]

DEAR FRANK

Would you have the kindness to ask Mr Ryde for my
quarters salary & place it in the hands of the bearer of this note
who will deliver it safely to me—my wife not being able to get
over for it herself & I have been so very unwell myself as
scarcely to be able to write†

---

* C. W. Chalklen.   † Letter unfinished.

ASYLUM LETTERS
1837–1864

Some say that Happiness is not good for Mortals, and they ought to be answered that sorrow is not good for Immortals, a blight never does good to a tree, and if a blight kill not a tree, but it shall bear fruit, let none say that the fruit was in consequence of the blight.—WILLIAM BLAKE

LEPPIT'S HILL LODGE
HIGH BEECH

ASYLUM LETTERS
1837–1864

To Patty

MY DEAR WIFE

I write to tell you I am getting better I cant write a long letter but wish to know how you all are the place here is beautiful* & I meet with great kindness the country† is the finest I have seen write & tell me how you all are I cant write a long letter but I shall do better God bless you all kiss them all for me

     Yours ever

       my dear wife

         JOHN CLARE

To Mary Joyce[1]

[1841]

MY DEAR WIFE MARY[2]

I might have said my first wife first love & first everything— but I shall never forget my second wife & second love for I loved her once as dearly as yourself & almost do so now so I determined to keep you both for ever—& when I write to you I am writing to her at the same time & in the same letter God bless

---

* Dr. Matthew Allen's private asylum at High Beech, Essex.
† Epping Forest.

289

you both for ever & both your families also I still keep writing though you do not write to me for if a man has a wife & I have two—but I tell it in a couplet with variations as my poetry has been the world's Hornbook for many years—

> *For if a husband will not let us know*
> *That he's alive—he's dead—or maybe so*

No one knows how sick I am of this confinement possessing two wives that ought to be my own & cannot see either one of the other If I was in prison for felony I could not be served worse than I am Wives ought to be allowed to see their husbands anywhere religion forbids them being parted but I have not even religion on my side & more's the pity I have been rather poorly I might say ill for 8 or 9 days before hay making & to get myself better I went a few evenings on Fern Hill & wrote a new Canto of 'Child Harold'³ & now I am better I sat under the Elm trees in old Mathew's Homestead Leppits Hill where I now am—2 or 3 evenings & wrote a new canto of Don Juan³—merely to pass the time away but nothing seemed to shorten it in the least & I fear I shall not be able to wear it away—nature to me seems dead & her very pulse seems frozen to an icicle in the summer sun—

What is the use of shutting me up from women in a petty paltry place as this merely because I am a married man & I daresay though I have two wives if I got away I should soon have a third & I think I should serve you both right in the bargain by doing so for I dont care a damn about coming home now—so you need not flatter yourselves with many expectations of seeing me nor do I expect you want to see me or you would have contrived to have done it before now [a change in the writing suggests the letter was finished off on another occasion]

My dear Mary take all the good wishes from me as heart can feel for your own husband & kiss all your dear family for their abscent father & Pattys childern also & tell Patty that her husband is the same man as he was when she married him 20 years ago in heart & good intentions God bless you both & your familys also I wish you both to keep in good health & be happy as I shall soon be when I have the good luck to be with you all at home once again—the love I have for you my dear Mary was never altered by time but was always increased by abscence

I am my dear Mary

Your affectionate husband

JOHN CLARE

To Eliza Phillips[1]

[1841]

MY DEAR ELIZA PHILLIPS

Having been cooped up in this Hell of a Madhouse till I seem to be disowned & even forgot by my enemies, for there is none to accept my challenges which I have from time to time given to the public I am almost mad in waiting for a better place & better company & all to no purpose It is well known that I am a prize-fighter by profession & a man that never feared anybody in my life either in the ring or out of it—I do not much like to write love letters but this which I am now writing to you is a true one—you know that we have met before & the first oppertunity that offers we will meet again—I am now writing a New Canto of Don Juan which I have taken the liberty to dedicate to you in remembrance of Days gone bye & when I have finished it I would send you the vol if I knew how in which there is a new Canto of Child Harold also—I am my dear Eliza

Yours sincerely

JOHN CLARE

To Patty

[sent]

Leppits Hill[1] March 17 1841

MY DEAR WIFE PATTY

It Makes Me More Than Happy To Hear That You & My Dear Family Are All Well—And You Will Be As Well Pleased To Hear That I Have Been So Long In Good Health & Spirits As To Have Forgotten That I Ever Was Any Otherwise—My Situation Here Has Been Even From The Beginning More Than

Irksome But I Shake Hands With Misfortune & Wear Through The Storm—The Spring Smiles & So Shall I—But Not While I Am Here—I Am Very Happy To Hear My Dear Boy Mention His 'Brother's & Sister's So Kindly As I Feel Assured That They Love One Another As They Ever Have Done—It Was My Lot To Seem As Living Without Friends Untill I Met With You & Though We Are Now Parted My Affection Is Un-altered—& We Shall Meet Again I Would Sooner Wear The Trouble's Of Life Away Single Handed Than Share Them With Others—As Soon As I Get Relieved On Duty Here I Shall Be In Northamptonshire—Though Essex Is A Very Pleasant County —Yet To Me 'There Is No Place Like Home'—As My Children Are All Well—To Keep Them So Be Sure & Keep Them In Good Company & Then They Will Be Not Only Well But Happy—For What Reason They Keep Me Here I Cannot Tell For I Have Been No Otherwise Than Well A Couple Of Year's At The Least & Never Was Very Ill Only Harrassed By Perpetual Bother—& It Would Seem By Keeping Me Here One Year After Another That I Was Destined For The Same Fate Agen & I Would Sooner Be Packed On A Slave Ship For Africa Than Belong To The Destiny Of Mock Friends & Real Enemies—Honest Men & Modest Women Are My Friends

Give My Best Love To My Dear Children & Kiss The Little One's For Me Good Bye & God Be With You All For Ever

I Had Three Seperate Dream's About Three Of Your Boys Frederick John & William—Not Any Ways Remarkable Only I Was In A Wreck With The Latter—Such Things Never Trouble Me Now In Fact Nothing Troubles Me & Thank God It Is So—I Hope The Time Is Not Long Ere I Shall See You All By Your Own Fireside Though Every Day In Abscence Seem's To Me Longer Than Year's

I Am My Dear Wife Your Affectionate Husband

JOHN CLARE

P.S. Give My Love To The Dear Boy Who Wrote To Me & To Her Who Is Never Forgotten

God Bless You All

J. CLARE

To Mrs Martha Turner Clare

292

To Mary Joyce [?]

[1841]

MY DEAREST MARY*

As This Will Be My Last Letter To You Or Any One Else
—Let My Stay In Prison Be As Long Or As Short As It May—
I Will Write To You & My Dear Patty In The Same Letter†

To Mary Joyce‡

Northborough
July 27 1841

MY DEAR WIFE

I have written an account of my journey or rather escape
from Essex for your amusement & hope it may divert your
leisure hours—I would have told you before now that I got here
to Northborough last Friday night but not being able to see you
or hear where you were I soon began to feel homeless at home
& shall bye & bye feel nearly hopeless but not so lonely as I did
in Essex for here I can see Glinton Church & feeling that Mary
is safe if not happy I am gratified Though my home is no home
to me my hopes are not entirely hopeless while even the memory
of Mary lives so near me God bless you my dear Mary give my
love to your dear beautifull family & to your Mother—& believe
me as I ever have been & ever shall be

My dearest Mary
Your affectionate Husband

JOHN CLARE

* This letter is from the small High Beech notebook.
† Letter unfinished.
‡ On 24 July 1841, the day after his arrival at Northborough, Clare made
this entry in his notebook:
' Returned home out of Essex & found no Mary. She & her family are nothing
to me now though she herself was once the dearest of all—& how can I forget.'
For three days he was occupied in writing the story of his journey. When
finished, he added the above letter, addressed 'To Mary Clare—Glinton'.

To Dr. Matthew Allen[1]

dear Sir

[August 1841]

My dear Sir

Having left the Forest in a hurry & not time to take my leave of you & your family but I intended to write & that before now but dullness & dissapointment prevented me for I found your words true on my return here having neither friends or home left but as it is called the 'Poet's Cottage' I claimed a lodging in it where I now am—one of my fancys I found here with her family & all well—they met me on this side Werrington[2] with a horse & cart & found me all but knocked up for I had travelled from Essex to Northamptonshire without ever eating & drinking all the way safe one pennyworth of beer which was given me by a farm servant near an old house called the Plough I eat grass to keep me going—but on the last day I chewed tobacco & never felt hungry afterwards—where my poetical fancy is I cannot say for the people in the neighbourhood tell me that the one called Mary has been dead these eight years but I can be miserably happy in any situation & in any place & could have staid in yours in the Forest if any of my friends had noticed me or come to see me but the greatest annoyance in such places as yours are those servants & stupid keepers who often assumed as much authority over me as if I had been their prisoner & not liking to quarrel I put up with it till I was weary of the place altogether so I heard the voice of freedom & started & could have travelled to York with a penny loaf & a pint of beer for I should not have been fagged in body only one of my old shoes had nearly lost the sole before I started & let in the water & silt the first day & made me crippled & lame to the end of my journey

I had Eleven Books sent me from How & Parsons Booksellers some lent & some given me—out of the Eleven I only brought 5 Vols back & as I dont want any part of Essex in Northamptonshire agen I wish you would have the kindness to send a servant to get them for me I should be very thankfull Not that I care about the books altogether only it may be an

* See Biographical Memoranda.

excuse to see me & get me into company that I do not want to be acquainted with one of your labourer's pretty wifes borrowed Childe Harold & Mrs Fishers daughter has two or three more all Lord Byrons poems—Mrs King late of the Owl Public house at Leppits Hill & now of Enfield Highway has two or three all Lord Byrons Poems & The Hours of Idleness

You told me something before haytime about the Queen alowing me a yearly sallery of £100 & that the first quarter had then commensed or else I dreamed so—if I have the mistake is not of much consequence to anyone save myself & if true I wish you would get the Quarter³ for me if due as I want to be independant & pay for board & lodging while I remain here—I look upon myself as a widow or bachelor I dont know which—I care nothing about the women now for they are faithless & deceitfull & the first woman where there was no man but her husband found out means to cucold him by the aid & assistance of the Devil. but women being more righteous now & men more plentiful they have found out a more godly way to do it without the devil's assistance. & a man who possesses a woman possesses loss without gain the worst is the road to ruin & the best is nothing like a good cow—man I never did like much & woman has long sickened me I should [like?] to be to myself a few years & lead the life of a hermit—but even there I should wish for one whom I am always thinking of & almost every song I write has some sighs or wishes in Ink about Mary If I have not made your head weary by reading this I have tired my own by writing it so I will bid you goodbye

I am my dear Doctor
Yours very sincerely
JOHN CLARE

Give my best respects to Mrs Allen & Miss Allen & to Dr Stedman also to Campbell⁴ & Hayward & Howard at Leopards Hill or in fact to any of the others who may think it worth while to inquire about me.

To George Reid, of Glasgow*

[sent]

Northborough 17. Nov. 1841

MY DEAR SIR

When your letter reached Northborough I was there also—having left Essex or rather made my escape from it on the 23 July since which time I have never seen any company or made any visits anywhere Solitude being my chief society & Nature my best companion Your enquiry to Patty after my health leaves me to say that I am very well, that is, as well as middling, for my mind is, as it always has been from a boy—a disappointment I have never had the perusal of a Newspaper for some years & if you have any entertaining incidents in your Scotch papers I should thank you for the loan of one now & then Could you give me any literary news I myself left my Byron Poems behind me but I did not stay to know or hear what became of them & I have written some since I returned with an account of my escape from Essex. I was three nights & four days on the road without food & lodging, but being used to rough voyages all my life it did not affect my health much, only it made me very lame in one foot from having on a bad shoe. The sole was nearly off when I started & its keeping on till I got here was little less than a miracle I am now more comfortable & remain

my dear Sir
Yours sincerely
JOHN CLARE

To Charles Clare

[sent]

Northampton Asylum June 15 1847

MY DEAR BOY

I am very happy to have a letter from you in your own handwriting & to see you write so well I am also glad that your

* This letter is from a transcript which has found its way into the Brooke-Taylor manuscripts.

Brothers & Sisters are all in good health & your Mother also
be sure to give my love to her but I am very sorry to hear the
News about your Grandfather¹ but we must all die—& I must
[say?] that Frederick & John² had better not come unless they
wish to do so for its a *bad Place* & I have fears that they may
get trapped as prisoners as I hear some have been I may not
see them nor ever hear they have been here I only tell them &
leave them to do as they like best—its called the Bastile by
some & not with[out?] reasons—how does the flowers get on
I often wish to see them—& are the young children at home I
understand there are some I have not yet seen kiss them & give
my love to them & to your Mother & Brothers & Sisters & my
respects to John Bellars³ & to your neighbours on each side of
you Mr & Mrs Sefton⁴ & Mr & Mrs Bellars & others who
enquire after me I have never been ill since I have been here
save a cold now & then of which I take no notice
Believe me my dear Boy
that I remain your affectionate Father
JOHN CLARE

To Charles Clare

[*sent*]
Northampton Asylum
Feb^r 1848

MY DEAR SON

I was very happy to recieve your Letter to hear you was all in
good health—your Mother & Brothers & Sisters & as satisfactory to tell you I am as well myself thank God for it

When I first came here I saw some of your little Brothers &
Sisters little Boys & Girls with red heads & others also dirty
& healthy which satisfied me very well some of them were with
your own Sisters which left home before you were born—my
dear Boy it does not signifye to a good boy or Girl how they
are drest or of what colour the hair is when you are men you
will know so—the warmth of our clothing & not the show is all
thats required—Pride is an unnessesary evil—I readily excuse
your Brothers John & William for not coming here & in fact

beg them not to trouble themselves at all about it unless it would give them pleasure to do so—I tell you all Brothers & Sisters to love truth be Honest & fear Nobody—Amuse yourselves in reading & writing—you all have the Bible & other suitable books—I would advise you to study Mathematics Astronomy Languages & Botany as the best amusements for instruction—Angling is a Recreation I was fond of myself & there is no harm in it if your taste is the same—for in those things I have often broke the Sabbath when a boy & perhaps it was better then keeping it in the village hearing Scandal & learning tipplers frothy conversation—'The fields his study nature was his book' I seldom succeeded in Angling but I wrote or rather thought Poems made botanical arrangements when a little Boy which men read & admired I loved nature & painted her both in words & colours better than many Poets & Painters & by Perseverance & Attention you may all do the same—in my boyhood Solitude was the most talkative vision I met with Birds bees trees flowers all talked to me incessantly louder than the busy hum of men & who so wise as nature out of doors on the green grass by woods & streams under the beautiful sunny sky daily communing with God & not a word spoken—The best books on Angling are by Piscator[1] & Henry Phillips[2] & Sir Humphrey Davies[3] though we must not over look the Father of Anglers Isaac Walton 'Art of Angling or the Contemplative Mans Recreation' a choice book with all Fishermen & there is many others every way as good—I had hopes I should have seen the Garden & Flowers [by?] now—but we cannot reckon on any thing before hand—The future is with providence & unknown till it comes to pass—Like old Muck Rake in the Pilgrims Progress I know nothing in other peoples business & less in whats to come or happen—'There is nothing like home' give my love to Mr & Mrs Bellars & Mrs Sefton & remember me to all your neighbours who enquire after me particularly old John Green whose words came true & who was the only Person who persuaded me not to come here—you never mentioned your Grandfather give my love to him & believe my love to you all while I remain my dear Children

your affectionate Father

JOHN CLARE

To Patty

[sent]

July 1848

My dear Wife

I have not written to you a long while but here I am in the land of Sodom where all the peoples brains are turned the wrong way I was glad to see John[1] yesterday & should like to have gone back with him for I am very weary of being here—You might come & fetch me away for I think I have been here long enough I write this in a green meadow [by?] the side of the river agen Stokes Mill[2] & I see three of your daughters & a Son now & then—The confusion & roar of Mill-dams & locks is sounding very pleasant while I write it & its a very beautiful evening—the meadows are greener that usual after the shower & the meadows are brimful I think it is about two years[3] since I was first sent up to this Hell & not allowed to go out of the gates—There never was a more disgraceful deception than this place

Keep yourselves happy & comfortable & love one another—Bye & bye I shall be with you perhaps before you expect me—there has been a great storm here with thunder & hail that did much damage to the glass in the neighbourhood—Hail-stones the size of Hen's eggs fell in some places—did your brother John come to Northborough or go to Barnack His uncle John Riddle came the next morning but did not stay I thought I was coming home but I got cheated—I see many of your little brothers & sisters at Northampton weary & dirty with hard work some of them with red hands but all in ruddy good health

To Charles Clare

[sent]

Northampton Asylum Oct 17 1848

My dear Son

I am glad to hear from you & write agen directly to say I am quite well & never was better in my life thank God for it. I am very glad to hear that your Mother & Brothers & Sisters are quite well also your Aunt Sophy Uncle & Aunt Riddle[1] & make them all the same return from me

We have had a very large Flood here the largest that has been known for many years & it seems not to have gone down yet—I think I shall not be long now before I see you & as I have so particularly enquired after each & all of you so lately in my last I shall only say God bless you all now & forever—live happy & comfortable together in your old house at home for go where we will & be as we may *always* remember 'there is no place like Home' be good children & be kind to your Mother & always obey her wishes & you will never do wrong I always found it so myself & never got into error when I did it

Your Brother John promised Mr Knight to send him with your Brothers & Sisters consent the loan of a Volume of MS Poems in your Possesion—You have my free consent to do so as soon as you like[2]

I am my dear Charles
Your affectionate Father
JOHN CLARE

To Charles Clare

[*sent*]
Northampton Asylum April 2 1849

MY DEAR SON CHARLES

I am happy to hear from you at any time but more particularly now as I am quite lost in reveries & false hums[1] I am now in the ninth year of my captivity among the Babylonians & any news from Home is a Godsend of blessing I am glad to hear your Mother & Brothers & Sisters are all well as this letter leaves me at present thank God for it & also my Grand Children God bless them kiss all the little ones for me & tell them it was sent from their father for I have no money to send them sweetmeats or Playthings or Books—The Sherwood Foresters name is Mr S. C. Hall[2] & not Knight as you write he has been here & said he would call & see you he left me the same little book 'The Upland Hamlet & other Poems'

I know of no 'Three or four Volumes of MS. Poems that have not been published' as we searched them all over & completed every fragment for the Press but if you think otherwise you may send them when you like & where you like—for I know nothing but of one Vol which I partly filled the last five months I was at Home & I think I reccolect something of the others which I brought home with me send them by all means—I know of none which he prefers but cant you send the 'Three or Four Volumes' of MSS. as they are & let him see what he wanted himself—do just as you please & you will do right enough— you tell me you will write to me again before long Do so as soon as you can & let it be about home & those who live there tell me how the flowers go on & read books of knowledge dont forget your Latin & Greek & Hebrew nor your Mathematics & Astronomy for in them you have Truth When I was a day Labourer at Bridge Casterton & courted your Mother I knew nine languages & could talk of them to Parsons & Gentlemen & Foreigners but never opened my Mouth about them to the Vulgar—for I always lived to myself—dont forget you have Bibles & Prayer Books—& never act Hypocrisy for Deception is the most odious Knavery in the World—Stick to truth & 'Shame the Devil'—Learning is your only wealth Mathematics Astronomy & Mechanics should be your 'Common Place Book' God Bless you all together & believe me my dear Children your

Affectionate Father

JOHN CLARE

To Charles Clare

[sent]

Asylum near Northampton June 1 1849

MY DEAR BOY

I was very happy to have so long a letter from you & to hear that you was all well & to hear that the Garden is prosperous & that you & your neighbours are all well & happy—Spring & Summer came in beautifull & the crops of Grass & Corn are plentifull & give promise of Haytime & Harvest in Plenty

You told me to enquire of you about my old Neighbours & Labouring Companions of my single Days—There is William

& John Close do they live at Helpstone yet & how are they—
How is John Cobbler of Helpstone I worked with him when a
single Man & Tom Clare we used to sit in the Fields over a
Bottle of Beer & they used to sing capital songs & we were all
merry together how is John & Mary Brown & their Daughter
Lucy & John Woodward & his Wife & daughter William
Bradford & his Wife & A. & E. Nottingham & Old John
Nottingham & his Wife Sally Frisby & James Bain & Old
Otter the Fiddler & Charles Otter & John & Jim Crowson—
most of us Boys & Girls together—There is also John & James
Billings & Will Bloodworth & Tom & Sam Ward & John
Fell & his Wife & John King & Mr & Miss Large & Mr &
Miss Bellars on the Hill & Mr Bull & all enquiring Friends &
Mrs Crowson many are dead & some forgotten & John & Mrs
Bullimore the village Schoolmistress & Robin Oliver & Henry
Snow & his Wife & Frank Jackson & his Wife Richard Royce &
his Wife & Daughter & Jonathan Burbidge & his Wife &
Daughter & all I have forgotten remember me kindly to—for I
have been a long time in Hell—how is Ben Price & Will
Dolby for I liked Helpstone well[1]—& all that lived in it &
about it for it was my Native Place—How is Thomas Parker of
Ashton he used to be my Companion in my single Days when
we loved Books & flowers together & how is Charles Welsh of
Bainton—my fondness for flowers made me acquainted with
him which has wore many years & his Wife too & Daughters
for they are all old Friends—Give my love to your Brothers &
Sisters & Grandfather & neighbours & ever [believe?] me your
Affectionate Father

JOHN CLARE

To Charles Clare

[sent]
Northampton Asylum October 15th 1849

MY DEAR CHARLES

I wrote to you sometime back & I never got any answer to
my Letter & thinking you might not get it I write agen hoping
this will reach you safely

I very much want to get back & see after the garden & hunt in the Woods for yellow hyacinths Polyanthuses & blue Primroses as usual & go in the Meadows a fishing with Henry Phillips in my Pocket—how are your Brothers & Sisters & your Grandfather & how is your neighbour Robin Smith we used to go & make ourselves 'welcome at the Bell' at Stone Brig how is your neighbours Seftons & Bellars & old Green & all the rest of Northborough People & how are they at Helpstone & how is Charles Welsh & Jonas Porter how do you get on with Latin Greek Hebrew & Mathematics—you must not forget Learning—Ainslies Land-surveying—& Cobbins Arithmetic are your Schoolbooks—you should read them still—& *think*—how is your old Schoolmaster Kenney[1]—I shall be glad to get out o' thought & out o' sight in the Fens as usual—I shall not trouble you with a long letter as it is nothing more than an inquiry after the other I am my dear Children

Your sincere Father

JOHN CLARE

To Charles Clare

[*sent*]

Nov 7th [1849]

Asylum

Northampton

MY DEAR CHARLES

I ought to have answered your Letter before now but I have to go down below for Ink & Paper & forgot all about it till this Morning—You never tell me my dear Boy when I am to come Home I have been here Nine years or Nearly & want to come Home very much—You need not mind about writing often only in your next say when Johnny is coming to fetch me away from this Bastile—Have you four Boys got each an Hebrew Bible & a Harry Phillips on Angling—How do you get on with the Flowers—how are your Sisters & your Mother & Grandfather your Three Brothers & your Neighbours Give my Love to them all & Helpston People likewise—Take care of my

Books & M.S.S. till I come—to your Neighbours on each side of you give my best respects—& to Mary Buzley & old Mr Buzley if alive—& believe me my dear Son

Your Affectionate Father

JOHN CLARE

To Mary Collingwood

Dec. 26. 1849

MY DEAR MARY COLLINGWOOD[1]

I long to see you & have Loved from the first night of my Capture here Betsey Averey[1] Mary Ann Averey

My dear Mary but there is no faith here so I hold my tongue & wait the end out without attention or intention—'I am that I am'—& done nothing yet

J. CLARE

Sally Mason[1]
Betsy Ashby[1]
Mary Bolland[1]
     Ashby

        Gently John gently John

To Frederick Clare

1849

MY DEAR FRED

It is so long since I have ever heard of or seen you* that I feel inclined to write to you on 'Just before Christmas' to enquire how you are & how you are getting on—are you at Barnack or Northborough or anywhere else—How is John & William & Charles & your three Sisters—

Mary Piggin

Are you fond of Reading—There is Gunters Works & Laybourns Works of Astronomy these writers or such as these best illustrate the Scriptures & first Know Thyself—& keep the

---

* Frederick Clare, born 1824, intelligent, but never strong, died in 1843, as we have said. It was he whom the Emmersons tried, unsuccessfully, in 1830, to get into Christ's Hospital.

Commandments—not like an Hypocrite but a Man 'Love Truth'
fear God Honour the king. This is from your bible & not my
own Words—they are plagarisms from the Scriptures—Read
them—& think Fred—for yourself—Do you spend any of your
time with your Brothers & Sisters & Mother at Northborough
I am glad you are there this Christmas give my love to them &
to your Barnack Friends. Also believe me my Dear Fred
Your Affectionate Father

JOHN CLARE

To Eliza Dadford

MY DEAR ELIZA*
    How I long to see you & kiss that pretty Face—I mean
'Eliza Dadford'† How I should like to walk with you in the
Snow where I helped to shake your carpets & take the opper-
tunity we neglected then to kiss on the green grass & love you
even better than before Some promises are broke as soon as
made & silent love is sweet thats never spoken
    The churchyard grass looks pleasant where the maid Looked
Love in smiles in Memory's pleasing Token
I am my dear Eliza Dadford

Yours forever

J. CLARE

To Charles Clare

[sent]

April 24th 1850

MY DEAR SON CHARLES
    I shall just write to tell you that I am quite well & never was
better—I imagine you have been to the Post Office every Day
since you wrote—I thought you had forgotten me altogether—

---

    * The manuscript of this letter is from the 'Ha'penny Ballad' notebook. There
is no other reason for placing it immediately after the previous.
    † Eliza Dadford exists only as a name. Like that of Eliza Phillips, it is not
known in Helpstone, nor in the near vicinity.

till I heard from you—I have got nothing to write about at all for I see nobody & hear nothing—give my best love to your Mother Brothers & Sisters—neighbours [gap] get on for I am still fond of flowers

I rather fancy I shall see you shortly & in the mean time believe me

my Dear Charles
Your Affectionate Father
JOHN CLARE

He that is down need fear no fall
He that is low no pride
He that is humble ever shall
Have God to be his Guide.

John Bunyan

To Charles Clare

[*sent*]

Asylum Northampton July 8th 1850

MY DEAR BOY

You must excuse me for not writing sooner I am glad to hear you are all well as for myself I seldom was better—Mr Knight is gone to Birmingham & the other that took his place is a Mr Wing I am very sorry Mr Henderson has left the neighbourhood before I get back as I thought of going to see him—when I got home—You may give him my best respects when you write to him & tell him I am still fond of Flowers & Birdnesting & all old amusements as usual Give my respects & love to your Grandfather & to your Brothers & Sisters & to Betsy Adams do you ever hear of your sister Anna Maria* or is she still at home with you

I would write you a long letter only I have nothing to write about for I see Nothing & hear nothing—It is now fine weather

* Anna died in 1844.
306

for the Haytime—& hope you will get your little well—give
my love to all your Friends & Neighbours at Northborough &
elsewhere & ever believe my Dear Charles

Your Affectionate Father

JOHN CLARE

P.S. I forgot to be kindly remembered to your Mother—&
agen yours sincerely

J.C.

To Charles Clare

[*sent*]

July 25th 1851

MY DEAR SON

I got your Letter safe & was pleased to hear from U as I
thought it a long while since I heard from any of U—How are
your Brothers & Sisters & your Grandfather & Neighbours—
& 'Country Cousins'

How is your Mother & Uncle & Aunt at Barnack I hope U
send the young ones to School—be sure not to forget that—how
is your Grandfather—tell John I shall be glad to see him—Give
my Love to all your Brothers & Sisters & believe me my Dear
Charles Your sincere Father

JOHN CLARE

P.S. I wrote so far the day before yesterday & then left off
thinking to finish it in Ink—but I can ask a few more Questions
with my Pencil how is Mary Buzley & is Miss Parkinson at
Northborough still—How is John Woodward his wife &
Daughter How is Peach Large Mary Large & her 4 or 5
Sisters how is Mary Burbidge & her Mother & Father & does
your Brother John ever see Jane Sisson[1] & her Brother William
or her Father or Mother tell Jhon to remember me to Dame
Porter & Ann & Thomas & also to Betsey Newbon & her
brother & Father & Mother[2] & believe me my Dear Boy

Your Affectionate Father

JOHN CLARE

307

To Sophia Clare

[*sent*]

Northampton
8th Oct 1852

MY DEAR DAUGHTER SOPHY

I am very glad to hear from you, and that the family are in good health—I hope that Charles will soon be better* and that he will be very soon able to write me a letter, and give me the same good news of my family which will be always dear to me

To Miss Sophy Clare
Northborough

I am happy at all times to hear of their welfare

I am very happy to inform, that I also am in very good health, and I think that I never have felt myself in better

You must not suppose me to be at all ailing because this is not in my own writing but a Gentleman who is here is very fond of writing, and therefore I have given him a copy and thank him for writing for me—You will understand it is only that I do not write so fluent & quick as he does that I have asked him to write for me

Give my love to your Grandfather your Mother and brothers and Sisters and believe me

My dear Sophy
Your affectionate Father
JOHN CLARE

To Patty

[*sent*]

March 7th 1860

MY DEAR WIFE

This comes with my kind love to you & the Childern & my Father & Mother hoping it will find you all well I would have written sooner but had no oppertunity is Mr Sefton & Mrs

---

* Charles died a little later in this same year, aged nineteen.

Sefton living & the two sons Well how is William & his wife[1]
& also the neighbours give my love to Wm & Sophy Kettle[2]
also to their two Sons & the Daughter—How is Champion
John Jun[r] & Frederick & also William Parker Clare &
Frederick & Anna Maria Eliza Louisa Sophia & Julia. give
my love to Mrs Kettle,[2] Fanny Kemp[3] & to all inquiring friends

Your loving husband till Death

JOHN CLARE

To Mr. Jas. Hipkins*

[*sent*]

March 8 1860

DEAR SIR
I am in a Madhouse & quite forget your Name or who you
are You must excuse me for I have nothing to communicate or
tell of & why I am shut up I dont know I have nothing to say
so I conclude

Yours respectfully

JOHN CLARE

---

* An unknown inquirer from the outside world.

CHRONOLOGICAL LIST
OF LETTERS

'A Gentleman Unknown' [1817]
(Isaiah Knowles Holland)
'The Gentleman at Mrs. Clarks
  Northborough' [1817]
  (I. K. Holland)
I. K. Holland [1817]
I. K. Holland [1817]
I. K. Holland [1818]
John Taylor
  Taylor's date: 24 November
  1818
Edward Bell Drury [1819]
John Taylor about 20 December
  1819
I. K. Holland [1819]
I. K. Holland [1819]
I. K. Holland
  Holland's date: 1819
Octavius Gilchrist [January 1820]
Gilchrist [January 1820]
Taylor 17 January 1820
Gilchrist 21 January 1820
Gilchrist Winter [1820]
Taylor 24 February 1820
Taylor [March 1820]
Taylor 19 March 1820
Gilchrist [April 1820]
Chauncy Hare Townshend
  [March] 1820
James Augustus Hessey
  2 April 1820

Townshend 10 April 1820
Taylor [April 1820]
Taylor 19 April 1820
Taylor May 1820
Townshend May 1820
Taylor 16 May 1820
Taylor 20 May 1820
Taylor 10 June 1820
Hessey 29 June 1820
Taylor June 1820
Hessey 4 July 1820
Hessey [July 1820]
Hessey 16 July 1820
Taylor p.m. 31 August 1820
Taylor 27 August 1820
Taylor [Autumn 1820]
Taylor [1820]
Gilchrist September 1820
Townshend 12 September 1820
Hessey September or October
  1820
Taylor 3 October 1820
Hessey 28 November 1820
Hessey 1 December 1820
Taylor [1820]
Taylor 14 December 1820
Taylor 18 December 1820
Taylor 21 December 1820
Taylor 30 December 1820
Taylor 2 January 1821
Hessey p.m. January 1821
Taylor 3 January 1821

311

Taylor	7 January 1821	Taylor	20 April 1822
Taylor	16 January 1821	Hessey	p.m. 11 May 1822
Taylor	23 January 1821	His Family	May 1822
Taylor	[Early 1821]	His Family	[May–June] 1822
Taylor	7 February 1821	Henry Francis Cary	
Taylor	8 February 1821		23 August 1822
Taylor	13 February 1821	Hessey	p.m. 4 January 1823
Taylor	15 February 1821	Hessey	
Taylor	p.m. 17 February 1821	Taylor's date: 17 January 1823	
Taylor	p.m. 24 February 1821	Hessey	
Taylor		Taylor's date: 20 January 1823	
Taylor's date: March 1821		Taylor	28 February 1823
Taylor		Hessey	[February–March 1823]
Taylor's date: about 7 March 1821		Hessey	[April 1823]
Hessey	17 March 1821	Taylor	8 May 1823
Taylor	[March 1821]	Hessey	p.m. 17 May 1823
Taylor	24 March 1821	Hessey	June 1823
Taylor	[March–April 1821]	Taylor	July 1823
Taylor	3 April 1821	Taylor	31 July 1823
Taylor	18 April 1821	Hessey	[August 1823]
Taylor	24 April 1821	Hessey	[1823]
Taylor	p.m. 3 May [1821]	Hessey	p.m. August 1823
Taylor	[June 1821]	Hessey	11 September 1823
Taylor	9 June 1821	Taylor	p.m. 5 January 1824
Hessey	26 June 1821	Thomas Inskip	
Hessey	8 July [1821]		[p.m. 10] August 1824
Taylor	10 July 1821	Taylor	[August 1824]
Taylor	12 July 1821	Hessey	20 August 1824
Taylor	[1821]	Cary	18 September 1824
Taylor	11 August 1821	Artis	[September 1824]
Taylor	p.m. 18 August 1821	Charles Abraham Elton	
Taylor	6 September 1821		18 December 1824
Gilchrist	[1822]	Cary	30 December 1824
Taylor	24 January 1822	James Montgomery	
Taylor	31 January 1822		5 January 1825
Gilchrist	31 January 1822	Joseph Weston	7 March 1825
Taylor	8 February [1822]	Artis	[March or April 1825]
Taylor	[21 February 1822]	Hessey	17 April [1825]
Edmund Tyrell Artis		Taylor	5 May 1825
	9 March 1822	Taylor	19 June 1825
Hessey	16 March 1822	Hessey	7 July 1825
Hessey	2 April 1822	William Hone	2 August 1825

Jane Mossop	August 1832	Taylor	5 May 1837
Cary	August 1832	Frank Simpson	[1835–7]
Taylor	6 September 1832	Patty Clare	23 November 1837
Charles Mossop	September 1832	Mary Joyce	[1841]
Charles Wentworth Dilke		Eliza Phillips	[1841]
(Editor of *The Athenaeum*)		Patty Clare	17 March 1841
	[Autumn 1832]	Mary Joyce (?)	[1841]
Cunningham	11 November 1832	Mary Joyce	27 July 1841
Eliza L. Emmerson		Dr. Matthew Allen	
	13 November 1832		[August 1841]
J. Henderson	22 April 1833	George Reid	17 November 1841
John Taylor of Northampton		Charles Clare	15 June 1847
	September 1833	Charles Clare	February 1848
Thomas Emmerson	1834	Patty Clare	July 1848
Taylor	12 April 1834	Charles Clare	17 October 1848
Eliza L. Emmerson	May 1834	Charles Clare	2 April 1849
How of Whittaker's		Charles Clare	1 June 1849
	p.m. 13 or 25 June 1834	Charles Clare	15 October 1849
Taylor	10 July 1834	Charles Clare	7 November [1849]
Behnes Burlowe	12 November	Mary Collingwood	
	1834		26 December 1849
Henderson	November 1834	Frederick Clare	1849
Taylor	1 December 1834	Eliza Dadford	1849
Taylor	6 January 1835	Charles Clare	24 April 1850
Earl Spencer	12 January 1835	Charles Clare	8 July 1850
Taylor	15 January 1835	Charles Clare	25 July 1851
Taylor	27 August 1835	Sophia Clare	8 October 1852
Dr. Darling	[Autumn 1835]	Patty Clare	7 March 1860
Henderson	13 January 1836	Mr. Jas. Hipkins	8 March 1860
Taylor	16 February 1837		

INDEX TO CORRESPONDENTS

with dates and whereabouts of letters

[August 1823]
[1823]
p.m.   August 1823
11 September 1823   } Northampton Brooke-Taylor mss.
20 August 1824
17 April [1825]   Peterborough mss.
7 July 1825
8 December 1825
21 January 1827   } Northampton Brooke-Taylor mss.
Taylor's date: October 1830?

HIPKINS, JAS.
8 March 1860   Northampton mss.

HOLLAND, THE REV. ISAIAH KNOWLES
[1817]
[1817]
[1817]
[1817]   } The Norris Library, St. Ives,
[1818]   Huntingdon.
[1819]
[1819]
Holland's date: 1819

HONE, WILLIAM
2 August 1825   Peterborough mss.
HOW (of Whittaker's)
p.m. 13 or 25 June 1834   Northampton Brooke-Taylor mss.

INSKIP, THOMAS
p.m. 10 August 1824   Published by Charles Clark in
                         Three Very Interesting Letters
                         (1837)

JOYCE, MARY
1841
[1841]
27 July 1841
MARSH, MRS. MARIANNE   } Northampton mss.
19 October 1829
[Spring 1832]

MONTGOMERY, JAMES
5 January 1825   Peterborough mss.
8 May 1826   Published by J. L. Cherry in *Life
                         and Remains of John Clare* (1873)

MOSSOP, THE REV. CHARLES
[January 1832]   Northampton mss.

28 April 1832
1 August 1832
September 1832
MOSSOP, MISS JANE
9 September 1830
[Spring 1832]
[Spring 1832]
August 1832
PHILLIPS, ELIZA
1841
POWER, J.
24 September 1825
PRINGLE, THOMAS
29 August 1829
}Northampton mss.

REID, GEORGE
17 November 1841   Northampton Brooke-Taylor mss.

SHARPE, W.
October 1829
SIMPSON, FRANK
9 April 1828
[Spring 1832]
[1835–7]
}Northampton mss.

SPENCER, EARL
12 January 1835   Peterborough mss.

TAYLOR, JOHN
Taylor's date:

24 November 1818	Northampton Brooke-Taylor mss.
About 20 December 1819	ms. lent by Mr. R. N. Green-Armytage
17 January 1820	ms. lent by Messrs. J. Thornton and Son
24 February 1820	Northampton Brooke-Taylor mss.
[March 1820]	ms. lent by Mr. M. Buxton-Forman
19 March 1820	Northampton Brooke-Taylor mss.
[April 1820]	Northampton Brooke-Taylor mss.
19 April 1820	ms. lent by Mr. R. N. Green-Armytage
May 1820	ms. lent by Mr. R. N. Green-Armytage
16 May 1820	Northampton Brooke-Taylor mss.
20 May 1820	Northampton Brooke-Taylor mss.

x

INDEX TO CORRESPONDENTS

BIOGRAPHICAL MEMORANDA
of the more Important of Clare's Correspondents

ARTIS, EDMUND TYRELL. Archaeologist-artist, F.S.A., F.G.S., and butler to Lord Milton. Artis was the discoverer of Durobrivae, the Roman site at Castor. Clare helped with Artis's excavations at Water Newton between 1822 and Artis's publication of *The Durobrivæ of Antoninus* in 1828. He also helped Artis (and Henderson, the Milton head-gardener botanist) in their hunts round the Pailgrounds and Oxey Wood near Helpstone. An account of Castor's fine mosaic pavements, baths, villas, and pottery is in *The New Monthly Magazine*, October 1826. They were then 'by far the most curious and extensive that have been explored in Britain'. The coloured plates, lithographed sketches, *Artis del*, collected under the title *Antediluvian Phytology*, is one of those rare, beautiful books that reveal the devotion of the artist as well as the zeal of the archaeologist.

ALLEN, DR. MATTHEW, M.D. (died 1845). Asylum physician, writer, and one of the reformers for the treatment of the insane in the early nineteenth century. He was superintendent at York (1819–24), after which he decided to apply his theories of comfort, diversity of occupation, amusement, and pure air, at High Beech, Epping. He wrote *Cases of Insanity* (1830), *Classification of the Insane* (1837). Went bankrupt (1843) over a scheme for wood carving with Tennyson. See *John Clare: A Life*, p. 408; as also *Alfred Tennyson*, by Charles Tennyson.

BEHNES BURLOWE, HENRY. Sculptor. (died 1837). His real name was Behnes. It was to avoid confusion with his more gifted but degenerate brother that, setting out, in 1828, to make his name as a sculptor, Behnes took the added name 'Burlowe'.

CARY, THE REV. HENRY FRANCIS (1772–1844). Author and parson, whose 'authorship and priesthood', says Clare, in the best contemporary verbal portrait of Cary extant, sat upon him 'very meekly': see *Life*, p. 193. Lamb's 'model of a country Parson, lean, (as a curate ought to be), modest, sensible'; Procter's 'mildest and most amiable of men'; Hood's 'mild and modest Cary'. The second edition of Cary's translation of Dante was published by Taylor in 1819. Cary reviewed French and Italian poets for *The London*, and translated 'The Birds' of Aristophanes. He was given place in Poets' Corner in Westminster Abbey.

CUNNINGHAM, ALLAN (1784–1842). Writer and poet. He was born in a Nithsdale village and came to London in 1810. He was given 'one bound copy', as remuneration, by Cromek the engraver, on publication of the well-received *Nithsdale and Galloway Song*. These ballads were his own composition, and not traditional, as Cunningham told Cromek. He then became assistant to Francis Chantrey, the rising young sculptor. Besides contributing to *Blackwood's* and *The London*, Cunningham wrote: *Sir Marmaduke Maxwell*, a tragedy, two volumes of *Traditional Tales of the English and Scottish Peasantry*, *The Songs of Scotland* (which included the undying 'A wet sheet and a flowing sea'), *Paul Jones*, a romance in the Scottish vernacular, the supernatural *Sir Michael Scott*, two three-volume romances, *Lord Roldan* and *The Maid of Elvar*, six volumes of *The Lives of the Most Eminent British Painters, Sculptors, and Architects*, and eight volumes of the *Works of Robert Burns*. When he died, he was revising the proofs of his *Life of Sir David Wilkie*, published after his death. Among his friends, who included the Carlyles, Scott, and George Darley, he was known as 'honest Allan', retaining, as he did to the end, his rusticity. William Jerdan, of the *Literary Gazette*, said he was 'straightforward, right-minded, and conscientious, true to himself and others', and it may have been these qualities which endeared him to Clare, with whom his dealings were all of the happiest. Cunningham, with others of the period, still waits for a little of posterity's attention.

DARLEY, GEORGE (1795–1846). Scholar, mathematician, and lyrical poet of importance in the history of English prosody. Darley's 'impediment', his stutter, isolated him, because of his excessive sensitiveness on its account, from many friends. Lack of recognition for his poetry lost him hope. He is Edmund Blunden's 'sometimes glorious poet'. But, according to Darley's only biographer, he was 'a shy and disappointed man, whose achievements, at his death, were known only to the few'. So passionately desirous of fame, so curiously athwart his age, with such a high standard for friendship, poetry, and critical integrity, he tried, by poetry, mathematics, and criticism, to eke out a very small private income. His complete works, besides anonymous contributions to Taylor's educational list, consist of *The Errors of Ecstasie* (1822), *The Labours of Idleness* (by 'Guy Penseval') (1826), *Sylvia* (1827) (which, he wrote to B. W. Procter, 'ranked me among the small poets only'; together with *A System of Popular Geometry*, *A System of Popular Trigonometry*, *Familiar Astronomy*, *The Geometrical Companion*, *Thomas à Becket* (a lyrical drama), and *Ethelstan* (also a lyrical drama). He also printed for private circulation: *Nepenthe*, *Olympian Revels*, and *The Lammergeier*. Darley was for years art critic to *The Athenaeum*. He was *The London*'s 'John Lacy'. But in spite of his 'Ryghte Pythie Songe'—'It is not beautie I demande—' and of the popularity of 'I've been roaming', as well as of his Syren Chorus in 'The Sea Bride' from Lenima Laburum—'Troop home to silent grots and caves'—neither his own day, nor Palgrave, accorded Darley a just hearing: he waited for R. A. Streatfeild, 1904, and Professor Colleer Abbott, 1928.

DARLING, DR. GEORGE, M.D. (1782(?)–1862). A Scotsman who came to London to doctor literary men. He was the friend of Taylor, benefactor to the National Gallery, and a contributor to *The London*. He bled Keats 'copiously', prescribed pills and gave advice gratis for Clare, and otherwise doctored Wilkie, Haydon, Chantrey, and Taylor himself.

ELTON, (SIR) CHARLES BARAHAM. 6th baronet (1778–1853), whom Crabb Robinson saw in 1824 as 'a sturdy fellow more like a huntsman than a scholar'. Yet Elton was, as well as a scholar, a man of passionately held religious convictions, as his excellent Introduction to his translation of Hesiod shows. He was author of *The Brothers* (1820), *Boyhood and other Poems* (1835), besides contributing to *The London Magazine*. His house at Clevedon was a literary centre.

EMMERSON, ELIZA LOUISA (1782–1847). The wife of Thomas Emmerson, an importer of pictures. His will, 1855, does not betray that he shared his wife's literary leanings. E. L. Emmerson herself was an invalid from about the time of Clare's own collapse. Clare's shrewd character sketch of her is given in full in *John Clare: A Life* (p. 132). She wrote fluent (far too fluent, Clare said, and he *should* know) verse for the annuals and other minor papers. But only her interest in Clare entitles her to consideration.

GILCHRIST, OCTAVIUS GRAHAM (died 1823). Grocer of Stamford, and friend of Gifford of *The Quarterly* and John Scott of *The London*. Gilchrist published a volume of verse (1805), edited Bishop Corbet's poems (1807), wrote *Examination of the Charges of Enmity of Ben Jonson towards Shakespeare* (1808), was an authority on the Elizabethan dramatists, contemplated a 'Select Collection of Old Plays', contributed to Leigh Hunt's *Reflector*, and wrote the article on Clare in *The London* (January 1820). In that year he was busy with the Letters to the Rev. William Lisle Bowles concerning Pope's moral character. For years he was editor of *Drakar a's Stamford News*, and was the author of the article on military flogging which led to the publisher being imprisoned. His vindications of Ben Jonson and Pope are perhaps worthiest of remembrance, but he was, for a long time, Clare's only immediate source of literary companionship.

HESSEY, JAMES AUGUSTUS (died 1870). John Taylor's partner in the enterprising publishing firm which flourished between 1806 and 1825. J. H. Reynolds thought him 'a very respectable person'. Clare once thought him 'miserly, cautious', but had sincere regard for him. In 1825 Hessey set up on his own as a publisher of religious books, failed in 1829, and the next year set up as a print auctioneer. In 1833 he turned schoolmaster, and had an establishment three miles outside London. See *Keats's Publisher*, by Edmund Blunden.

HOLLAND, THE REV. ISAIAH KNOWLES (died 1873). Not 'Isaac' Knowles Holland, as recorded in *John Clare: A Life*. Presbyterian minister of Northborough and then of St. Ives, Huntingdon, and one of Clare's earliest supporters. His friendship with Clare, 1817–20, did not survive Holland's removal to St. Ives. If he heard of Clare's difficulties, he did not, because of Clare's adherence to Taylor, come a second time to his help.

HONE, WILLIAM (1780–1842). Miscellaneous writer and Lamb's 'needy and clever friend', whose *Political House that Jack Built*, in 1819, ran into 54 editions. The 'ingenuous' Hone was also editor of the *Every-Day Book* (1826–7), that compendium of Recreations, Information, and morbid curiosities, in less bustling but prophetic days immediately before cheap literature, cheap press, film, and radio. In 1827 Hone began his *Table Book* and in 1828 his *Year Book*, but for his political squibs against the Government he was prosecuted. The mental vigour of his own defence at his trial created much public sympathy for him. He must be remembered chiefly for his contributions to (*a*) the fight for the freedom of the Press, and (*b*) cheap literature. The abuse of the second, Q. D. Leavis's searching analysis revealed no more than a century later.

INSKIP, THOMAS (died 1849). Watchmaker of Shefford, and friend of Robert Bloomfield. Inskip's one publication was *Cant. A Satire* (1843). But his friendship with Clare during the first lonely eight years of Clare's Northampton incarceration testifies to Inskip's inspiriting kindness. Unfortunately, the important Asylum letters from Clare to Thomas Inskip are still untraced.

BIOGRAPHICAL MEMORANDA

MONTGOMERY, JAMES (1780–1854). Poet and hymn-writer. Editor of *The Sheffield Iris* for 31 years, during which he was twice imprisoned for political libel in York Castle, though his life and character had the exemplary quality of Cowper's. He befriended Ebenezer Elliot, the Corn Law Rhymer.

PRINGLE, THOMAS (1789–1834). Writer, and editor of the annual *Friendship's Offering*. Pringle was a Scotsman, the friend of Hogg and Cunningham, and secretary to the Anti-Slavery Society. Pringle published *The Autumnal Excursion, or Sketches in Teviotdale* (1819), *African Sketches* and *Afar in the Desert,* as well as editing various newspapers, Scottish and African.

RIPPINGILLE, EDWARD VILLIERS (1798[?]–1859). Self-taught painter of rural and domestic life. 'A pleasant fellow over the bottle, & a strong dealer in puns', Clare said. Later Rippingille became a champion of orthodoxy against the Pre-Raphaelites. For list of his pictures, and for Clare's admiring description of him, see *John Clare: A Life* (pp. 181–2).

TAYLOR, JOHN (1781–1864). Publisher and son of a bookseller. John Taylor was in London in 1803, and took service, first with Lackington at the Temple of the Muses, then with Vernor and Hood. With James Augustus Hessey, he formed the progressive partnership of the firm which was to publish Keats, Hazlitt, Reynolds, Cary, Lamb, De Quincey, Landor, and Clare. Taylor was himself a writer, as well as editor of *The London* (1820–25). His identification of Junius with Sir Philip Francis is still considered the best solution. He was also a student of theology and of the Great Pyramid, as well as a philologist. See *Keats's Publisher*, by Edmund Blunden.

TOWNSHEND, THE REV. CHAUNCY HARE (1798–1868). Friend and adorer of Dickens. Fitzgerald suggests he was the original of Cousin Feenix and Mr. Twemlow. *Great Expectations* was dedicated to him, and he appointed Dickens his literary executor, which involved Dickens in editing *The Religious Opinions of Chauncey Hare Townshend*. Townshend seems undecided about the 'e' in his first name and the 'h' of his second. Though he took Holy Orders, he was disabled by illness, and spent much of his time travelling. Though his *Poems* in 1821 received generous applause, Townshend showed no anxiety for fame, and his next poems, *Sermons in Sonnets*, were not published till 1851. Townshend drew and painted, collected and wrote on jewels, and also on mesmerism.

VENTOUILLAC, L. T. (1796–1834). Writer and Professor of French Literature and Language at King's College, London. Ventouillac was born in Calais. He supplied the topographical and historical descriptions for Pugin's *Paris and its Environs* (1829), wrote *French Poetry for Children* and *Rudiments of the French Language* (1831). He edited, with the Rev. Thomas Dale, the annual *The Offering*.

WATTS, ALARIC ALEXANDER (1797–1864). Author, and editor of *The Manchester Courier*. In 1824 Watts edited *The Literary Souvenir*, confessedly an imitation of German Literary Almanacks. *The Literary Souvenir* gained the position of the parent of the 'annuals' and 'pocket books', which absorbed so much of English art and literature for the next fifteen years. Watts also wrote *Poetic Sketches* (1822), *Scenes of Life and Shades of Character* (1831), and *Lyrics of the Heart* (1851).

DE WINT, PETER (1784–1849). English landscape painter of Dutch extraction, and brother-in-law of William Hilton. He himself usually wrote his name 'de Wint'. He delighted in the Fen landscapes, and 'was never so happy as when looking at nature'. This peace is reflected in all his work. See Mr. Geoffrey Harmsworth's article on de Wint in *Country Life* (July 1949).

NOTES

Page 25. Letter to HOLLAND. 1817.

[1] The poems sent to Holland which still remain in the Clare manuscript in the Norris Library, St. Ives, Huntingdon (though these are not the only copies) are:

> 'The Jewell of all' (unpublished).
> 'To an April Daisy' (*Poems Descriptive of Rural Life and Scenery*).
> 'My love thou art a Nosegay sweet' (*Poems Descriptive*).

On this sheet Clare has written: 'I had great hopes in my fragment of "Helpstone" [*Poems Descriptive*], my native Village—that spot so belovd in my Infancy & masterpiece (it may be) but my hopes are vanishd since I am told that Nat Bloomfield has far outdone me in a piece of a similar subject—"Honington Green" Your information would be thankfully Recd'

> "To the Gloworm" [*Poems Descriptive*].

'Please to keep the M.S.S. as some are the only Copies'

> "The Suprise"

'The "Death of Dobbin" [unpublished] mentioned in Lett need not be expected—there is anew [dialect for 'enough'] without it—I shall finish it at leisure (perhaps) before long

> "To the Winds" [*Poems Descriptive*]
> Sonnet "Well have I learnt the Value of Vain Life" [unpublished]

'Sir You perceive I take little Notice of the Mechanism which all Sonneteers in general are particular to Notice—They are the Wild notes of a Labour[er] & the unpolishd heartfelt feelings of a Lowly Clown who is not aquainted with the craft and Subtlety of Art to make them agreeable to the tastfull Eye

> "A Simple Effusion Adressd to my Lame Father" [unpublished]

330

'SIR
' You hinted a loss in the "Fate of Amy" [*Poems Descriptive*] of the
Omission in that Dreadful Castrophy where the victim takes the
Plunge from this mortal Scene to unknown Eternity—I here send the
scene from the Tale now composing—But as you say Kirke White
has done it before me I am in great Diffidence as to its Merit—

"O who can paint the anguish of the heart . . ."

'SIR
'It would greatly Oblige if you would Condecend to give me (some
time at leisure in writing) a Paraphrase of the 3 ch Job particularly
8, 14, 15, 23, 24, 25, and 26 Ver.'
" Epistle to a Friend" [*Poems Descriptive*]
[signed] 'RANDOM JACK'

PAGE 26. Letter to HOLLAND. 1818.
¹ Clare had read Allan Ramsay (1686–1758)—author of *The Gentle
Shepherd*, and father of the well-known portrait-painter to George
III—much earlier than this. His poem on 'Ale' and his 'Address to
a Lark' (1814–15) are in the Ramsay–Burns metre.
² 'Familiar Epistle, to a Friend' (*Poems Descriptive*).

PAGE 27. Letter to JOHN TAYLOR. Taylor's date Nov. 24 1818.
¹ There is the first indication of the beginnings of trouble—on this
letter, a note by Edward Drury, the Stamford Bookseller, who introduced Clare's poems to his cousin, John Taylor, the publisher.
'I am almost jealous of O.G. I think he woud not willingly miss
being in the book' wished to ask T. many things which may 'look
to my discredit on paper'. The 'book' is *Poems Descriptive of Rural
Life and Scenery* (1820).

PAGE 28. Letter to EDWARD BELL DRURY. [1819.]
¹ *Poems Descriptive of Rural Life and Scenery.*
² See note 1 on Messing, of letter to Octavius Gilchrist, September
1820.

PAGE 28. Letter to JOHN TAYLOR. About 20 December 1819.
¹ Cf. the version of this poem in the Introduction to *Poems Descriptive of Rural Life and Scenery.*

PAGE 29. Letter to HOLLAND. [1819.]
¹ Clare returned to Casterton, after lime-burning there in 1817, in
the spring of 1819, to work in the garden of his employer Wilders.
² Holland did. *The Village Minstrel* (1821).
³ *The Village Minstrel.*
⁴ It is impossible to be certain, without the first lines, as well as
the titles, whether these poems are published or not.

331

PAGE 30. Letter to HOLLAND. [1819.]

[1] Robert Bloomfield's *The Farmer's Boy* had gone through many editions since 1800. His *Rural Tales* (1802), *Wild Flowers* (1806), and *Banks of Wye* were not so popular. For Bloomfield's *May Day with the Muses*, see Clare's letter to Hessey (p.m. May 1822) and notes 2 and 3 to that letter.

PAGE 31. Letter to HOLLAND. (Dated by Holland '1819. on the eve of his first pub. of his Poems'.)

[1] It seems to have been already decided among Clare's Stamford friends that he was not fitted for a schoolmaster.

[2] Unpublished.

[3] Drury had criticized Holland's presbyterianism.

[4] *Poems Descriptive of Rural Life and Scenery.*

PAGE 32. Letter to OCTAVIUS GILCHRIST. [January 1820.]

[1] The manuscript of this letter is in the handwriting of James Simpson, father of Frank Simpson, Mrs. Gilchrist's nephew.

[2] *Poems Descriptive of Rural Life and Scenery* were published 16 January 1820. This fact dates the above letter as early January.

PAGE 32. Letter to GILCHRIST. [January 1820.]

[1] The manuscript of this letter, but not the note, is in the 'copperplate' with many flourishes, Clare learnt from John Turnill with such pleasure as a child, and later used in the letter to Patty, though *there* with capitals throughout, from 'Leppit's Hill', 17 March 1841.

[2] Under John Scott; Gilchrist, friend of Scott and Gifford, had an article about Clare in the first issue of *The London Magazine* (January 1820).

PAGE 35. Letter to TAYLOR. 24 February 1820.

[1] Admiral the Hon. William Waldegrave, first Baron Radstock, and friend of Nelson, had written to the vicar of Helpstone about Clare, and was ready to become a patron.

[2] Joseph Warton's edition. See also p. 39, Hayley's (poems).

PAGE 36. Letter to TAYLOR. [March 1820.]

[1] Clare returned to Helpstone from his first visit to London at the end of the first week in March 1820, and married 'Patty' Turner immediately after.

[2] This miniature was acquired by the Royal Naval Museum, Greenwich, during the last war.

[3] Taylor had written (16 March) '. . . Keats came to dine with me the Day before yesterday. . . . He was very sorry he did not see you—' Keats and Clare did not meet.

⁴ John Hamilton Reynolds, divided between poetry and solicitoring, who wrote to Keats, 'Do you get Fame, and I shall have it in being your affectionate and steady friend', was, according to Clare, the 'three in one of wit and punning personified': although they did not correspond, Clare greatly admired Reynolds's poetry. Reynolds wrote: *Safie, an Eastern Tale, The Naiad, Peter Bell, a Lyrical Ballad, The Fancy, The Garden of Florence,* and anonymously (!) in collaboration with Hood, the popular *Odes and Addresses to Great People.*

⁵ Richard Woodhouse, also a friend of Keats, a studious young barrister who, at this time, was acting in some capacity as literary assistant or adviser to the firm of Taylor and Hessey.

⁶ The Rev. John Percival, yet another friend of Taylor and of Keats, contributor to *The London* and one of those who advanced £10 each towards the expense of Keats's voyage to Italy.

⁷ William Hilton, painter, was elected R.A. in 1819, and Keeper of the Academy in 1826. His paintings of both Keats and Clare have never received quite their due of praise; nor, says Mr. Geoffrey Harmsworth (*Country Life,* 1949) has his work in general, 'owing to his unfortunate liking for bitumen', been fully recognized.

⁸ Lady Fitzwilliam, wife of Charles William Wentworth, third Earl Fitzwilliam. The Fitzwilliams had sent £100 to Taylor, for Clare, in February 1820.

PAGE 39. Letter to GILCHRIST. [April 1820.]

¹ The Marquis of Exeter had given Clare £15 a year.

² Dialect: use of 'till' meaning 'whilst'.

³ See next letter, which also dates this one.

PAGE 40. Letter to HESSEY. 2 April 1820.

¹ Hoare was a rich banker who had written in approval of *Poems Descriptive.*

² James Currie's edition of Burns went through many reprints between 1800 and Cunningham's edition.

³ *The Village Minstrel* (1821).

⁴ *The Rural Muse* (1835).

⁵ *The Shepherd's Calendar* (1827).

PAGE 43. Letter to TAYLOR. [April 1820.]

¹ Taylor's date for the above letter is July 1820. But, dating some time afterwards, Taylor is not in every case accurate. The postmark looks like '22 Ju', but is not clear enough to admit of no doubt whatsoever. The 'gentleman from Cambridge' was presumably Chauncy Hare Townshend; his first visit was, as we know, in March, though he may have been twice, or even three times, and Clare, also writing

later in his memoirs, dates Townshend's visit as 'summer, 1820'. But Taylor, writing to his brother (31 May 1820) says: 'we have published the 3rd edition of Clare . . .'; so that Clare's reference to the '2nd Edit' dates the above letter clearly as before May. Also, Gilchrist's 'Review' (of *Poems Descriptive*) was in the May *Quarterly*. Finally, the fact that 'O.G.' (Gilchrist) has the manuscripts for the 'new vol.' (*The Village Minstrel*), and is to send them on to Taylor, whilst in the next letter, clearly dated 'April 19', he has presumably sent them, dates the above as not long before that; we have placed it here.

PAGE 50. Letter to TAYLOR. 20 May 1820.

¹ To Clare.

² *The Village Minstrel.*

³ The manuscript, though difficult in places enough to be open to conjecture, certainly reads 'hardship' here and not 'Lordship'. In connection with Hilton's portrait of Clare, see also Note 2 to Letter to Taylor (15 November 1829).

PAGE 51. Letter to TAYLOR. 10 June 1820.

¹ J. H. Reynolds's witty farewell to youth, poetry, and pugilism, *The Fancy*, had just been published by Taylor. It was subtitled 'The Poetic Remains of the late Peter Corcoran'.

² Clare's song, set to music by Haydn Corri, was sung by Madame Vestris.

PAGE 58. Letter to HESSEY. [July 1820.]

¹ Clare's letter (16 May), or Radstock's, must have arrived too late to effect the 'expunging' of the offensive lines in Helpstone ('Accursed wealth . . .' and 'When ease and plenty, known but now to few . . .') as well as ' . . . that necessary tool of wealth and pride', in 'Dawnings of Genius'. The third edition of *Poems Descriptive* which, Taylor wrote to his brother, 'seems likely to go off with as much spirit, as its predecessors', appeared in May, without 'My Mary' and 'Ways of the Wake' ('Dolly's Mistake'). It had many minor alterations, but no omissions from the two poems 'Helpstone' or 'Dawnings of Genius'. Clare had reason to be 'mad' at Taylor's judgement. He was willing to omit the odd dozen lines out of gratitude for what Radstock had done for the Subscription List, but was prepared to stand by the poems.

² Dialectal meaning, 'fanned'.

³ Edward Scriven (1775–1841) engraved Hilton's portrait of Clare for *The Village Minstrel.*

⁴ 'inserted'? This 'young friend' may have been William Cowen, landscape painter and the friend of E. T. Artis, archaeologist-butler of Milton. Clare was at this time just getting to know Artis. On the other hand, since Clare refers to Cowen later (17 January 1823) as

'Mr' Cowen, this 'young' friend may have been Frank Simpson, Mrs. Gilchrist's nephew, an art-student at this time; or even Hankinson, Clare's 'old' friend and friend of Townshend, who would not be old in years.

⁵ The original, unrecast 'Hyperion'—last poem in *Lamia, Isabella, and Other Poems*.

PAGE 60. Letter to HESSEY. 16 July 1820.

¹ Drury.

² Unpublished.

³ In the *Village Minstrel*, not *The Rural Muse* (1835). There are at least two poems of this latter name.

PAGE 60. Letter to TAYLOR. p.m. 31 August 1820.

¹ Unknown: or else it is 'Hopkinson *of* Morton' (Lincs.), a J.P.

² Reynolds. See 'The Fields of Tothill' in *The Fancy*. The poem is in the Byron stanza. Note, also, Clare's later Asylum poem 'Don Juan', and his confusion of his 'identity' with Byron's and with Jack Randall's, the pugilist.

PAGE 61. Letter to TAYLOR. August 1820.

¹ The letter was from some reader who pointed out that by internal evidence 'Helpstone' was written when its author was 20, and yet the Introduction claimed it to have been written at 17:

London August 27 1820

SIR

   In reading over a volum of your Poems I discovered a contridiction which I humbly wish you to explain. If you please to look at the of Page 22 of the Introduction you will find that the poem Helpstone was Written before you were seventeen years old now sir if look on to Page 5 of that poem in the 5th and 6th lines you will find the following words

Dear nature spot! which length of time endears
The sweet retreat of twenty lingering years.

Now sir if you had felt the sweets of rural Helpstone twenty years when you wrote this Poem how coud it be written before you was seventeen

——————

N B Sir an answer with an explanation to the above will be most thankfully Received

H B	By your most
'No. 31 Garden Row'	obedient
London Road	and Humble
near the Oblisque	Servant
London . .	

[Clare had written:]

This d–d impertinent coxcomb of your fine city would sooner have an answer from my cudgel than pen if I was nigh him I assure you

It is wretched writing—smell him out if done with little trouble if not let him lye neglected & unanswered & that will be punishment enough for one of his assurance Ill be bound

Yours &c &c

JOHN CLARE

PAGE 64. Letter to GILCHRIST. September 1820.

[1] -poet? This was probably the S. Messing, later of Langham, Rutlandshire, whose prospectus Clare mentions in the letter to Drury, 1819. Messing had sent Clare (March 1820, British Museum Correspondence), with a very condescending letter, a copy of his *Rural Walks* (1820?). Messing also published—the proofs of which Clare is speaking of in the above—*Poems on Various Subjects*, printed by T. Drakard, Stamford, 1821. Clare's estimate of Messing is not unjust. His verses have a certain country freshness—nothing more.

[2] 'left'?

[3] *Essays Moral and Literary*. As evidence of the deeply savouring reading habits of his day, see *Journal* for Thursday, 28 October 1824, when, together with the Cary-recommended Bacon *Essays*, he was still picking up Knox.

PAGE 71. Letter to HESSEY. 28 November 1820.

[1] We have not traced the advertisement Clare refers to, but it looks like one of Taylor's moves under the pressure we know Lord Radstock to have been putting on him concerning his secrecy and highhanded dilatoriness in Clare's affairs during the autumn of 1820. See *Life*, pp. 157–9. Clare's own criticism of Taylor at this early date was not so much concerning money and written agreements as concerning the text and publication of poems.

Hessey replied (28 November, British Museum Correspondence): 'The announcement is in fact merely intended to inform the Public that such a Volume is in Preparation, and to keep alive the interest...' (Taylor was away. No mention of the cottage sketch by Clare's 'young friend'.) '... of course we should not think of sending them into the world without your seeing the Proofs...' Clare's date for his letter, the 28th, the same as Hessey's reply, must be a day or two late.

PAGE 78. Letter to TAYLOR. 18 December 1820.

[1] Radstock's criticisms of Taylor's methods had resulted in a break between the two and an angry letter from Taylor to Clare (16 December, British Museum Correspondence) together with an appeal from him to Clare's loyalty.

[2] Dialectal meaning, 'pull'.

PAGE 82. Letter to TAYLOR. 30 December 1820.

¹ Gilchrist's brother-in-law, a London jeweller.

² See, later, undated letter to Taylor placed in August 1821.

³ *The Fall of Jerusalem*, a dramatic poem, by the Rev. Henry Hart Milman, had been published by Murray earlier in 1820.

⁴ *The Village Minstrel.*

PAGE 86. Letter to TAYLOR. 3 January 1821.

¹ The second Earl, George John Spencer, Trustee of the British Museum, and collector of the then finest library in Europe, had given Clare £10 a year for life, after the publication of *Poems Descriptive.*

² A doctor in the army, and editor of *The Banisher of the Blue Devils*, a jest book. Clare met him at Drury's in 1819, and Bell it was who wrote to Earl Spencer about him.

³ A paragraph sent with the poem 'The Woodman'. Taylor (December 1820, British Museum Correspondence) thought it 'more correct than your prose usually is'.

PAGE 88. Letter to TAYLOR. 7 January 1821.

¹ See Cowper's 'On Observing Some Names of Little Note in the *Biographia Britannia.*'

PAGE 89. Letter to TAYLOR. 16 January 1821.

¹ 'My Mary' and 'Ways of the Wake' ('Dolly's Mistake') which Radstock considered 'indelicate', and which had been omitted from the third edition of *Poems Descriptive*, were not restored in the fourth edition. 'The Country Girl' had appeared only in the first edition. Its Burns-like challenge and outspokenness evidently offended Taylor. 'Friend Lubin', a poem with a like realistic flavour, was also only in the first, second, and third editions.

² Unpublished.

³ *The Village Minstrel.*

PAGE 91. Letter to TAYLOR. [Early 1821.]

¹ Thomas Mounsey, second master of the Stamford Free Grammar School, who taught 'the Greek and Latin Languages and every branch of Commercial and Mathematical learning'. See Asylum letter of 15 October 1849, and note on Kenney.

² Vicar of Ufford, three miles from Helpstone.

³ Mrs. Emmerson? Taylor was collecting information of Clare's benefactors for his Introduction to *The Village Minstrel.*

⁴ Dawson Turner, botanist, antiquary, indefatigable writer of books, and friend of John Sell Cotman.

⁵ Reynolds's *The Garden of Florence and other Poems* (1821) was published under the name 'John Hamilton' only. In his introduction to the unfinished canto of 'The Romance of Youth', Reynolds refutes

the charge that the poem, in Spenserian stanza, is based on Beattie's *Minstrel*, but the similarity among the three poets' childhood experiences is strong.

PAGE 95. Letter to TAYLOR. 13 February 1821.
[1] 'I'll be bound for it', i.e., 'I'm sure'.

PAGE 97. Letter to TAYLOR. 15 February 1821.
[1] The Honourable Henry Manvers Pierrepont was brother-in-law to the Marquis of Exeter.

PAGE 99. Letter to TAYLOR. p.m. 17 February 1821.
[1] W. Sharpe, who visited Clare in January 1824, and in 1828 and 1829 tried to extract from S. C. Hall what Hall then owed Clare.

PAGE 101. Letter to TAYLOR. Taylor's date: March 1821.
[1] Clare's letter about the fate of the Elms quoted by Taylor in his Introduction to *The Village Minstrel*, and evidently immediately preceding the above, is not in the Brooke-Taylor manuscripts, and we have no draft-letter.
[2] *Collected Poems.*
[3] Published 1818.
[4] *The Village Minstrel.*

PAGE 104. Letter to TAYLOR. About 7 March 1821.
[1] It is still not known exactly where the froghopper, to which Clare is referring, lays the eggs from which next spring's insect appears about cuckoo time. The froth in which it protects itself is called 'cockoo-spit'—sometimes 'snake-spit'. Clare's name, 'woodseer', is, Miss Baker says, not found elsewhere than Northants. For poem 'Woodseers', see *The Village Minstrel*.
[2] John Scott, able editor of *The London Magazine*, died of wounds in February of this year after a duel with Christie.
[3] The 'Battle of the Pamphlets', between Lisle Bowles on one side and Byron, Gilchrist, and Campbell on the other, had been raging since 1806.
[4] *The Village Minstrel.*

PAGE 106. Letter to TAYLOR. [March 1821.]
[1] *John Clare: Poems chiefly from Manuscript*, ed. Edmund Blunden and Alan Porter (1920).
[2] Clare is not mistaken. Milman's poetic drama does not *quite* deserve the oblivion meted out.
[3] The publisher Murray's place.
[4] Diffusers of the cheap 'literature' just beginning.
[5] Lord Radstock's *The Cottagers Friend: or a word in Season to him*

who is so fortunate as to possess a Bible . . .' was in its twentieth edition in 1816.

⁶ A periodical of the 'Cheap Repository' order, with 'allowances' even on the penny, 'to hawkers'—published by the Moral and Religious Tract Society. Issues like 'Black Giles the Poacher' were very circumspect, and the country mind very much written down to. Hannah More contributed to this publication.

PAGE 108. Letter to TAYLOR. 24 March 1821.

¹ The one which, as Severn recorded when hope of Keats's recovery was nearly gone, Keats himself chose, from the phrase in *Philaster*: 'Here lies one whose name was writ in water': or was it, as Mr. R. N. Green-Armytage suggests, from *Catullus*?

PAGE 110. Letter to TAYLOR. 3 April 1821.

¹ This is the *Sketches in the Life of John Clare by Himself*, edited by Mr. Edmund Blunden in 1931. The original was used judiciously by Taylor in the Introduction to *The Village Minstrel*, and passed on by him to Frederick Martin for use in his 1865 biography.

² Lolham Bridges, half a dozen old stone arches, carry the Roman road called King Street over flood meadows of the Welland. The place is rich in flowers. Langley Bush is gone. See sketch map of Clare country. No reference to 'Lollius Ubiens' is to be found in Bridges's or Whellan's *History of Northamptonshire*, who give the first mention of the bridges as in the reign of Henry III. They are generally supposed to have been built by the Romans.

³ See Taylor's account of Clare's imagination revealed in this poem: *London Magazine* for November 1821.

PAGE 111. Letter to TAYLOR. 18 April 1821.

¹ 'The Rivals', in *The Shepherd's Calendar*, or 'Chub's Lament for Nanny', unpublished.

² *The Village Minstrel.*

³ Unknown.

⁴ *The Village Minstrel.*

PAGE 114. Letter to TAYLOR. p.m. 3 May [1821.]

¹ Impossible to decipher, but from the fact that 'Jockey and Jenny' was in progress about this time, as well as the proofs of *The Village Minstrel*, the letter most likely belongs here.

² 'The Fate of Genius', *Collected Poems.*

³ Clare's final fair copy of this poem, with Taylor's alterations, is in the Peterborough manuscripts. It was published (*The Shepherd's Calendar*) as 'Jockey and Jenney; or, The Progress of Love'.

PAGE 115. Letter to TAYLOR. [June 1821.]

[1] Taylor had written on 1 May 1821 saying he would like Clare to write an article for *The London Magazine*, and on 11 May he wrote saying he had taken the magazine over after John Scott's death. The above letter seems to be the answer to these.

[2] *The New Monthly Magazine and Universal Register* (1814–20) was now being continued in *The New Monthly Magazine and Literary Journal*, edited by Thomas Campbell.

[3] A second daughter was born to Patty on 2 June 1821, but died soon after.

PAGE 120. Letter to TAYLOR. 10 July 1821.

[1] Taylor's editorship of *The London* began with the June issue, 1821.

[2] *The Village Minstrel.*

[3] *The Village Minstrel.*

[4] Unpublished.

PAGE 123. Letter to TAYLOR. 11 August 1821.

[1] This is the last time Clare tells of seeing Mary Joyce, not 1816, as recorded in *The Life*. The poem was published in *The London* (September 1821).

[2] This may have been the criticism of *The Village Minstrel* which Taylor rejected for *The London* and sent to Clare—probably by Cunningham.

[3] Near Towcester in Northamptonshire.

[4] Unpublished.

[5] Taylor's last letter (June) had no criticism of 'Jockey and Jenny', but on 17 May he had listed a number of poems for *The Village Minstrel*.

PAGE 125. Letter to TAYLOR. p.m. 18 August 1821.

[1] Clare was not unreasonable in his impatience at the delay over the publication of *The Village Minstrel*. See *Life*. It appeared at the end of September.

[2] Charles Mathews, the London actor, whose wife, half-sister to Lamb's Fanny Kelly, recorded of Charles Lamb that 'his figure was small and mean; and no man certainly was ever less beholden to his tailor'. Clare did not meet Mathews.

[3] Joseph Bunney, Lieutenant, K.O.S.M.

[4] Benjamin West (1738–1820), author of *Poems, Translations and Imitations*, as well as painter of historical pictures.

PAGE 127. Letter to GILCHRIST. [1822.]

[1] From *The London*. 'Jockey and Jenny' was not published till *The Shepherd's Calendar*.

² *The Shepherd's Calendar.*

³ Owen Feltham's (Felltham) *Resolves* contains no 'Miseries of Human Life'. The humorously mock-pathetic *Miseries of Human Life, or Groans of Samuel Sensitive, and Timothy Testy,* in its seventh edition in 1806, by James Beresford, is what Clare has significantly confused it with. Radstock sent him Feltham's *Resolves* we know from Clare's library at Northampton; but the *Miseries of Human Life* was from Mrs. Emmerson; the fly-leaf says: 'to beguile his [Clare's] occasional melancholy hours'.

⁴ *The Cabinet of Poetry.*

⁵ Essays by Sir R. Steele, Joseph Addison, and others (1713).

⁶ *National Melodies and Other Poems*—Mrs. Emmerson's gift. She has written on the fly-leaf: 'The author was known to me . . . and I sympathized with his misfortunes. He was indeed born "under malignant star".'

PAGE 127. Letter to TAYLOR. 24 January 1822.

¹ Clare was not, this time, disappointed. 'The Dream' was published in *The London* of February 1822, and later in *The Shepherd's Calendar.*

² See *Biographical Memoranda.*

³ Dialectal meaning: 'until'.

PAGE 133. Letter to TAYLOR. 21 February 1822.

¹ The manuscript of the above letter is undated by Clare. It has 'Feb. 21' outside, so it most probably belongs here.

² Cf. Dr. Johnson's opinion of the Sonnet form.

³ This was probably too long for *The London. The Shepherd's Calendar.*

⁴ Clare did not, as far as we are aware, achieve this.

PAGE 136. Letter to HESSEY. 2 April 1822.

¹ Hessey had written: 'The last piece ['April'] bears evidence of having been written under unfavourable circumstances and we should certainly do you Injustice were we to print it.' (British Museum Correspondence.)

² *Sir Marmaduke Maxwell* (1822): criticized by Scott, and never acted, this was Cunningham's only attempt at drama.

PAGE 137. Letter to HESSEY. 11 May 1822.

¹ *The London Magazine,* July 1822: also *The Shepherd's Calendar.*

² This letter was delayed in the posting or else Bloomfield's was. He had actually sent Clare a copy of his *Mayday with the Muses* on the 3 May 1822, which fact helps to determine the month as well as the year of this letter.

[3] Bloomfield's publishers. It will be recalled that Bloomfield's affairs collapsed in bankruptcy not long before his death.

[4] *The Shepherd's Calendar.*

PAGE 140. Letter to HESSEY. p.m. 4 January 1823.

[1] Hessey had sent only the £5 from Earl Spencer's annuity— unnecessarily late, surely.

[2] *Collected Poems.*

PAGE 141. Letter to HESSEY. (Taylor's date: 17 January 1823.)

[1] Cowen's sketch of the cottage was finally engraved for the 'second edition' of *The Village Minstrel*, March 1823.

PAGE 142. Letter to HESSEY. 20 January 1823.

[1] On the 17th Hessey sent the £10. With injunctions to be economical, he added 'more if need be'. There is a note on this letter (British Museum Correspondence) in Clare's handwriting, '10£ Credit'.

[2] 'He has not been here yet—tell me how you like it.'

[3] Taylor's father had died (British Museum Correspondence).

PAGE 143. Letter to HESSEY. [February–March 1823.]

[1] The criticism of 'The Bride's Tragedy' (1822) was in *The London* for February 1823. With Hessey's thanks for the apples (31 March 1823, British Museum Correspondence), this dates the above letter as February-March 1823. The unsigned review hailed Beddoes's Websterian Tragedy as 'undoubtedly one of the most promising performances of this "poetical" age'.

[2] Unpublished.

PAGE 144. Letter to HESSEY. April 1823.

[1] Hessey wrote (31 March) announcing the 'second edition' of *The Village Minstrel*—really the second thousand of the first edition, reissued with an engraving of Cowen's sketch of the cottage in the second volume.

[2] Eventually part of the much longer 'To the Rural Muse'. *The Rural Muse.*

[3] 'Percy Green' was the pen-name Clare had first taken in a letter to Taylor in October 1822 (not in this collection unfortunately). By this he sought to escape what he felt was a falsifying stigma on his poetic relations with his public—the incubus of 'peasant poet'. Taylor himself for 'sales' reasons had helped to hang this round Clare's neck in his Introductions to both *Poems Descriptive of Rural Life and Scenery* and *The Village Minstrel*. However, Taylor published three of these 'Percy Green' poems in the *London* of 1823.

⁴ See letter for 2 April 1822.

PAGE 145. Letter to TAYLOR. 8 May 1823.

¹ Friend of Taylor, who lived at Retford. I. W. Brooks was author of a tract: 'The Word of God concerning all who are in trouble or affliction'.

² Cf. Keats's anguish during his illness from his inability to obtain comfort from orthodox beliefs.

³ I. J. Walker, essayist and author of *On the Larynscope and its Clinical Application* (died 1864), was surgeon of Peterborough Infirmary at this time.

PAGE 147. Letter to HESSEY. p.m. 17 May 1823.

¹ There had been the 'Hymn to Spring': ('Thou virgin bliss the seasons bring' . . .) in *The London* (January 1822), and 'The Approach of Spring' ('And once again thou lovely Spring . . .') (March 1822). This was also in *The Shepherd's Calendar*. What the third poem on spring, mentioned above, was, we are not sure. It may have been 'Impulses of Spring', published in *The Spirit and Manners of the Age*, and, later, in *The Rural Muse*.

² 'To xxxx' ('O lovely maid, though thou art all . . .') was in *The London* (February 1822). Whether this was the *first* part of what Clare here calls 'the Mary poem' is not clear. It looks as if he may have intended a long poem on Mary, much as he later wrote the 'Don Juan' over a long period (cf. *Poems of John Clare's Madness* and *Collected Poems*). Mr. Grigson publishes it as one poem, though it is as easily seen as short poems. The Mary poems, written over a quarter of a century, may have been intended by Clare as one long poem too. 'To an Early Friend' was published in *The Literary Receptacle* and, later, in *The Rural Muse*.

PAGE 148. Letter to HESSEY. June 1823.

¹ Thomas Bennion, Taylor and Hessey's porter?

² It is just possible that this is £17 in the manuscript. Clare is given the benefit of the doubt.

PAGE 149. Letter to TAYLOR. July 1823.

¹ Gilchrist, after a long illness, had just died.

² The Rev. W. Allen had written a critique of Clare's poetry in the form of *Four Letters to Lord Radstock*. Taylor declined either to publish them in *The London Magazine* or to mention the book in his list of new publications. Yet Allen's work remains the best contemporary account of Clare's poetry.

PAGE 152. Letter to HESSEY. [August 1823.]

¹ Taylor had written (1 August, British Museum Correspondence),

'I shall be very agreeable to the Publication of another Volume this ensuing Winter'; the above would seem to be written soon after that.

PAGE 154. Letter to HESSEY. [1823.]
¹ The *Four Letters to Lord Radstock* were published by Murray 1823.

PAGE 154. Letter to HESSEY. p.m. August 1823.
¹ Taylor's suggestion: *The Shepherd's Calendar*.
² 'enough'.
³ Southey, whom as poet Clare did not admire, and, as patron, he did not trust, had begun in 1808 to edit Kirke-White's 'Remains', in two volumes. In 1822 Southey added a third volume.
⁴ *Antediluvian Phytology* by Edmund Tyrell Artis. See Biographical Memoranda on Artis.
⁵ Engravers. Westall engraved for Southey.
⁶ Thomas Griffiths Wainewright, the 'Janus Weathercock' of *The London*, painted 'Paris in the Chamber of Helen' and 'The Milkmaid' from Walton's *Angler*. See J. Curling's *Life* of him.
⁷ Charles Robert Leslie (1794–1839), a Londoner born of American parents, was a Royal Academician, and wrote the celebrated life of Constable.

PAGE 157. Letter to THOMAS INSKIP. p.m. 10 August 1824.
¹ This letter, already printed in the curious *Mirth and Mocking on Sinner Stocking*, edited W. L. Hanchard (1932), was there in turn reprinted from an 'extremely scarce pamphlet' published by Charles Clark. Clark was a friend of Inskip, visited Clare in 1832, subscribed to 'Cottage Poems', which Clare was then projecting, published the above from Clare to Inskip, with one of Cowper and one of Bird, privately, in 1837, and later accused Dr. Matthew Allen, of High Beech, of 'neglect', while Clare was under Allen's care. The above text is from Clark's version (British Museum); the manuscript, like the Inskip Asylum letters, is lost.
² Bloomfield had died in 1823.
³ One of these ('Sweet unassuming Minstrel! not to thee . . .') was published in *The Literary Receptacle* and, later, in *The Rural Muse*. This, and a second ('The shepherd musing o'er his summer dreams. . .') in *Collected Poems*. The third ('Some feed on living fame with conscious pride') among the Bloomfield manuscripts (British Museum) is still unpublished.

PAGE 159. Letter to TAYLOR. [August 1824.]
¹ There is difficulty about the dates of both the above and the next letter, dated by Clare 20 August 1824. Clare returned from his third visit to London on the 8 August 1824. He had been there since about

the middle of May. 'I got all safe' looks like the acknowledgement of money, but it may not have been Clare's money due in July. Clearly this letter and the following one belong together, since Clare says 'I have not answered Hessey's last letter', and then does answer it, on the religious topic in question. But the following letter, clearly dated, almost looks as if it belonged to the period just *before* his third visit to London. The only solution open to us is that, feeling no improvement in health since his return, he wished, as quickly as a fortnight later, to go back to London for further help from Dr. Darling.

PAGE 164. Letter to CHARLES ABRAHAM ELTON. 18 December 1824.

1 We are indebted to Mr. Arthur Elton for the transcript of the above letter, and also for notes 2, 3, and part of 4.

2 The following words have been lightly scored out: 'to get this letter free for my'.

3 The letter is on two sides of a page. Some collector thief has cut the signature from the second page, at the same time shearing off the last line from the first page. This might have read ' . . . made such an offer—I only wish that I could . . .'

4 'The Idler's Epistle to J. Clare' (by C. A. Elton) was published in *The London Magazine* (August 1824). The two verses Clare felt flat had already been omitted by Taylor; the half-stanza about the opium-eaters' 'dreams of murkiest hell' and one in praise of Barry Cornwall were restored when C. A. Elton republished the 'Epistle' in *Boyhood* (1835). Deville was the phrenologist in the Strand.

5 '. . . in whose hot window seat I used to sit and read Cowley, with the grass-plot before, and the hum and flappings of that one *solitary wasp* that ever haunted it about me . . .' Elia's 'Blakesmoor in H–shire' (*The London Magazine*, September 1824).

6 De Quincey's indictment (*The London Magazine*, August–September 1824) is a brilliantly witty contribution to the controversy on Goethe's 'Germanism' and his position, on the publication of the English translation of *Wilhelm Meister*, beside Homer and Shakespeare.

PAGE 166. Letter to JAMES MONTGOMERY. 5 January 1825.

1 This attempt to deceive James Montgomery was apparently successful, and the poem appeared, Montgomery repeating the story of its origin on Clare's authority, and praising the 'felicity of language' (*The Sheffield Iris*, February 1825).

PAGE 168. Letter to ARTIS. March or April 1825.

1 Artis was in London in March 1825.

2 Unknown.

3 Harrison's pailgrounds, near Oxey Wood.

4 During this visit to London Artis called on Taylor and Hessey

three times, to urge them to get on with the printing of *The Shepherd's Calendar*.

PAGE 169. Letter to HESSEY. 17 April 1825.

[1] Clare first met Harry Stoe Van Dyk at Taylor's in 1824, and left his sketch of him (see *Life*, p. 216, etc.). Van Dyk, whose fortune in the West Indies was in peril, was trying to make a living by writing. For a year, 1824–5, he took over the editing of *The Shepherd's Calendar* but he may have been too friendly with Mrs. Emmerson for Taylor's liking: he himself wrote to Clare that fortune had 'knocked him backward' (October 1825, Peterborough manuscripts). He wrote *English Romances* and *Songs of the Six Minstrels*. He died in 1828, in poverty, though his last weeks were helped by Mrs. Emmerson, who had him removed to better quarters, and did much for him. Though we know, from Van Dyk's letters to Clare (British Museum Correspondence and Peterborough manuscripts) and from Clare's *Journal* entries, that Clare wrote to him a number of times, only one letter to Van Dyk has so far come to light.

PAGE 170. Letter to TAYLOR. 5 May 1825.

[1] Taylor had written (18 March 1825, British Museum Correspondence) that as Clare had mentioned 'hints' and 'cautions' (presumably from Mrs. Emmerson and Lord Radstock) ' . . . if you and they cannot find another publisher let me not have my Feelings of Distaste created by the Mention of Such Things. Better to terminate the Connection than Continue it in Distrust . . .'

[2] Unfortunately for some reason—let us hope not Clare's diffidence—Elizabeth Kent's third volume, this one on birds, was not made companion to her *Flora Domestica* (1823) and *Sylvan Sketches* (1825). Clare has, however—still unpublished—a very interesting manuscript (Peterborough) descriptive and enumerative of Northamptonshire birds.

PAGE 173. Letter to TAYLOR. 19 June 1825.

[1] 'Village Stories' in *The Shepherd's Calendar*.

[2] 'Ann', 'Anne', or 'Anna' Adcock evidently forsook poetry for schoolmarming. She is mentioned as principal of a school in the Market Place at Oakham in directories for 1846 and 1850. But *Cottage Stories* has not survived.

[3] We have also failed to trace Kenrick and his *Memory's Musings*.

[4] *Poems on Various Subjects*. See letter to Gilchrist for September 1820.

[5] The poems of Rose and Wilkinson do not appear to have reached the British Museum catalogue, nor has the Peterborough library anything to disclose.

[6] John Banton, of Teigh, in Rutlandshire, wrote *The Village Wreath* and *Excursions of Fancy*, managing to get both trite volumes published by subscription.

[7] Nicholas Stratton, who styles himself in his cheerfully ebullient preface a 'rustic farmer's son', seems also to have written *Poems on Various Subjects* (1824). But Stratton, too, has none of Clare's sensitive master-love and lore, and deserves, with Banton and Messing and the others, his oblivion.

[8] 'Droop': Baker's *Glossary of Northamptonshire*.

PAGE 175. Letter to HONE. 2 August 1825.

[1] Hone had accepted Clare's 'Death' by 'Andrew Marvell' without question, and it appeared as Marvell's, with, probably, Clare's valiant efforts at punctuation, in Hone's *Every-Day Book*, for 28 June 1826. The above attempt to father 'A Defiance to Love' on Sir Henry Wooten (Wotton) or, as Clare says in his *Journal* for 2 August 1825, on Sir John Harrington—his final decision in the letter he sent—did not deceive Hone. It appeared later in *The European Magazine* for March 1826.

[2] Thomas Moore, slick versifier though he was, wrote some Irish songs which have a perennial quality like those of the Elizabethans.

[3] See Moore's *Almanac* (1825). This curiosity, begun in 1697 by Francis Moore, to facilitate the sale of his 'Pills', was continued after his death by others, and to this day has a large sale! 'Tr of St. Mart = Trial of St. Margaret.'

PAGE 176. Letter to TAYLOR. 15 September 1825.

[1] Taylor had had brain fever. He was never the publishing venturer among poets again.

[2] The common name nowadays for Epimedium: according to Gerard's description, 'Dioscorides and Pliny do report, that it is without floure or seed'. It is interesting that Clare's experience of the plant seems to accord with that of these two writers. But Gerard found that, in most years, it 'bringeth seed to perfection'.

PAGE 177. Letter to J. POWER [?]. 24 September 1825.

[1] J. Power, of the Strand, had requested permission to publish 'The Banks of Broomsgrove', which a Mr. Barnett had set to music. Hessey, calling the poem 'The Maid of Bromsgrove', wrote (22 September) conveying the request, and advising Clare to ask for five guineas. Clare records in his *Journal* (7 September 1825) that he received the request from Power in October. Power wrote (29 September) enclosing £2, which is no doubt what Clare, with his

inexactness about dates, was remembering; the above letter is clearly dated, and Power almost without doubt its recipient.

PAGE 179. Letter to HESSEY. 8 December 1825.

[1] *The European Magazine* published 'Thoughts in a churchyard' ('Recall that strain! Whose harrowing spell'), 'Farewell to Love' ('I knew thee in thy cloudless sky') both anonymously, as 'Stanzas', as well as 'The Gipsy's Song' (August 1825–January 1826). Presumably the editor suspected the fathering of them on Sir Henry Wotton, Sir John Harington, and John [?] Davies respectively. The magazine also published in November of this year (1825) Clare's 'Popularity in Authorship', well punctuated to stress the interesting balance of the prose, but without even the customary initials.

[2] It is difficult to decide what Watts—proclaiming in his preface that he signed his own name and affixed those of most of his contributors, 'accentuated by no ostentatious motive'—printed in his 1825 *Literary Souvenir*, of Clare's—with *no* name affixed. It may have been 'To Mary'; but this is signed O, and is a sonnet. More likely it is 'The Last Adieu', which might be called a ballad, but has been carefully smoothed by Watts, till all individuality which might have marked it as Clare's is gone. And if Watts altered the first line, our index of Clare's unpublished poems ceases to be of value. We are left, for the time being, with our inadequate knowledge. But the theme is Clare's.

PAGE 189. Letter to TAYLOR. 11 April 1826.

[1] Taylor has written (8 April 1826, British Museum Correspondence) that Welch and Hames, who had published songs for Darley, had said they had paid Drury for the songs Clare wrote. See letters to Hessey [July 1820] and 16 July 1820.

PAGE 190. Letter to MONTGOMERY. 8 May 1826.

[1] This letter is printed from J. L. Cherry's *Life and Remains of John Clare* (1873).

[2] Montgomery had asked for definite proof of the authorship of 'The Vanitys of Life'; he wished to reprint it in *Christian Poetry*. See letter to Montgomery for 5 January 1825.

[3] Montgomery printed 'To John Milton, from his honoured friend, William Davenant', in *The Sheffield Iris*, 6 May 1826.

PAGE 194. Letter to TAYLOR. 15 July 1826.

[1] It had been published as 'Superstition's Dream' in *The London*. It was entitled 'The Dream' in *The Shepherd's Calendar*.

[2] This volume was never published.

PAGE 196. Letter to TAYLOR. 1 December 1826.

[1] There had been innumerable collections of 'Scotch Songs' since 1735. In 1826 there was a 'Popular Collection of Scottish Comic Songs, original and select', which may be the one Clare means.

[2] Watts published 'First Love's Recollections', another of the 'Mary' poems, in his 1826 *Souvenir*.

[3] David Roberts, painter and engraver (1796–1864).

[4] Unpublished. It is not clear what Clare means here. There is no manuscript 'Sea Songs Love Ballads etc.' at Peterborough or Northampton, as far as we know.

[5] 'John, son of John Clare, Poet', had been baptized on 18 June 1826.

PAGE 199. Letter to HESSEY. 21 January 1827.

[1] The gay, vivacious Elizabeth Ogilvy Benger (1778–1827) wrote *Memoirs of Anne Bolyn*, a couple of novels, a poem on the slave trade, and some other biographies. Madame de Staël thought her the most interesting woman she met in England. She was the person of whom Southey wrote: 'Mary Lamb and her brother have succeeded in talking Dyer into love with . . . but they have got him into a quagmire and can't get him out again, for they have failed in their attempt to talk her into love with him.' Elizabeth Benger died in poverty.

[2] The publisher, Henry Colburn (died 1855), was one of those responsible for the diffusion of light literature and the growth of circulating libraries in the first half of the nineteenth century. He published the *New Monthly* and speculated constantly in journalism.

[3] A reference to a popular boot-'blacking' of Clare's day.

[4] Manuscript may be 'singing'.

PAGE 202. Letter to DARLEY. 3 September 1827.

[1] Clare could not know the personal tragedy that was hidden behind Letitia Elizabeth Landon (1802–38) and her remarkably successful efforts (and genius, according to Jerdan) in supporting impecunious relatives by writing; but he did see clearly the dissipation of talent (even of genius itself) that could occur under too low a valuation of poetry. In his essay in *The European Magazine* (q.v.) he had shown the rigid demarcation-line between 'fame' and 'popularity'.

[2] Nor could he know how quickly the feminine over-sweetness of Mrs. Dorothea Hemans would pall on her readers, after Byron's, Lady Blessington's, and North's support. But he himself found *some* pleasure in her as late as the Inskip period of his stay at St. Andrew's, Northampton.

³ 'Dartford' has quite defeated us, though we have tried to take into consideration the names Clare might have misspelt, or those similar in looks to 'Dartford' the manuscript might intend. 'Morrison' is either James Morrison, writer of popular books on arithmetic (which would show again the serious reading-habits of Clare's day), or, less likely, Robert Morrison, D.D., missionary and writer on China and the Chinese.

⁴ Darley's first letter (2 March 1827) (British Museum Correspondence and *Life and Letters of George Darley*, C. Colleer Abbott), to which the above is the answer, does not indicate which poem Darley enclosed. Professor Colleer Abbott calls the measure of 'The Green of the Day' one of those 'almost vulgar rhythms that prance jauntily', into which Darley was betrayed by his metrical facility. But for Darley every 'true poet' had 'a song in his mind', and this 'dumb music'—rhythm—was what 'attuned', 'heart, and mind, and soul' to poetry; while in Clare, even as late as 1827, the re-creation, in words, of the mystery of leaf, scent, creature, and flower was more conscious than the music. With the others, Darley did not comprehend Clare's practical difficulties. He had written concerning Clare's ill health: 'What *can* be the matter with you, so healthfully situated and employed? Me thinks you should live the life of an oak tree or a sturdy elm, that groans in a storm but only for pleasure? . . . Do you meditate too much? . . . or sit too immovably? . . . Poetry—I mean the composition of it, does not always sweeten the mind as much as the reading . . .'

PAGE 205. Letter to TAYLOR. 17 November 1827.

¹ Shrub's Hill, home of the Hon. Henry Robert Westenra, M.P. for County Monaghan since 1818. Darley occasionally stayed there, and his friend Westenra 'franked' his letters.

² Josiah Conder, whose poems, *The Star in the East* (Taylor and Hessey, 1824), Clare also admired, was editor of *The Eclectic Review* (New Series, 1814–28) and had reviewed *The Shepherd's Calendar* himself. Conder's 'The Late Spring' has the same colloquial lilt as Darley's 'Green of the Day'. Only disappointment over *The Shepherd's Calendar* could have made Clare want to write like *that*.

³ Unknowns.

PAGE 206. Letter to [HARRY STOE VAN DYK]. November 1827.

¹ *The Country Literary Chronicle and Weekly Review* (1819–23) became *The Literary Chronicle* and then *The Athenaeum* (1828–1921). The laudatory but somewhat hasty review of *The Shepherd's Calendar* was by a friend of Van Dyk. This is our clue as to the recipient of the

above letter; the other, 'My dear Harry'—Henry Behnes Burlowe— Clare did not meet till his 1828 visit to London; and by that time (February-March) Harry Stoe Van Dyk was dying.

PAGE 207. Letter to TAYLOR. 10 December 1827.

[1] Darley had intended Taylor to send a copy of *Sylvia* explaining the gift as 'a mark of my regard and brotherly feeling'; evidently the letter was sent after the parcel, since it is among the Clare Correspondence.

[2] Despite handsome letters of recommendation from Lamb and Cary, Darley did not get this post at the new 'University of London', i.e., the institution which subsequently became University College, London, the foundation stone of which was laid on 30 April 1827. Taylor, however, succeeded where his only remaining friend (except Clare) of *The London Magazine* days, failed. Taylor became bookseller and publisher to the University, saying to his brother that he owed his success partly to Darley and partly 'to providence'.

[3] This letter is not now (1949) with the rest of the Martin manuscripts. It was published by Mr. Blunden in his *Sketches in the Life of John Clare* (1931) and has, therefore, been printed direct from that source.

PAGE 208. Letter to HIS WIFE PATTY. 25 February 1828.

[1] Clare's fourth visit to London lasted about five weeks, and soon after his return his third son, baptized in May, 'William Parker', was born.

[2] Towards the end of 1827 Clare's illness had taken a graver turn. Undoubtedly the failure of *The Shepherd's Calendar* had its effect. Dr. Darling still thought the eruptions on the body were due to eating more and working less, and apparently Mrs. Emmerson's doctor felt that acute mental distress, violent head-pain, loss of memory, chill numbness, were 'little or nothing'.

[3] Helpstone friends.

PAGE 209. Letter to ALARIC WATTS. 12 March 1828.

[1] Since *The Literary Souvenir* was edited by Alaric Watts, it is very likely that the above letter, without an addressee's name, is to him. There is, among the British Museum Correspondence, the following letter from Watts (18 February 1828).

'Dear Sir

I sent you the Literary Souvenir for 1828 at the time of its publication and cannot account for you not receiving it.

Having made use of a little Sonnet [?] I have no objection to make you some pecuniary return if you send me any poem worthy of yourself, but really those you have sent me of late are so very inferior, with the excepting (sic) of a little drinking song, which I shall probably print, that it would do you no service to insert them.

The Literary Magnet is discontinued.

I am Dear Sir

Yours truly

A. A. WATTS.'

Clare's letter seems to be the answer to this. He met Watts at Mrs. Emmerson's and later at Watts's own home in Torrington Square but felt 'like a fish out of water' (see letter to Taylor, 3 April 1828) though he had been represented in Watts's 1828 volume, and Watt s by 22 September was asking for more contributions and returning others as unsatisfactory, as well as saying 'the books shall be sent', there is no mention of payment. It is, however, possible, since Clare says Watts 'behaved very well', that Watts paid him in London, and —it should be added—Watts was one of the few to notice *The Rural Muse* in 1835.

PAGE 210. Letter to TAYLOR. 3 April 1828.

¹ There are two copies of this letter, the second unsent, and neither published. The one sent is among the Martin manuscripts at Northampton, probably given to Frederick Martin, for use in his biography, just before John Taylor's death. Though for reasons of his own Martin altered both month and year of this letter, it clearly belongs to April 1828.

² *Poems Descriptive* and *The Shepherd's Calendar*, remaining copies of which Clare was going to try to sell locally.

³ Clare stayed with the Emmersons on his fourth visit to London. Hence, Taylor would not know of his visit to Watts.

PAGE 212. Letter to FRANK SIMPSON. 9 April 1828.

¹ Mrs. Octavius Gilchrist's nephew, the art-student, had inherited Gilchrist's grocery business at Stamford.

² An unknown.

³ This was not Harry Behnes Burlowe, Clare's friend, but William Behnes (Behnes Burlowe's brother), who had asked Clare to write a verse for his bust of Princess Victoria, engraved for Mrs. S. C. Hall's *Juvenile Forget-Me-Not* (1829). Clare managed to comply.

⁴ *The Evergreen—a Selection of Religious and Perceptive Poetry* (1830) may have been edited by S. C. Hall's wife, but Clare has evidently confused the two. His 'Grasshopper' appeared in her *Juvenile Forget-Me-Not*.

⁵ Mr. Henry Ryde, estate agent of Burghley, had offered to get Clare a cottage, but nothing came of it. We cannot find that Ryde's 'Classical or Heathen Dictionary' was ever published either.

PAGE 215. Letter to TAYLOR. 12 April 1828.

¹ Unpublished.

PAGE 215. Letter to THOMAS PRINGLE. 29 August 1828.

¹ *Ephemerides or Occasional Poems written in Scotland and South Africa* (1828).

² This was a reprint of Pringle's *The Autumnal Excursion* (1819) with added Songs and Sonnets.

³ F. W. N. Bayley (1808–53) was a miscellaneous writer who conducted the publication *Omnibus*. He also was the first editor of the *Illustrated London News*. His *Four Years in the West Indies*, of which Clare is surely speaking, is dated 1830, and published by William Kidd. Bayley's other book on the West Indies, *The Island Bagatelle*, is 1829. But it does not seem that we can call the date of the above letter into question because of this puzzle.

⁴ Manuscript torn.

PAGE 221. Letter to TAYLOR. 3 January 1829.

¹ Taylor had suggested drinking at Boston was the cause of Clare's illness. This fallacy about drink being the chief cause of his ills dogged Clare a very long way. Writing to Martin (1865), P. R. Nesbitt, fourteen years Medical Superintendent at Northampton, said 'I was always led to believe C's mental affliction had its origin in dissipation'.

² Taylor had written that *Pleasures of Spring* would be too like poems already published. Darley had suggested—though not world-loving enough to follow his own counsel in his own poetical dramas—it would need 'action'. See *Poetry and the People*, by Kenneth Richmond.

³ Cunningham edited *The Anniversary* in 1829 and 1830 for the publisher, John Sharpe, in an effort to outshine the popular *Keepsake*. It sold 6,000 copies before publication, but though it counted among its contributors, Southey, Wilson, Lockhart, Montgomery, Hogg, Bryan Waller Procter ('Barry Cornwall'), Darley, Clare, and Cunningham himself, it lasted only two years.

⁴ Hessey's prospectus ran: 'On the 13 January 1829 will be published . . . the Library of Religious Knowledge, Consisting of a series of original treatises, written in a popular and familiar style, relating to "Revealed Religion".'

⁵ William Burke, murderer and supplier of bodies to Dr. Knox's school of anatomy, came up for trial in Edinburgh on 24 December 1828. Burke's story caused a great sensation, as did those of Orator Hunt the Radical and of John Thurtell the murderer at their trials, in 1819 and 1824 respectively.

PAGE 223. Letter to CARY. January 1829.

¹ This letter is printed from the transcripts of Mr. R. W. King, author of *The Translator of Dante*.

² William Hayley, whose reputation in the eighteenth century on *The Triumphs of Temper* (1791) was greater than Erasmus Darwin's on *Loves of the Plants, The Botanic Garden*, and *The Temple of Nature*, is remembered now chiefly as the good-natured friend of Cowper, Blake, and Charlotte Smith. Hayley refused the Laureateship on the death of Thomas Warton and, in his 'Essay on Epic Poetry' (1782) translated Dante's *Inferno* (Cantos I–III) in terza-rima.

³ Cary had been made 'Assistant Keeper of the Printed Books' (assistant librarian) at the British Museum in 1826.

⁴ This was the poem Hone had accepted without question as the work of Marvell, and printed in the *Every-Day Book* (1825).

PAGE 225. Letter to ALLAN CUNNINGHAM. 22 February 1829.

¹ Clare's *Journal* for Tuesday, 21 September 1824, records: 'The Statute & a very wet day for it . . . wrote a poem on the "Statute" last year lookd it over & think it a good one Taylor is of another opinion & thinks it not but it is true like the "Lodge House" and others he dislikes. . . .'

'Helpstone Statute' remained unpublished till *The Collected Poems* (1935). We have not been able to trace what the poem sent by request was.

² 'Glow-worm', by 'A Ferguson, Esq.', is a poem after Clare's own heart—twenty-eight sensitive-descriptive verses in the Burns's stanza by an impecunious country Scot.

PAGE 226. Letter to MRS. EMMERSON. [April 1829.]

¹ Cunningham's letter (6 April 1829, British Museum Correspondence) is our evidence for placing the above letter in April 1829.

² Henry Behnes Burlowe's bronze bust of Clare, now in Northampton Library, remained the property of Taylor till the sale of his effects in 1865, when it was bought by Frederick Martin.

PAGE 227. Letter to ELIZA L. EMMERSON. 1 August 1829.

¹ 20 Stratford Place, London.

² than?

PAGE 229. Letter to [BEHNES BURLOWE]. 1 August 1829.

[1] *The Spirit and Manners of the Age*, a 'Christian and Literary Miscellany', was edited and published by Frederick Westley and A. H. Davis. Though a non-flamboyant publication, it paid nearly as poorly as S. C. Hall's. But Westley and Davis had sent money in July of this year.

[2] S. C. Hall, editor of *The Amulet*, had sent £5 (4 November 1828) for Clare's contributions to *The Amulet* and *The Juvenile Forget-Me-Not*. But, added Hall, 'I am still £2 in your debt £7 being the sum I had set aside for you—How shall I forward to you the remaining £2?' There seems no record that he found a way. But Hall's *Book of Gems* (1838) contained a tardy appeal for Clare, with a description, as Hall saw him in 1828. Behnes Burlowe did much to help Clare in this matter of payment during these years.

[3] *Poor Humphrey's Calendar:* 'Prophecies concerning the signs of the times'; a fictitious almanac, known as Hone's 'Poor Humphrey'—another of the 'ingenious' Hone's publications.

PAGE 229. Letter to [WILLIAM] SHARPE. October 1829.

[1] Sharpe, who worked in the Dead Letter Office, not Sharpe (John), the publisher. With Behnes Burlowe, Sharpe sought to extract money from Hall and other editors for Clare.

PAGE 231. Letter to MRS. MARIANNE MARSH. 19 October 1829.

[1] The kindly German wife of Herbert Marsh, critical theologian and Bishop of Peterborough, had been Clare's acquaintance since 1820.

[2] We have unfortunately not traced which Book of Epitaphs this was; perhaps *Churchyard Gleanings*, by William Pulleyn.

[3] We cannot say whether Clare's is a misquotation of the more usual version of Browne of Tavistock's epitaph, or the older form.

[4] A friend of the Bishop and Mrs. Marsh.

[5] George Henry Marsh, Mrs. Marsh's second son. Their eldest son went mad—which may account for Mrs. Marsh's quite exceptional understanding of Clare, and her kindly sympathy after his violent cursing of Shylock in the theatre incident of 1830.

PAGE 233. Letter to L. T. VENTOUILLAC. 7 November 1829.

[1] Clare may have been using 'Almanack' as a general name. The Annual edited by Ventouillac and the Rev. Thomas Dale was, as far as we can discover, *The Offering*, 'to illustrate the connection between polite literature and religion', begun 1828. L. T. Ventouillac seems to have paid Clare well (£10 a sheet, 32 pages), and promptly; his letters—those sky-lights on character (British Museum Correspondence)—are of a sensitive, scholarly person.

PAGE 235. Letter to TAYLOR. 15 November 1829.

[1] There are four attempts at this letter, which Clare found so uncongenial and difficult a task. The above is the one sent.

[2] In justice to Taylor it should be mentioned that Cherry, writing in 1873, says it was at Gilchrist's desire that Hilton painted the portrait which now hangs in the National Portrait Gallery. In the letter to Taylor for 20 May 1820, Clare had written gaily: '... got Hilton's sketch ... pay him at my account ...' The picture, *not* the 'sketch', remained in Taylor's possession till his death, when it was sold at Christie's. In Account D. 1829, Clare was charged fifteen guineas for it. Whether, at Clare's mention of the matter in the above letter, Taylor retracted the charge, is not clear. But, again, in strict justice to Taylor, it should be added that there are notes of Clare's (Peterborough manuscripts, small memorandum books) which state that he had £85 'credit' from Taylor between 1821–9. His childlike dependence and trust, coupled with his desire for independence, must have been a snare and an exasperation for Taylor, as well as his ignorance of what paintings, sketches, even books, cost.

[3] Clare may have meant the *drawing* Taylor rejected. De Wint made two for *The Shepherd's Calendar*. And after all, as the accounts record (Peterborough manuscripts) de Wint *gave* the accepted one.

[4] Published anonymously (1827). A book of Aphorisms and wisdom by the brothers Augustus and Julius (afterwards Archdeacon) Hare.

[5] Hessey, like so many other booksellers of this period, less cautious than Taylor, had gone bankrupt.

PAGE 238. Letter to DE WINT. 19 December 1829.

[1] This letter, like that to de Wint (October 1829) is in the collection of Geoffrey Harmsworth, Esq.

[2] This may have been either the sketch of Clare Hilton did at the same time as the portrait, or the 'wise bird the owl' (see also p. 252), now in the possession of Mr. Edmund Blunden.

[3] Not, as far as we have been able to discover, did de Wint, his wife, or daughter, ever grant Clare's request—even on the publication of the sonnet to de Wint in *The Rural Muse*. And the accepted original of the drawing for *The Shepherd's Calendar* apparently remained with Taylor, now de Wint's near neighbour in Gower Street.

PAGE 241. Letter to CARY. 25 January 1830.

[1] This letter is printed from the transcripts of Mr. R. W. King, author of *The Translator of Dante*.

NOTES TO PAGES 242–45

PAGE 242. Letter to TAYLOR. [January–February 1830.]

¹ Since Clare was writing to thank Taylor for the 'annuity' which Taylor, as trustee, sent in January and July, and since the two letters for the 1831 receipt of 'annuity' are fortunately both dated, and, also, since Clare had a cold, unlikely in summer, but was otherwise in good health, the above would seem to belong to late January–February, or even March 1830, and not 1831 as listed in the *Life*. This gives the facts of the death of Sir Thomas Lawrence—1830 as obviously very recent, more recent than in the next letter, also undated. Clare was late in acknowledging, but he was never *very* late. See also note on next letter.

PAGE 244. Letter to DARLEY. [1830.]

¹ We do not know who gave or lent Clare *Humphry Clinker*, the novel Thackeray thought 'the most laughable story that has ever been written'. Clare wrote of Smollett (Peterborough manuscripts) 'what a soul has that man for satire, ridicule and genuine humour—his Winifred Jenkins is the truest & most humorous picture of low life I have ever met with'. There are hints of Smollett in his 'Bone and Cleaver Club' and other manuscripts of these years.

² Since Sir Thomas Lawrence's successor as President of the Academy has been decided upon, this fact is the chief clue to the place of the above letter. But, since Clare was ill again after July 1830, and since the tone of the letter and of the following one to Cunningham (also undated) suggest he was still in the reasonably good health he had been enjoying when he wrote the previous letter to Taylor, it seems that the above and the following should belong to January–July 1830. On account of Darley's strictures, Cunningham and Darley were no longer the friends they had been.

³ (Afterwards Sir) Martin Archer Shee (1769–1850), historical painter.

⁴ The Scottish painter (1785–1841) received only two votes for the presidency.

⁵ William Etty (1797–1840), fellow-student of Hilton, and R.A. in 1828, was not in the running, either.

PAGE 245. Letter to CUNNINGHAM. [1830?]

¹ We have failed to trace Mr. Nell. The R. Nell, of Grantham, who in 1831 requested permission to publish songs of Clare's, may have been a relative.

² Francis Chantrey, of as humble origin as Cunningham and Clare, was created R.A. and knighted; he left a fortune from his sculpture.

Cunningham, who had the physique of the Scottish peasant, and believed in the sweat of the brow as a pecuniary aid to literary endeavour, worked as Chantrey's assistant most of his London life.

³ When Hogg came to London, Cunningham and he had had a tiff, and neither would go to see the other. Clare did not ever meet Hogg, whose *Confessions of a Self-justified Sinner* (1828) (after an enviably determined list of publications in verse) would have delighted him.

PAGE 246. Letter to MISS JANE MOSSOP. 9 September 1830.
¹ Sister to the Vicar of Etton and Helpstone.

PAGE 247. Letter to TAYLOR. [Late September 1830.]
¹ The manuscript of this letter is in the collection of Geoffrey Harmsworth, Esq.
² Clare's sixth surviving child, Sophia, was born in September 1830. Clare's mention of her is our chief clue to the date of this letter.
³ A severe attack of mental and physical illness followed Clare's rising to curse Shylock in the middle of a performance of *The Merchant of Venice*, which he had attended as the guest of Mrs. Marsh and the Bishop, at the Peterborough theatre. The attack lasted two months— July and August. The seton was part of Dr. Darling's prescription, together with leeches, poultices, and admonitions to eat little and drink only water.

PAGE 249. Letter to HESSEY. ? October 1830.
¹ Since the failure of his publishing of religious books, Hessey had set up as a book and print auctioneer.

PAGE 251. Letter to TAYLOR. 15 January 1831.
¹ Taylor had sent Clare's annuity in the form of a bill which Drakard and Wilson of Stamford owed *him*, and which Clare was to present!
² This visitor who admired Spenser and Burton, and knew Keats, remains unknown, unfortunately.

PAGE 253. Letter to TAYLOR. 7 March 1831.
¹ Dialect for 'throbbing'.
² There had been published, in 1830: *Attempts in Verse, by John Jones, an old Servant, with some account of the writer by himself, and an Introductory Essay on the Lives and Works of our Uneducated Poets*, by R. Southey. John Jones (1788–1855?) was a butler, and the first poem of his which had attracted Southey's attention was 'To a Robin Redbreast', which *has* a certain similarity to Clare's, but not enough to justify any accusation of plagiarism. Southey's selective and con-

descending account of 'uneducated poets' in *The Quarterly* (1831) taking note of Taylor the Water Poet, Bloomfield, Cunningham, Stephen Duck, and Burns, has no mention of Clare, or the many other 'uneducated poets', prior or contemporary.

PAGE 255. Letter to TAYLOR. 24 July 1831.

[1] Taylor wanted him to make an anthology of Seventeenth-century Minor Poets. It was a practical idea, if Clare could have carried it out. Romantic interest in the past was still strong.

[2] They were never sent but remain among the Peterborough manuscripts, many of them unfinished, all uncorrected, but full of sound, poetic common sense.

[3] William Browne (c. 1590–1645?) in 1613 and 1616 published the first and second parts of *Britannia's Pastorals*.

PAGE 258. Letter to TAYLOR. [January 1832.]

[1] This looks like a reference to the receipt of the January annuity, which Clare was particular about acknowledging; the fact that he asks Taylor for Fund money, telling him of the Northborough cottage, and adding that he has not heard from Taylor (see later in letter), dates the letter as before Taylor's reply of 13 January.

[2] He had—in the preceding October. Taylor replied (13 January 1832), as we have said.

PAGE 259. Letter to TAYLOR. [January 1832.]

[1] Taylor had replied to Clare's request of the previous letter—for money from the Fund, to cover the removal to Northborough—via Parson Mossop. He did not write to Clare between July 1831 and January 1832. On the 13 January 1832 he wrote that 'a Multiplicity of avocations' had prevented his writing before. He could do nothing about the Fund money until the other trustee, Richard Woodhouse, returned from Italy in May. He did not think the Principal could be touched. He did not reply about publishing Clare's new poems.

PAGE 260. Letter to REV. CHARLES MOSSOP. [January 1832.]

[1] Bachelor Rector of Etton and Vicar of Helpstone (1817–53), and afterwards Rector of Etton. He visited Helpstone every day, on horseback, to look after his farm there, but his home was at Etton (two miles distant).

PAGE 262. Letter to MARIANNE MARSH. [Spring 1832.]

[1] The 'Lady' remains untraced.
[2] *Madrigals and Chronicles* (1924).
[3] Unpublished.

PAGE 264. Letter to CHARLES MOSSOP. 28 April 1832.

[1] Pamphlet on the Roman and Anglican Churches.

PAGE 265. Letter to ARTIS. May 1832.

[1] He proposed to print *The Midsummer Cushion* by subscription at 7s. 6d. a copy.

PAGE 265. Letter to CHARLES MOSSOP. August 1832.

[1] *The Athenaeum* (25 August 1832) stated that Clare's Northborough cottage had been bestowed on him for life rent-free. A further notice appeared in the London *Alfred*, giving the correct facts about the cottage, but suggesting Clare had been cheated out of his profits by his publishers, and that he had, at that time, £15 a year on which to keep himself, wife, and 14 children! The *Stamford Bee* repeated this story on the 5th October, and on the 13th *The Athenaeum* corrected its story about the cottage, but repeated the *Alfred* story of Clare's poverty. The originator of these misstatements appears to have been a Peterborough printer, Charles Jacob, and the second *Athenaeum* notice, at least, was by Allan Cunningham.

PAGE 268. Letter to CARY. August 1832.

[1] May be 'memory'.

[2] Wilson of Drakard and Wilson, Booksellers of Stamford, wrote of his debt to them, 'you need not be under any apprehension that I could, as one of the agents for the spreading of literature, attempt to lay the iron hand of oppression on a son of the Genius of poetry . . .'

PAGE 269. Letter to TAYLOR. 6 September 1832.

[1] This letter is written on the prospectus of *The Midsummer Cushion*.

[2] Probably the untraced 'Lady' referred to in the letter to Marianne Marsh, spring 1832.

[3] Taylor eventually gave £5 for two pigs, and the Emmersons had opened a subscription list with £10 for a cow, but the Fund money was not drawn upon.

[4] The Charles Clark, Inskip's friend, who published Clare's letter to Inskip of August 1824 ('Three Very Interesting Letters. Clare, Cowper and Bird' (1837)). See note to the Inskip letter. Not Clark, the editor of *The Stamford Bee*.

PAGE 271. Letter to the EDITOR of *The Athenaeum*. [Autumn 1832.]

[1] Charles Wentworth Dilke (1789–1864) was the energetic editor of *The Athenaeum* at this time, and for many years afterwards. John Sterling had bought it in 1828 from James Silk Buckingham, but did not make of it a success. Dilke did.

There is a second attempt at the above letter, showing Clare's never-conquered perturbation at having to clear up such misunderstandings; it is almost identical with the first half of the above. Whether there was a 'sent' letter to Dilke, we do not know.

2 The origin of this second article in *The Athenaeum*—the *Alfred* one—was a violent condemnation of publishers and patrons, as if from the mouth or pen of Clare. *The Athenaeum* article, for 13 October, corrected its information about the cottage thus: 'We are sorry both for the Noble Lord and the humble poet to find we were misinformed . . .' The Editor of The *Alfred* adds: 'What we are sorry to hear is that his [Clare's] poems yielded him no profit: and that £15 a year . . .' etc. And so the confusion Clare hated grew—between his struggle with poverty and his poetic worth.

PAGE 272. Letter to CUNNINGHAM. 11 November 1832.

1 From the punctuated transcript by Francis Cunningham.

2 Henry Behnes Burlowe was trying to find another publisher for Clare. Taylor, writing sternly (July 1832), having heard, or assumed, from an interview with Mrs. Emmerson, Clare's comments to them on the 1829 Accounts and on the tying up of the Fund money, had declared: 'If you have not had sufficient remuneration from your Poems, let it be remembered that I am out of pocket by them.'

3 *The Maid of Elvar*, which appeared soon after *Lord Roldan*. Both were little regarded. Cunningham was writing much and hurriedly.

PAGE 277. Letter to JOHN TAYLOR. September 1833.

1 Publisher, antiquary, compiler of bibliographies, and editor of *Northamptonshire Notes and Queries*, but no relative of the London John Taylor. He did great service, later, in collecting Clare manuscripts for the Northampton Library.

PAGE 278. Letter to THOMAS EMMERSON. 1834.

1 Clare had decided *The Midsummer Cushion* must be published in London. He had sent the manuscripts to Mrs. Emmerson in August 1833. Mrs. Emmerson changed the title to *The Rural Muse*, and her husband obtained J. How's solemn promise to bring the book out in 1834. How was connected with the publishing firm of Whittaker. Although the Northborough cottage had now its cow and two pigs, debts had accumulated. The £40 for the copyright of *The Rural Muse*, finally sent by Thomas Emmerson in March 1834, was a long-needed relief to Clare.

PAGE 279. Letter to HOW OF WHITTAKER'S. 13 or 25 June 1834.

1 Whittaker's.

² Taylor had, by July 1833, been moved by Clare's determined friendly regard', and by their 'early and long-continued acquaintance' to drop the libel action against *The Athenaeum* and *The Alfred.* Though he would not publish nor help Mrs. Emmerson to edit, he promised to look over the proofs of the new poems.

³ The manuscript of the preface to *The Rural Muse* is with this letter. With some omissions (chiefly of repetitions that reveal the confused state of Clare's mind), Taylor allowed it to stand, as he had Clare's preface to *The Shepherd's Calendar.*

⁴ How, in his connection with the firm of Whittaker, was publishing Mudie's *British Birds.*

PAGE 282. Letter to TAYLOR. 6 January 1835.

¹ We had thought, hitherto, that the youngest of Clare's children to survive infancy was Charles, who died in 1852, aged 19, and the first to die (after infancy) was Fred, but not till 1843. There is no record of any birth or burial in 1835 or late 1834. All we can go upon, then, is the tenacious 'village-chat', or hearsay, which recalls Patty's ninth child, which died almost at birth, in early 1835. The church records, not extravagantly well-kept, even at that date, fail to record either birth or death of the unbaptized child, as they failed to record the birth and death of Clare's sister, who died in infancy.

PAGE 282. Letter to TAYLOR. 15 January 1835.

¹ The second Earl, Clare's patron since 1820, had died. The new Earl responded to Clare's letter, finally finished and sent, and the annuity went on as before.

² Taylor had written on 9 January: ' . . . Poor Charles Lamb is dead—perhaps you had not heard of it before—He fell down and cut his Face against the Gravel on the Turnpike Road, which brought on the Erisypelas, and in a few days carried him off.—Our Friend Reynolds also has had such an Affliction as you mention in your own Case—he has lost a Child—but she was his only Child, a Daughter, 10 years of Age, and I understand he grieves much for her Loss.'

PAGE 283. Letter to TAYLOR. 27 August 1835.

¹ 'Blackwood's'. Taylor, in his letter of 3 August (British Museum Correspondence) said the review was 'very Scotch and very much inferior to what it should have been'.

PAGE 284. Letter to TAYLOR. 16 February 1837.

¹ George Reid (later of Glasgow), formerly a 'bookseller's clerk', had first written to Clare in 1834. In 1837, he wrote in appreciation of *The Rural Muse.* He worked in the Western Bank of Alloa.

PAGE 285. Letter to FRANK SIMPSON. [1835-7.]
¹ There is a note on the manuscript of this draft-letter :

'April 19. The last of my Poor Stock doves got murdered in the cage under the Eldern Tree in the Garden by a Dog after I had kept it seven years.'

But this note probably belongs to 1824-5 and *The Journal*, and is no indication of the date (day-month) of the above letter. Clare was using this book for draft-letters in the Northborough period. There was no 'Eldern Tree' in the Northborough garden as there was at the bottom of the Helpstone garden, and though the present Clares recall the landing window from which he watched the birds, he kept no doves at Northborough. The only indications of the year-date of this letter are the tone and the unfinished state, which should place it in 1835-6, or later 1837, when his illness overtook him again after the short lightening of mental conflict discernible in the two letters preceding this.

PAGE 289. Letter to MARY JOYCE. [1841.]
¹ The manuscript of this draft-letter is in a notebook of the High Beech period inscribed 'John Clare's Poems Feby. 1841'. There are two drafts of the letter. The first reaches only to *
² Mary Joyce died unmarried, 1838.
³ See *Poems of John Clare's Madness*, edited Geoffrey Grigson, 1950.

PAGE 291. Letter to ELIZA PHILLIPS. [1841.]
¹ The manuscript of the draft-letter is in the same notebook of the High Beech period as the previous letter. We have no evidence that Eliza Phillips was, as Mr. Geoffrey Grigson says, an 'old love' of Clare's. She may have been no more than a name (cf. letter to Mary Collingwood). This notebook and the *Ha'penny Ballad Book* of the St. Andrew's period have many women's names. Some may have been people he met outside the asylum. The point is, we must not, without clear evidence, add to the myth that Clare was, in his youth, a roué among women, which, like the myth about his excessive drinking, is so wide of the mark.

PAGE 291. Letter to PATTY. 17 March 1841.
¹ One of the three separate buildings of High Beech, Leppit's Hill Lodge housed the incipients, the convalescents, and the partially deranged. The immediate vicinity is now known as Lippit's Hill, an interesting place-name derived from the leap of the Epping deer.

PAGE 294. Letter to DR. MATTHEW ALLEN. [August 1841.]
¹ The manuscript of this draft-letter, together with one stanza 'Sweet comes the misty mornings in September' is written round the

margin of *The Lincolnshire Chronicle and General Advertizer* for Friday,
27 August 1841. We have not seen the sent letter to which Allen
replied so kindly (18 November 1841). The stanza, with two others,
was published in *Collected Poems* (1934), as 'September Mornings', and
later, as more likely Clare intended it, as part of 'Child Harold', in
Poems of John Clare's Madness, since Clare retranscribed it as part of
that poem.

² Three miles south of Northborough.

³ This request is not as aberrant as it looks at first glance. Allen
had been attempting, since 1840, to raise £500 by subscription on
Clare's behalf, in order that he might go home, since he was so much
recovered. The sum finally collected fell far short of £500. The
scheme had been commended by Cyrus Redding (*English Journal*,
May 1841) and, according to a later notice, the Queen Dowager sent
twenty guineas. In his reply to Clare, Allen said Clare had been mistaken about the annuity; it was a single donation. What finally hap-
pened to the money collected is not clear.

⁴ Son of the poet Campbell, Thomas Campbell was an inmate of
High Beech, with Clare.

PAGE 297. Letter to CHARLES CLARE. 15 June 1847.

¹ Parker Clare, who had moved with the family to Northborough,
lived to be eighty-two, dying in 1846.

² Clare's first and second sons: Frederick had been dead since 1843,
but John visited his father at Northampton in 1848.

³ Life-long friends who lived at Woodcroft Castle.

⁴ Eliza Louisa, Clare's second daughter, married Samuel Sefton,
after his first daughter Anna, who had also been married to Sefton,
died in 1844.

PAGE 298. Letter to CHARLES CLARE. February 1848.

¹ 'Piscator' (T. P. Lathy) wrote *The Angler: A Poem in ten cantos*
(1819). 'Piscator' also wrote *Observations on the Public right of
Fishing* (1826) and *The Practical Angler* (1842); but we are not sure
whether these two later books are by Lathy; nor is it clear to which
book Clare was referring.

² No confusion here. Henry Phillips, the popular singer and song-
writer—to whom Mrs. Emmerson gave a copy of *The Rural Muse* in
1835—also wrote *The True Enjoyment of Angling* (1843).

³ And no irrationality here. Humphry Davy, as a young man, added
poetry to science. Later, as antidote to science, he turned back
to nature. Though little known, his *Salmonia, or Days of Fly Fishing*,
had been published in 1827. Clare read much during this fertile period

of the friendship with Thomas Inskip, and he may have met these books now for the first time.

PAGE 299. Letter to PATTY. July 1848.

[1] No confusion. John had been, as we have said.

[2] Spokes's Mill, near Western Favell, about a mile from St. Andrew's, most probably. Clare had considerable freedom in this early period at Northampton under Dr. Prichard—in spite of his non-sequitur a few lines further on in this letter.

[3] Nearly seven, of course.

PAGE 300. Letter to CHARLES CLARE. 17 October 1848.

[1] Clare's grandchildren testify to 'Uncle and Aunt Riddle, of Barnack'. But we have failed to clear up whether this was Clare's sister or not. If it was she married twice because Clare speaks in his will-draft of 'my sister Sophia Hetwell'.

[2] No factual confusion here, either. To W. F. Knight, the Steward at Northampton, we owe the preservation of those Asylum Poems of Clare which, as Mr. Grigson so truly says, push him 'over the border-land between the pathetically interesting and exquisite into the great; however circumscribed his greatness'. The manuscript was sent by Patty, but though we hear of Knight's project for a volume to be published for Clare by subscription, even after Knight left St. Andrew's in 1850, it was one more of those good intentions that bear no fruit.

PAGE 300. Letter to CHARLES CLARE. 2 April 1849.

[1] This word, though difficult to decipher, is surely 'hums'.

[2] Not S. C. Hall, but Spencer T. Hall, mesmerist, and self-taught author of the book Clare mentions.

PAGE 302. Letter to CHARLES CLARE. 1 June 1849.

[1] The only Northborough name in this list of real Helpstone families is perhaps 'Robin Oliver'. The place-name, though spelt in old O.S. maps 'Rice' wood, recalls the farmer's name 'Richard Royce'. The family of 'Old Otter the Fiddler' was one of very clever masons.

PAGE 303. Letter to CHARLES CLARE. 15 October 1849.

[1] Clare had always been ambitious for his children's minds. He did not wish them to have the ignorance of some in the class from which, as he said in 1820, he had 'struggled upward as one struggling from the nightmare in his sleep'. Ainslie's *Land Surveying* and Ingram Cobbin's *Elements of Arithmetic for Children* may have been among the formidable list of books he had sent to Mrs. Emmerson and to Taylor, in 1833, for his children's education, asking Taylor to deduct the cost

from his next dividend. And Kenney was certainly the promising Charles's schoolmaster at Northborough—though without either Greek or Hebrew. Charles was at this time apprenticed with a firm of solicitors at Market Deeping. It will be recalled that Clare's first subscriber in 1818 was Thomas Mounsey, who taught 'the Greek and Latin Languages and every branch of Commercial and Mathematical Learning'. See letter to Taylor (early 1820).

PAGE 304. Letter to MARY COLLINGWOOD. 26 December 1849.

[1] This letter is from the pocket-book marked 'Ha'penny Ballads by John Clare', dated 'Dec. 26. 1849', and used by him at St. Andrew's. The book has many girls' or women's names in it. The Averys and the Masons were Helpstone families of Clare's youth, but the other names are not known. Names of people, like 'pleasant names of places', may have had an attraction for him, feeling friendless.

PAGE 307. Letter to CHARLES CLARE. 25 July 1851.

[1] The Sissons were a farming family near Stamford.

[2] Elizabeth Newborn, of Ashton, with whom Clare had a chequered love-affair before that with Patty. Elizabeth's father, a religious, well-read countryman, inspired Clare's poem 'The Cottager'.

PAGE 309. Letter to PATTY. 7 March 1860.

[1] Clare's third son, William Parker, was now married and living at home.

[2] The Kettle family were Helpstone labourers, but some members moved to Northborough.

[3] Also of near Helpstone. The name remains in 'Kemp's Corner'.

INDEX

INDEX

Brooke-Taylor MSS. (*seealso* Robinson-Brooke-Taylor MSS). 63 *n.*, 296.

Brooks, Rev. I. W., 145, 343 *n.*

Browne, William, 255, 358 *n.*

Buck (*see also* Back), 67 *and n.*

Budd and Calkin, Messrs., 155.

Bull Inn, 117.

Bunney, Joseph, 125, 340 *n.*

Bunyan, John, 306.

Burghley, 119, 120, 133.

Burke, W., 223, 354 *n.*

Burkhardt, J. C., 82.

Burns, Robert, 17, 18, 26, 29, 41, 43, 75, 215, 333 *n.*

Burton, Robert, 252.

Byron, Lord, 32, 88, 98, 175, 295, 338 *n.*

Cabinet, The, 127, 341 *n.*

Cambridge, 43; (University of), 173.

Campbell, T., 56, 195, 338 *n.*; (his son), 295, 364 *n.*

Carborough, Lord, 281, 285.

Caroline (Queen), 72, 73, 125.

Cary, H. F., Biog. Mem., 14, 15, 17, 139, 162, 163, 165, 220, 223, 354 *n.*, 241, 257, 266, 285.

Casterton, 29, 31, 102, 301.

Castor (Durobrivae), 205.

Centaur, The (Hood's), 127.

Chancery, 181.

Chantrey, F., 246, 357 *n.*

Chatterton, Thomas, 163.

Chaucer, 43, 57, 251.

Cherry, J. L., *Life and Remains of John Clare*, 348 *n.*

Childe Harold (Byron's), 295.

Chiswick, 139.

Christian Poetry, 193, 348 *n.*

Christ's College, Cambridge, 72, 85.

Clare, Anna Maria, 138, 151, 208, 306 *and n.*, 309.

Clare, Charles, 296, 297, 299, 300-8 *and n.*

Clare, Eliza Louisa, 139 *n.*, 151, 208, 209, 363 *n.*

Clare, Frederick, 208, 210, 250, 292 304 *and n.*, 305, 309.

Clare, John (son of the poet), 208, 292, 297, 300, 304, 309.

Clare, John (*see also under* Poems):

manuscripts, present state and where abouts of, 13.

autobiography, 16-17; biography, *John Clare: A Life*, 16; *Sketches in the Life of John Clare, by Himself*, 16.

Mr. Grigson's analysis of his mind, 19.

friendship and encouragement of Isaiah Knowles Holland, 23-6, 29-31.

criticism of Shenstone and pastoral poetry, 27.

estimate of Burns, 26.

dedication of *Poems Descriptive of Rural Life and Scenery*, 27.

friendship and relations with John Taylor (*see also under* Taylor); receives books from, 33; admiration for, 35, 69, 103, 222; dependence on, 37, 45, 46, 67, 76, 87, 108, 132, 136; sends all MSS. to Taylor, 64, 74, 78, 89.

agrees with Taylor's emendations, 62, 68, 81, 93, 103, 106.

placates Taylor concerning other patrons, 78, 79, 80, 180, 275, 361 *n.*

wishes Taylor to publish his (C.'s) Letters and write his (C.'s) Life, 95.

sends Sketches of his life to Taylor, 110, 111.

collects coins for Taylor, 210, 219, 221.

friendship with J. A. Hessey, *see under* Hessey.

friendship with the Emmersons, *see under* Emmerson Mrs., *and* Emmerson, Thomas.

publication of *Poems Descriptive*, 29, 31.

INDEX

INDEX

INDEX

INDEX

INDEX

INDEX

INDEX

375

INDEX

INDEX

INDEX

INDEX

83
85